HITLER
MILITARY COMMANDER

ARRAS
Noyelles
CAMBRAI
La Quesnoy

HITLER
MILITARY COMMANDER

RUPERT MATTHEWS

Skyhorse Publishing

First Skyhorse Publishing Edition 2018

Visit our website at www.skyhorsepublishing.com.

10 9 8 7 6 5 4 3 2 1

Library of Congress Cataloging-in-Publication Data is available on file.

Cover design by Dani Leigh
Cartography © Peter Harper
Photographs © Robert Hunt Library except pp. 85, 87, 178, 179, courtesy of Wharton Military
Collectables from film exposed until 2002, probably personal photographs from Operation
Barbarossa June/July 1941

ISBN: 978-1-5107-3394-7
E-Book ISBN: 978-1-5107-3400-5

Printed in the United States of America

CONTENTS

FURTHEST GERMAN
ADVANCES 1941–42

Sphere of Axis
influence

ALLIED CONVOY ROUTES

CONVOYS TO RUSSIA

ICELAND

ARCHANGEL

NORWAY

SWEDEN

FINLAND

LENINGRAD

RUSSIA

Strategic objective of
Operation Barbarossa

MOSCOW

ATLANTIC OCEAN

U.K.

ASTRAKHAN

CASPIAN SEA

GERMANY

POLAND

KURSK

KIEV

FRANCE

CZECH.

AUS.

HUN.

RUMANIA

BLACK SEA

VICHY
FRANCE

ITALY

YUGO.

BULG.

OPERATION TORCH
ALLIED LANDINGS

PORT.

SPAIN

GREECE

TURKEY

GERMAN ARMY
GROUP A
REACH THE
CAUCASUS

MOROCCO

ALGERIA

MEDITERRANEAN SEA

A F R I C A

LIBYA

EGYPT

INTRODUCTION

"Hitler is the greatest military commander of all time."
– Field Marshal Wilhelm Keitel

"Hitler is a jumped up Bohemian Corporal."
– Field Marshal Paul von Hindenburg

As a military man Hitler won victories that many professionals considered impossible to achieve. He formulated plans that were bold to the point of rashness. He enthused his men with a confidence and morale that took them through defeats and reverses that would have broken other armies. The sheer scale of Hitler's military achievement is breathtaking.

Yet Hitler led his superb armed forces to total and crushing defeat. With the world seemingly at his feet, Hitler threw it all away and ended his days as the demented commander of a few square yards of rubble in what had once been his capital city. Whatever qualities Hitler had for good or for bad, he had them in abundance: for Hitler there was rarely a middle way or a reason to compromise. That is what brought him his successes and what caused his downfall.

There are many attributes which are essential in a military commander. Napoleon, for instance, thought that luck was the most important asset in a general. Hitler had plenty of luck, but other qualities essential to a commander were entirely lacking. He had no real empathy with the men he commanded. Despite having served in the trenches of the First World War, Hitler could without any remorse send an

By December 1941 the Nazi flag of Germany dominated Europe

entire army to their deaths, as at Stalingrad. The sufferings of those he commanded were as nothing to him, and as a result he had no real idea of their morale and abilities. Nor did he have any real competence in the business of moving his forces and getting them into action. Supply lines and logistics were closed books to Hitler. Where he relied on his staff officers to work out these mundane practicalities, and listened to their opinions of what was and was not possible, Hitler did well. But where he organized these matters for himself, his efforts were doomed to failure.

HITLER'S GIFTS

Yet there can be no doubting Hitler's gifts. His grasp of strategy was, almost to the end, superb. He could correctly identify the essential objectives for his attacks and, very often, the best way to secure them. Even during his last days in Berlin, Hitler could foresee that the continent of Europe would soon be split between capitalist west and communist east, and that Germany would eventually rise again to hold the balance between the two.

His ability to foresee the reactions of his opponents was also highly developed. He correctly predicted that the French would not oppose the remilitarization of the Rhineland and that Austria would welcome the German troops when they marched over the border. Not until 1940 was he confounded. He expected the British to make peace once France was defeated, but these expectations were disappointed: Hitler had failed to take Winston Churchill into account.

Perhaps what Hitler had working for him most was the tremendous influence of his willpower and personality on the performance of the German armed forces. He could inspire devotion in the hardest of men and stir thoughts of victory in those

facing abject defeat. More than once it was Hitler's blind refusal to accept defeat that held the German army together. But then it was that same refusal to accept the inevitable that caused him to take Germany down to ultimate destruction.

Hitler was in reality a better politician than military commander. It was when he was using military force to resolve political disputes that he was at his best and when attempting to use politics to solve military problems that he was at his most useless. He was also a better soldier than he was a

commander. In the trenches of the Great War, Hitler excelled as a front line infantryman. His courage and skills were never in doubt, though it is telling that despite being awarded the Iron Cross Second and First Class, he was never put forward for promotion above the rank of corporal.

Nor can the true evil of the uses to which he put his military gifts be overlooked. Hitler did not use his gifts to save a peaceful nation from sudden danger nor to overcome tyranny. He used his military abilities, and the superb fighting machine

Hitler studying a map with his Staff, whom he treated more as underlings than assistants

of the German Wehrmacht, to spread evil, death and destruction across Europe. Even if Hitler had been a far greater military figure than in truth he was, these facts could be neither forgotten nor forgiven.

For Hitler military power was merely a means of furthering his agenda of retribution, extermination and conquest. He was always a Nazi first and a commander second.

DOVER
Ostende
BRUGGE
DOVER
Folkestone
St Omer
Valery-en Caux
Neufâchtel

1

HITLER'S HIGH COMMAND

Germany's senior generals were initially suspicious of Hitler's military abilities, but his early successes kept them quiet while his appointment of loyal men to key positions ensured obedience

When Hitler became Führer in 1933 he automatically became the head of the German armed forces. At that time the high command of the armed forces was a complex mixture of planners, staff officers and field commanders held together by a feeling of solidarity among the officer corps. There was space for group decision making, discussion and even dissent, although once a decision had been made the command structure was such that it could be carried out quickly and efficiently. Hitler was to change everything. He wanted absolute power over the military. The way he achieved this was to drive some officers to resign, others to question their duties and some to attempt the murder of the Führer.

During the Nazi rise to power, the army officer corps were not wholly hostile to Hitler and his party. Indeed, Hitler's failed 1923 putsch in Munich numbered the Great War hero General Erich von Ludendorff among its leaders. Nor were the generals opposed to one of the Nazi Party's central policies, that the Versailles Treaty which ended the Great War was unfair and needed revising. The treaty had put severe constraints on the German military and many senior officers wanted to shake these off.

The men of the Sturmabteilung on parade in Berlin. The SA was the enforcement arm of the Nazi Party

ABSOLUTE POWER

Once Hitler came to power, his desire to win over the military to whole-hearted support of himself was a dominant influence in persuading him to destroy the power of the Nazi storm troopers, the brown-shirted *Sturmabteilungen* or SA. The army officers jealously guarded the army's traditional right to be the only body in Germany authorized to carry arms and, as such, the ultimate guarantors of the constitution. Under the Versailles Treaty the army was allowed to be only 100,000 men strong. Ernst Röhm, the SA leader, had the basis of the armed might of Nazi Germany.

On the night of 30 June 1934, in an action that was to become infamous as the "Night of the Long Knives", Hitler ordered the murders of Röhm and dozens of other leading SA men, together with the disbanding of large numbers of stormtroopers. The immediate reaction of the army officers was to support Hitler's actions and welcome the overthrow of the SA. Some officers opposed the brutal and illegal methods used but most were prepared to overlook them.

One of the officers who turned a blind eye to what was done to the SA on the Night of the Long Knives was General Ludwig Beck. As adjutant general in the War Ministry, Beck was second to the Chief of the Army Staff, Kurt von Hammerstein-Equord. In the days preceding the murders of Röhm and others, Beck had taken Hitler's comments to mean that the members of the SA leadership were to be arrested on charges of treason and put in prison. He had, therefore, offered the army as an instrument to arrest the SA leaders and disarm the members, an offer that won Hitler's favor. Although in the event the SS

Ernst Röhm (left) and Edmund Heines led the SA and had ambitions to merge it with the army

was used to carry out the killings, that they had logistical support and weapons supplied by the army is undeniable; it is highly likely that the army was passed lists of those to be executed, and was able to confirm or veto a number of names.

Ludwig Beck was Chief of Staff 1936–38 but became disillusioned with Hitler

At the time this decision of Hitler's seemed unimportant, but by 1936 it was clear that the SS had come to include a number of paramilitary units armed in similar fashion to the regular army. In 1938 Hitler grouped these various units together to be the Waffen-SS, or armed SS, as a private army under the orders of himself, through Heinrich Himmler. Thus the army ended by getting, in the shape of the Waffen-SS, the rival to their monopoly of armed power that they had feared from the SA. The following years saw endless disputes between Himmler and the army high command as both tried to get the best of the new panzers and other equipment for their troops.

These difficulties were exacerbated by the very different internal morale of the two organizations. The army was officered by professional soldiers who were classically trained and usually came from aristocratic or wealthy families. The Waffen-SS took in recruits at the lowest level from all classes, and promoted exclusively from within. Even the most senior officers had worked their way up through the ranks and, unlike their army counterparts, were often from working class families. Nor were Waffen-SS relations with the army helped by the fanatical Nazism of the SS men, a fanaticism often considered "poor form" amongst the aristocratic Prussian officer class.

Hitler himself resolved the dispute when war broke out. He gave Himmler the task of administrating the Waffen-SS, but put the combat troops under direct army command. In time the Waffen-SS would grow in numbers. When the invasion of France took place about 120,000 men served in the Waffen-SS. When Russia was invaded there were about 210,000 and by autumn 1944 over half a million men were Waffen-SS. Friction with the army continued throughout the war. Hitler's obvious preference for SS men did little to help his increasingly strained relationship with the army commanders.

In 1934 the German President and aging hero Field Marshal Paul von Hindenburg died. Within hours, Goebbels had announced the abolition of the office of president. Supreme political power in Germany now rested in the person of the Führer: Adolf Hitler. At the same time, Hitler appointed himself head of the armed forces, changing the traditional oath taken by army officers from one of loyalty to the "people and the fatherland" to one of personal loyalty to "the Führer and Chancellor."

At the time the change was opposed by only a few officers, but this new focus of loyalty was later to be used as the basis for a ruthless imposition of Hitler's will on the army.

Hitler reorganized the armed forces. Under the new regime at the top was the *Oberkommando der Wehrmacht*, the OKW, of which he was head, responsible for the armed forces on behalf of the War Ministry. Detailed organization and planning for each service were undertaken by their own staff. *The Oberkommando des Heeres*, OKH, ran the army; the *Oberkommando der Luftwaffe*, OKL, ran the air force and the *Oberkommando der Kriegsmarine*, OKK, ran the navy.

Minister of Defense Werner von Blomberg, a conservative aristocrat, along with Beck, now chief

Werner von Blomberg resigned as Minister of War after a scandal

of the general staff of the army, formulated plans to expand the army to about 30 divisions, with many more trained men in reserve. This, the two generals calculated, would be enough to defend the Reich against an attack by any two neighboring countries. Their plans had barely begun to be implemented when in 1936 Hitler marched troops into the Rhineland. Beck and Blomberg both warned Hitler against the move, explaining that the army would be unable to defend Germany if France retaliated. France did not retaliate, so the credibility of Beck and Blomberg in Hitler's eyes was seriously damaged.

In the views of the senior, more conservative army officers, the Beck–Blomberg years were looked back on with favor. The army had been formulating its doctrine of Blitzkrieg (lit. lightning war) and was expanding rapidly, but the senior generals had still been in control. At this time the top generals were able to speak up against Hitler at meetings and to formulate their own plans. Perhaps more importantly, the Nazis were kept out of internal army matters including discipline. All that changed in 1938.

In February of that year Blomberg was forced to resign after Hitler discovered that the general's new, and much younger, wife was a former prostitute. At the same time, the commander-in-chief of the army, General Werner von Fritsch, was forced to resign over allegations of homosexuality, charges trumped up by Himmler and the SS. Both generals had been opposed to Hitler's military adventures in the Saarland and the Rhineland, and Hitler was glad to be rid of them; they were altogether too independent for his taste. In the wake of these resignations, the true extent of Hitler's plans for political and military dominance and for foreign conquests was becoming clear to Beck, but it was not until the crisis over the

Willhelm Keitel, Hitler's Chief of Staff throughout the war

Sudetenland in September of 1938 that Beck finally became disillusioned with Hitler. Friends of General Fritsch had appealed to him to persuade generals to mass resignation in support of Fritsch, and General Franz Halder, his soon-to-be successor as army chief of staff even went so far as to urge a raid on Gestapo headquarters, only to be bluntly told by Beck: "Mutiny and revolution are not words in the dictionary of a German officer!' In August he resigned, after submitting a paper highly critical of Hitler's apparent war intentions, but continued to keep in touch with the more traditional army officers.

The new figures then placed in the high command were more congenial to Hitler, and were more in tune with the views of the majority of junior army officers. Tens of thousands of young men were brought into the armed forces during the massive German rearmament of 1934 to 1938. Most of these saw only the growing confidence of the German nation and the way Hitler seemed to overcome insuperable odds and great obstacles.

Hitler chose as the new head of OKW the leader of Blomberg's private staff, an officer named Wilhelm Keitel. Keitel came from the proud class of old landowning families known as the Junkers, as did most of the conservative, professional officers. Until 1933, Keitel had shared most of the views and opinions of Blomberg and his fellow professionals, but after meeting Hitler for the first time, Keitel became overwhelmed by the sheer force of the Führer's personality. At one point, as the invasion of Russia seemed to be going well, Keitel described Hitler as the "grosster Feldherr aller Zeiten" (the greatest military leader of all time), a term contemptuously abbreviated by many of the great leader's soldiers to "Grofaz."

One observer said of Keitel, "Constantly in Hitler's presence after war began, he succumbed to his influence. From being an honorable, respectable general he developed into a servile flatterer." Others were less kind. They called the new head of OKW not Keitel but *Lakeitel*, or "toady." Keitel, was, however, an efficient staff officer who was able to ensure that even the more bizarre of Hitler's plans were carefully transformed into detailed orders for the army commanders and officers to follow. Keitel was to remain as head of OKW until after Hitler's death, being promoted to Field Marshal in 1940.

Another key appointment at OKW was the chief of the planning staff, responsible for the strategic planning and supervision of campaigns. Hitler gave

Field Marshal Alfred Jodl was deputy to Keitel and, like him, was hanged after the war

the job to General Alfred Jodl, a professional soldier who had served with distinction in the trenches. Jodl had known Hitler since 1923, though he was never close to the Führer and always avoided getting involved in politics. Even in his new post, he would severely reprimand any officer who talked politics on duty. For Jodl the task of OKW, and himself, was simply to carry out the wishes of the Führer in the military sphere.

Like Keitel, Jodl retained his position right to the end of the Third Reich, but in the later years his job became almost redundant. As Hitler took a greater and greater role in the detailed planning of operations, Jodl had less to do. He was completely excluded from the planning of Operation *Barbarossa*, the attack on Russia in 1941, and was rarely consulted about events on the Eastern Front. He did however continue to serve Hitler loyally by planning campaigns elsewhere, such as the invasion of Greece and the Ardennes Offensive of 1944.

NAZI CONNECTIONS

As head of OKH, Hitler chose another outwardly conservative officer who in reality could be relied upon to do as Hitler wanted. This was Walther von Brauchitsch, born in 1881 to one of the proudest of the Prussian military families. Like Hitler, Brauchitsch won the Iron Cross 1st Class in the trenches of the Great War. Unlike Hitler, he stayed in the army during peace time rising to become a senior figure at OKH, and was thus conveniently on hand in 1938 when Hitler was suddenly in need of a new head of OKH.

Hitler seems to have picked Brauchitsch not because the man was any more or less gifted than other officers, but because Hitler knew Frau Brauchitsch. The general's wife was a fanatical Nazi and besotted admirer of Hitler's. Nevertheless,

Hitler meets (l to r) Goering, Brauchitsch and Raeder, commanders of the Luftwaffe, army and navy, early in the war

Brauchitsch began his career at OKH by voicing concerns about the practicality of Hitler's plans to take over Austria. Although the army did, indeed, suffer some logistical problems as Brauchitsch had predicted, the overwhelming success of the operation made his earlier caution seem excessive. In March 1939 he again voiced private doubts to Hitler about the invasion of Czechoslovakia. Hitler attacked Brauchitsch with a furious tirade of words and insults. Again, Brauchitsch was proved to be wrong.

After being wrong twice, Brauchitsch decided to keep quiet in future. In the build up to the attack on Russia, Brauchitsch loyally drew up the details needed by Hitler's general strategy. In the height of summer 1941, when the panzers were being repaired, he urged Hitler to launch a single drive on Moscow to end the war quickly. Hitler ignored him and thereafter treated his advice with some contempt. In December 1941, Brauchitsch took advantage of heart trouble to resign.

With Brauchitsch gone as head of OKH, Hitler decided to take the position himself

Halder led the Army General Staff until Hitler sacked him in 1942

As a replacement for Halder at OKH, Hitler chose a youthful officer several ranks junior to Halder named Kurt von Zeitzler. Zeitzler came from the section in OKH which dealt with logistical planning and supply lines. His skills were great, but were largely limited to calculating the payloads of truck convoys or rail networks. He was a straightforward, efficient staff officer who, in the opinion of his contemporaries, lacked any gifts at handling armies or at planning campaigns. There can be little doubt that this was one of the main reasons Hitler chose him. By late 1943 however, Zeitzler had been sharp enough to realize that his main task was simply to carry out the wishes of the Führer, and then be blamed if events did not go according to plan. Wisely he managed to be conveniently ill during most of the crisis meetings of early 1944, staying in his quarters to recover rather than attending.

rather than entrust it to anyone else. Given his responsibilities elsewhere, Hitler was not on hand full time to act as head of OKH, so much responsibility fell to his deputy, Franz Halder. Like Jodl, Keitel and Brauchitsch, Halder came from a distinguished military family, though Halder was a Bavarian. Unlike the others, however, Halder was not handpicked by Hitler. Indeed, Hitler had been dubious about making Halder Brauchitsch's deputy in 1938 due to Halder's strict Catholicism and support for the old German royal family. Hitler would certainly not have appointed Halder had he known the general routinely referred to him in the mid-1930s as "the Austrian lunatic." However, Halder was a good professional soldier who kept his private political opinions outside his job. This did not stop him from voicing his disquiet to Hitler at private meetings about the attack on Russia. In September 1942 Halder and Hitler disagreed openly about the strategy to be employed at Stalingrad, and Halder resigned. Hitler never really forgave him for being right on this occasion.

Kurt Zeitzler, a master of logistics, became head of the Army General Staff in 1942

It was through these senior men in the high command of the armed forces that Hitler sought to control the Wehrmacht. After the resignation of Brauchitsch it was only Hitler, Keitel and, to an extént, Jodl, who had access to reports and analysis from every front. Only they knew what was really going on. Even the most senior of Field Marshals knew only what was happening in the area where they were operating, and were kept totally in the dark about what was happening elsewhere. Hitler hoped that he would therefore be in a position to control absolutely the Wehrmacht and its commanders.

The traditions of the German officer class dated back to the Prussian army, but they were fundamentally at odds with Nazi doctrine

Despite this degree of control, Hitler still had to deal with the various Field Marshals and Generals who held operational control on the ground. At the outbreak of the war the two most senior army commanders were Gerd von Rundstedt and Fedor von Bock. Both men were superbly trained Prussian officers of the old school who had served with distinction in the Great War. Between them, these two men commanded the main attacking forces which

Von Rundstedt retired in 1938, but was recalled by Hitler, only to be sacked in 1941, recalled in 1942 and sacked again in 1945

crushed Poland in 1939 and France in 1940. In 1941 the same two men, now promoted to be Field Marshals, led the central and southern army groups in Operation *Barbarossa*. The northern Army Group was led by Wilhelm von Leeb, a career officer from Bavaria.

None of these three Field Marshals were close to Hitler and all were viewed with some suspicion by the Führer. Most distrusted of all was Leeb, who in 1923 had been the commander who was instrumental in suppressing the Nazi putsch in Munich. As soon as Hitler came to power, the Gestapo investigated Leeb for subversive activities and he was removed from his post. But Leeb was careful to stay out of politics and was so well regarded by Brauchitsch that he regained high command.

After the initial failure of Operation *Barbarossa* to destroy Russia before winter, Hitler looked for scapegoats and found them in Leeb, Rundstedt and Bock. All three were sacked. Leeb retired to his estate in Bavaria and Bock was later killed in an air raid. Only Rundstedt was not dispensed with completely and was given command of reserve forces in Germany. A few months later, Rundstedt was put in charge of the Germans occupying France. By 1944 this was proving to be a crucial command. When Rundstedt suggested that, with the British and Americans ashore in Normandy, it would be a wise decision to make peace, Hitler sacked him once again.

These dismissals of high-profile, competent commanders served several purposes for Hitler. They ensured the removal of men who were rather too quick to criticize. They ensured that the men promoted to take their places were grateful to the Führer. Finally, the sackings sent a very clear signal throughout the officer corps that those who opposed the will of Hitler could expect similarly abrupt treatment.

Wilhelm von Leeb was a dedicated anti-Nazi but a talented commander who did well in Poland and France

In any case, Hitler preferred younger and more daring men. There can be no doubt that his favorite general in the first years of war was Erwin Rommel. Born the son of a schoolteacher, Rommel was very different from the stuffy aristocratic army officers that Hitler disliked. He was lucky

Von Rundstedt (left) and Rommel commanded the Western Front in 1944 and were sacked for warning the Allies would win

Rommel's hero status was enhanced by numerous anecdotes. During one advance he spotted a field hospital and ordered his driver to pull up so he could visit the wounded. Rommel strode into the tents, lined with beds holding troops of both sides. Spotting a German soldier gawping at him, Rommel went to speak to him. The wounded man hissed, "Herr General, this is a British hospital!" Glancing around, Rommel realized that the only armed men in sight were, indeed, British. Saluting the doctors cheerfully, Rommel walked back to his car and told the driver, "I think we had better leave." The British had, apparently, mistaken Rommel's German for Polish.

After the final defeat of the Afrika Korps in 1943 by overwhelming Allied forces, Rommel took sick leave. With time to catch up with information about the war outside North Africa, Rommel became pessimistic. His earlier admiration for Hitler waned abruptly as he saw the blunders occurring in the east and Hitler's growing refusal

enough to have been appointed to the command of Hitler's personal guard during the invasions of Czechoslovakia and Poland. Hitler liked Rommel and gave him command of the 7th Panzer Division in the invasion of France. In February 1941 Hitler put Rommel at the head of the Afrika Korps. For the next 18 months Rommel led his troops in campaigns of swift movement across the deserts of North Africa, earning for himself the nickname Desert Fox.

"Fast Heinz" Guderian was a superlative panzer commander

to accept reality. In 1944 Hitler sent Rommel to defend Normandy. When D-Day put the western Allies into France, Rommel advised Hitler to make peace. Only the fact that Rommel was injured in an air raid saved him from being sacked. He travelled back to Germany to recover from his wounds.

The type of swift-moving panzer warfare at which Rommel excelled had actually been developed by another younger officer, Heinz Guderian, who earned himself the nickname of "Fast Heinz." When Hitler came to power, opinion in the German army was split between those who saw future wars in terms of the static defenses and fortifications that had dominated the Great War and those, led by Guderian, who foresaw wars of movement spearheaded by tanks and aircraft. It was Hitler who settled the dispute in favor of Guderian's ideas and who ordered the rearming of Germany with panzers and Stuka dive-bombers. Guderian commanded panzer groups in Poland, France and in Russia with startling success. In December 1941, however, he disobeyed a direct order from Hitler and withdrew troops from an exposed position. Hitler sacked him.

Probably the finest German strategist of the war, Erich von Manstein was sacked in 1944 when he disagreed with Hitler

WARNING IGNORED

In March 1943, Hitler reinstated Guderian as the inspector general of all panzer divisions, charged with equipping and supplying the crucial armored units. Guderian again performed his task well, ensuring the new Panther and Tiger tanks were supplied to the front line troops as speedily as possible. By March 1944, however, Guderian had become convinced the war was going to be lost. Although he tried to advise Hitler that even the new panzers would not counteract the Russian superiority in numbers, he was ignored.

Almost the same age as Guderian was Erich von Manstein, another early supporter of the Blitzkrieg doctrine. It was Manstein who produced the detailed plan for the invasion of France in 1940 which led to spectacular victory. He was rewarded by Hitler with an independent command, LVI Panzer Corps, in the invasion of Russia. Unlike many other senior officers, Manstein kept his command through the winter of 1941, largely by not arguing openly with Hitler. After his defeat at Kursk in 1943, however, Manstein too came to believe that the war with Russia could not be won and lost his faith in Hitler's military leadership.

At a conference of senior officers in March 1944, Hitler was making a speech outlining his plans for the coming summer campaign. As usual by this stage in the war, Hitler's plans had more to do with wishful thinking than actual reality. As usual the officers were listening with dutiful attention, whatever their private views. When Hitler paused after delivering himself of some high flown piece of rhetoric, Manstein's sarcastic voice cut the silence, "Oh yes, my Führer. I am certain it will be so." There was a long silence while Hitler glared at Manstein before storming from the room. Manstein went home.

By the early summer of 1944 most of the senior generals, even those who had been among Hitler's most open admirers, thought that the war was lost. Many of them were in despair at Hitler's actions and words, foreseeing only disaster for Germany. But Hitler's absolute grip on the levers of power made it impossible for the generals to oust him. They could advise Hitler, but if he ignored them, as he often did, they had no real choices except to carry out his orders or resign. Relations between Hitler and his senior officers were disastrous. Most generals were disillusioned, but felt powerless to do anything other than watch Germany's slow slide to defeat.

A few army officers, however, were determined to do something to save Germany. Their plans varied greatly, but all involved the death of Adolf Hitler. Between September 1943 and February 1944 there were four failed assassination attempts, after which the Gestapo arrested or placed under surveillance many of those known to be anti-Nazi.

One officer who escaped Gestapo attention was Colonel Count Claus von Stauffenberg, a career officer from one of Prussia's oldest military families. In the early war years, Stauffenberg had been an admirer of Hitler but by December 1943 he was a staff officer, having lost a hand and an eye in action. Seeing Hitler at close quarters cured Stauffenberg of his admiration and convinced him that Hitler had to be overthrown.

Stauffenberg contacted a number of other middle ranking officers in key positions throughout the Reich. Many agreed with him that the war should be ended and some said they would help bring this about. Stauffenberg had two main problems. First, he had to arrange for Hitler to be killed or arrested. Second, he had to have the means to seize control of the government before the fanatically Nazi SS could do so. In June Stauffenberg was promoted to be Chief of Staff of the Home Army, those Wehrmacht forces located in Germany itself. In his new position he would be able to give orders for the army to seize the SS and the government buildings. He was also in frequent personal contact with Hitler himself and could get close enough to kill him.

Stauffenberg hurriedly contacted his sympathizers in various commands and alerted them to the need to take swift action against the SS and Gestapo. Stauffenberg knew that many senior generals were disillusioned with Hitler, but that they were already under surveillance by the Gestapo. He decided to rely on these senior men to follow his lead, but did not contact them directly for fear of alerting the Gestapo. One senior figure who was brought into the conspiracy was General Ludwig Beck, the former chief of staff at OKH who had resigned in 1938. He was to be the interim head of state once Hitler was dead.

Stauffenberg contacted junior and staff officers. Some were fully aware of the conspiracy, others did not want to know details of what was going on but had assured Stauffenberg they would follow his instructions. The conspiracy was given the codeword Valkyrie.

On 20 July Stauffenberg, along with other high-ranking officers, attended a meeting with Hitler at the Wolf's Lair. He placed a briefcase packed with explosives on a 15-minute fuse under Hitler's desk and left. At 12.42pm the Führer's office exploded in flames and smoke. Hearing the explosion, Stauffenberg sent out the radio signals instructing his co-conspirators to begin seizing power. Then he raced back to Berlin to play his part.

Claus von Stauffenberg (left) came from an old, Catholic, military family. In 1944 he led the plot to assassinate Hitler

THE MANHUNT BEGINS

Hitler, however, had not been killed. By chance he had stepped around the desk and was shielded from the blast by its solid wooden frame.

Stauffenberg tried to put the Valkyrie plan into action anyway, but only some conspirators played their part. Others were too frightened to move now they knew Hitler was alive or hoped to evade punishment by betraying their colleagues. Only in Paris did the conspiracy take place as planned, with the army arresting the SS and Gestapo men before preparing for an armistice with the Allies.

By midnight the confusion caused by the attempted coup was over. Stauffenberg and his three closest allies at Home Army HQ were shot. Beck shot himself, but survived and was also executed out of hand. Before dawn Josef Goebbels, propaganda minister, and Heinrich Himmler, head of the SS, were firmly in control in Berlin. Stauffenberg had carelessly left written records of some of his agreements with other officers. The SS began the hunt for the conspirators.

As the weeks passed the SS and Hitler were amazed at how many army officers had been involved in the plot or had known something was about to happen. On 7 August the trial of Field Marshal von Witzleben and seven other officers began, in the *Volksgericht*, the so-called People's Court, under Roland Freisler. After a few days of abuse and insults, the men were found guilty and hanged. For months the investigations, sudden arrests and show trials continued as Himmler oversaw a reign of terror. About 5,000 people were arrested in the course of the investigations into the bomb plot and 200 officers, including over 50 generals, were executed. Many hundreds more died in prison or in concentration camps.

Some high profile names were involved. Franz Halder was arrested and had his earlier opposition

Von Stauffenberg was an aristocrat and staunch Catholic representing the old German values

to Hitler used against him, but he persuaded the Gestapo that he had known nothing about the Stauffenberg plot. He was sent to Dachau concentration camp for his views. Luckier was Heinz Guderian who had known about the plot, but had refused to join it. He was on a hunting trip when Stauffenberg exploded the bomb, so the Gestapo concluded he had not been involved at all.

The most high profile casualty of the purge that followed the failed coup was Field Marshal Erwin Rommel. The Desert Fox had been considering his own plan to arrest Hitler and put him on trial for war crimes when he had been approached by one of Stauffenberg's conspirators. Rommel had welcomed the approach, but had not committed himself before he was injured and put out of action. Hitler was astonished that Rommel, of all men, had been so deeply implicated. But Rommel was a hero to the German people. Hitler gave him the choice of committing suicide and being honored as a war hero, or being put on trial and executed along with his wife. Rommel chose to kill himself.

The July bomb plot of Stauffenberg marked the final break down of trust between Hitler and his army officers. After July 20 no army officer was allowed to enter the same room as Hitler without being relieved of his pistol by the ever-present SS guards. Hitler stopped believing anything the army officers told him, unless it was backed up by a report from the SS or Gestapo.

On August 15 Field Marshal von Kluge was on a trip to inspect his forward positions facing the British in France when a British bomber destroyed his radio truck. When Hitler sent a message to Kluge that evening, he was told the Field Marshal was at the front but out of radio contact. Hitler at once assumed that Kluge had been involved in the bomb plot and was sneaking off to surrender to the British. When Kluge got back to his headquarters he found that he had been relieved of command and was ominously ordered to return to Berlin for questioning. He committed suicide on the plane to Berlin, having a very good idea of what was awaiting him there.

As Hitler's distrust of the army grew, so the grip of the Nazi machine over the army strengthened. In September the Nazi salute became the obligatory replacement for the conventional army salute. The officers of the staff who worked with Hitler were redesignated as Nazi Party officers. Every senior officer had a Gestapo officer attached to his staff to supervise his actions and monitor his dedication to the Nazi Party and to Hitler. Increasingly, senior

officers were stripped of the power to command their forces. Every action, every disposition had to be approved by the Führer's staff before it could take place. And Hitler insisted his staff did nothing without his approval.

The slow paralysis which afflicted so many operations of the German army in the final year of war came directly from Hitler's distrust of his generals after the bomb plot. In February 1945 Hitler sent out a general order on the conduct of operations. Among other provisions it read:

*"**Divisional Commanders are personally responsible for reporting to me in good time any of the following:***

- **Every attack planned in divisional strength or above**
- **Every offensive in quiet sectors of the front of battalion strength or above**
- **Every plan for withdrawing forces**
- **Every plan to surrender a local strong point.**
- **They must ensure that I have time to consider the plan and to intervene in time for my orders to reach the front line.**
- **Commanders in chief, generals and all staff officers are personally responsible to me that every report made to me should contain nothing but the truth.**
- **I shall impose draconian punishments on any attempt at concealment from carelessness, oversight or deliberate action."**

Hitler was attempting to manage the war down to the actions of every battalion. Such a task was beyond the abilities of any one person, let alone a man so trapped by paranoia and distrust as Hitler. In the collapse of trust between Hitler and his commanders lay the collapse of the ability of the German army to wage war effectively.

Großadmiral Dr. h. c. Raeder

2

THE OTHER SERVICES

Hitler prided himself on his army career and knowledge, but neither the navy nor the air force really interested him. His failure to appreciate naval warfare led him fatally to underestimate Britain's power

Hitler was, first and foremost, an army man. He had served in the army during the four long years of the Great War when he lived in the trenches of the Western Front for months at a time, and the topic was never far from his mind. Even as the Russians closed in on Berlin, Hitler would treat his captive audience in the Führerbunker to long monologues on the good old days in the trenches. When he first became Führer, it was to the army that he first turned his attention. For Hitler the air force had interest only in so far as it served the army. The navy was barely of interest at all. And yet if Germany was to live up to Hitler's pretensions to world power, it would need a navy to project that power.

The German navy had been secretly re-equipping itself for war before Hitler came to power. Under the terms of the Versailles Treaty, the Germans were forbidden to have any submarines at all, and surface ships were restricted to 10,000 metric tons, less than a third the size considered necessary for a battleship and barely large enough for a light cruiser. The navy had no intention

Admiral Erich Raeder, head of the Kriegsmarine, 1935–43

of being bound by these restrictions, but through the 1920s were hindered by the politicians, who feared that the building of large warships could neither be hidden nor explained away.

CRUISER MAN

In 1928 Erich Raeder was appointed Commander-in-Chief of the Reichsmarine and given instructions to make the navy as effective as possible within the terms of Versailles. Significantly, during the 1920s, Raeder had been writing the official history of the cruiser operations of the First World War, having served in cruisers for most of the war. It was as a cruiser man that he looked at the problem.

In drawing up plans to make the German navy an effective weapon of war, Raeder made a number of assumptions. First he reasoned that German naval operations would be limited to inshore work in support of the army in the event of a war against any likely enemy, except Britain. Second, Raeder

believed that if Britain were the main enemy then Germany would have to aim to strangle Britain's sea supply routes. Germany could attempt to take on the Royal Navy and defeat it in open battle, but this would need the construction of large battleships, which Versailles forbade. Alternatively, Germany could develop a fleet of ships designed specifically to sink merchant ships and to avoid rather than defeat the Royal Navy.

The most obvious type of warship to achieve this was the U-boat, but again Germany was forbidden to have any submarines in its fleet. Not daunted, Raeder turned to the small team of engineers who had been recruited in 1925 by Wilhelm Canaris, the future head of the Abwehr, German military intelligence, to design U-boats in case Germany was ever allowed to own any. Under Raeder this team began building U-boats for

The tiny U1 of 1906 was the first of many submarines in German service

export to Turkey and Spain. Thus, the Germans gained the equipment and expertise necessary to build and operate a U-boat fleet but without contravening Versailles.

In 1931, Raeder recruited a former German naval U-boat captain named A.D. Bräutigam who had been implementing the Japanese submarine program. Bräutigam was put in charge of testing U-boat designs and training crews. During 1933 a submarine school was opened in Kiel-Wik on the Baltic coast. The school's first course began with eight officers and 75 seamen undergoing training in torpedo firing, convoy attack tactics and methods for evading enemy destroyers.

The equipment for this course verged on the farcical. Correct navigation with a periscope, for instance, was taught by building a shed on the deck of a tug. The navigation officer was put in the shed with a mirror mounted in a tube, which served as a periscope, and told to shout steering instructions to the tug helmsman through an open window. Such methods were improved in 1935 when Finland agreed to lend a submarine for training purposes.

Although Germany was acquiring trained crews and experience in U-boat design, its navy as yet had no actual submarines. In 1934 the steel parts for twelve U-boats were made in the Ruhr under conditions of such secrecy that the different teams making the various components had no idea what the parts were for. The following year the parts were put together in heavily guarded warehouses in Kiel and on 15 June 1935 the first of the U-boats was launched. This was the *U1*, a small coastal craft which would be unfit for the open ocean, but could raid merchant shipping off Europe's shores. By 1937 six U-boats were operational.

British concern at these moves was mollified by Hitler's foreign policy adviser, Joachim Ribbentrop, who signed a British proposal outlawing the type of unrestricted submarine warfare that had caused the Royal Navy so many problems in the First World War. Germany, like many other nations, was now pledged to the policy that U-boats would torpedo ships only after giving their crews due warning and time to take to their boats. This, of course, would give any other ships in the vicinity time to escape and seriously hampered the effectiveness of the submarine as a sinker of merchant ships. Hitler had no intention of sticking to Ribbentrop's promise if war with Britain ever came about, but it allowed him to continue to build up the undersea fleet.

In September 1935 the growing U-boat flotilla was put under the command of Captain Karl Dönitz. Unlike most other naval officers, Dönitz was to become close to Hitler and had a reputation for being able to placate the Führer even when he was in one of his most dangerous temper fits. In 1945, Hitler was to appoint Dönitz as his successor as Führer, over the heads of many other Nazi or military figures.

Born in 1891, Dönitz was a career naval officer who served in cruisers at the start of the First World War. In 1916, however, he transferred to the command of U68 and pioneered the tactic of coordinating attacks on convoys with two or more U-boats. In October 1918, his U-boat was sunk in the course of just such an attack. He was held prisoner by the British until 1919 and while in prison he further developed his concept of joint attack. He remained an officer in the much reduced German navy of the 1920s and by the time he took command of the new U-boat flotilla he had fully developed the attack strategy that was dubbed "the wolf pack."

Raeder (left) and Dönitz who followed him as head of the navy

Dönitz believed that U-boats should operate in groups up to a dozen strong. They would lie scattered across a wide area of ocean until one of them found a convoy. This U-boat would promptly dive and follow the convoy unseen. At night it would surface and radio the other U-boats in the pack to gather ahead of the convoy. Dönitz knew that the British had ASDIC, a method of using sound waves to locate a U-boat underwater. But he also knew it was ineffective if

the U-boat was on the surface. Dönitz therefore instructed his captains to attack on the surface at night when they would be virtually invisible to the eye and undetected by ASDIC.

By the time war broke out Dönitz had 55 operational U-boats under his command. He was blunt in his appraisal that to defeat Britain he would need 300, but he never got them.

While Dönitz was developing the U-boat service, Raeder had been closely studying the provisions of the Versailles Treaty regarding surface ships. He realized that although the total size of individual ships was limited, Versailles said nothing about their weaponry or other features. Raeder ordered the design of warships equipped with massive, battleship-sized guns mounted on a hull able to outrun the main Royal Navy battlefleet and small enough to be legal under Versailles. With these ships Raeder hoped to be able to destroy British merchant shipping while avoiding a full scale battle.

The first of these ships, dubbed "pocket-battleships," was the *Deutschland*, laid down in 1929. She displaced 11,700 metric tons, though Raeder claimed it was only 9,800 metric tons, and carried six 11 inch guns together with eight 5.9 inch guns, torpedoes and anti-aircraft guns. Equipped with eight enormous diesel engines, she could steam at 28 knots for sustained periods. By 1931 three such ships were under construction, entering service in 1933 and 1935 as *Deutschland*, *Admiral Scheer* and *Admiral Graf Spee*.

By the time the pocket-battleships were in service, Raeder had moved on to bigger and better things. When Hitler came to power in 1933 he made it very clear he expected the navy to be able

The pocket battleship Deutschland *in her peacetime paint scheme. In 1940 she was renamed the Lützow after she was damaged in the invasion of Norway, as Admiral Raeder worried that the loss of a ship with such a prestigious name as "Deutschland" might be taken as a bad omen*

Battle cruiser Gneisenau

to defeat the French and the British naval power. In response, Raeder put forward what he called "Plan Z." Announced in 1935, this ten year plan envisaged the construction of six battleships of 56,000 metric tons, four battleships of 42,000 metric tons, three battle cruisers of 31,000 metric tons, two aircraft carriers and a vast supporting fleet of cruisers and destroyers and 267 U-boats. Plan Z shifted the balance in types of warships because the main naval enemy was seen now as France, not Britain. While Britain could be strangled by the sinking of merchant ships, France would only be defeated if her battleships were destroyed.

The battle cruisers were laid down in 1935 and two of them were completed by the outbreak of war in 1939. These were the *Scharnhorst* and *Gneisenau*, both of 32,000 metric tons and equipped with nine 11-inch guns, twelve 6-inch guns and a variety of anti-aircraft guns. Hitler intervened in the construction of these ships. Raeder had wanted 14-inch guns for the main armament, but Hitler knew the British would view such massive guns on fast, well-armored warships as a direct challenge to the Royal Navy, and Hitler wanted to remain on amicable terms with Britain.

FAVORABLE TERMS

In 1935 Hitler had signed the Anglo-German Naval Treaty which allowed Germany a fleet of about a third the size of the Royal Navy. Not only was this a major increase in the German navy compared to the rules of the Versailles Treaty, but it also meant the two fleets would not be too different in size in European waters, as much of the Royal Navy was scattered around the Empire. Hitler, pleased with this treaty, thought Britain was proving to be very friendly. He instructed Raeder to use the smaller guns on the battle cruisers and to save the big guns for the battleships.

The battleship Bismarck with eight 15-inch guns was Germany's most powerful warship

In 1936 the first two of the big battleships were laid down, though they were not to be completed until 1940. These were *Bismarck* and *Tirpitz*, the two great ships that would dominate the thinking of the admirals while the actual fighting was largely left to the U-boats and smaller ships. These huge warships displaced 42,000 metric tons and were equipped with the mighty 15-inch guns, eight on each ship, as well as a variety of smaller guns and anti-aircraft weapons. The armor on these ships was formidable. There was one armored deck 2 inches thick, backed by a second 5 inches thick, while the gun turrets were encased in 14 inches of steel and the command bridge in 8 inches.

When war actually broke out in 1939, Raeder and the Kriegsmarine, as the war navy was by then known, were not even halfway through their rearmament program. In the event, Raeder was never called upon to sink the French battleships, as the army crushed France before the naval war got underway. The naval enemy was now Britain, as had been envisaged in the days before Plan Z. Painfully aware that his fleet was unable to compete with Britain's, Raeder persuaded Hitler to occupy the Atlantic coast of France to give his ships and U-boats forward bases from which to operate. The unequal fight against the Royal Navy was about to begin.

HMS Courageous was sunk by a U-boat in September 1939

The sea war had gotten off to a fair start for Germany. In September 1939 a U-boat torpedoed and sank the British aircraft carrier HMS *Courageous* and in October the battleship HMS *Royal Oak* also went to the bottom. In November the German heavy cruisers *Scharnhorst* and *Gneisenau* broke out into the Atlantic, sank the cruiser HMS *Rawalpindi* and got home again safely. In the Indian Ocean and South Atlantic the pocket battleship *Graf Spee* was sinking British merchant ships with ease.

Then, on 13 December 1939, the *Graf Spee* encountered three British cruisers, one from New Zealand. In the fight that followed, all four ships were damaged and the *Graf Spee* put into the neutral harbour of Montevideo for repairs. Convinced that a large British fleet was waiting just over the horizon, Admiral Langsdorf scuttled his ship, then committed suicide. Hitler was unimpressed. From his point of view, he had been persuaded to spend large sums of money on the navy by Raeder, money which could have been spent on panzers, and now the navy sank itself.

The U-boats were, however, doing better. By the end of 1939 they had sunk over 100 British merchant ships. When the U-boats began to operate out of ports in western France the kill rate went up considerably. Between June and December 1940 they sank 3 million metric tons of British shipping. In November the pocket battleship *Admiral Scheer* broke into the Atlantic, sinking 16 ships and causing the complete disruption of British convoys for two weeks before she returned to port. In December the trick was repeated by the cruiser *Hipper*.

In February 1941 Hitler stepped in to intervene. He ordered the U-boats to go to the Mediterranean to protect the transport of the Afrika Korps to Tripoli. Although Raeder protested and complained, Hitler insisted that several U-boats stay in the Mediterranean to protect supplies to Rommel. He did not authorize an increase in U-boat production nor crew training to take account of these increased responsibilities. That would have drained resources from the buildup for the coming war with Russia.

Raeder was furious. He and his U-boat commander Karl Dönitz estimated they needed 300 U-boats in the Atlantic to starve Britain into surrender by the end of the year. They had only 30. In May 1941 Raeder persuaded Hitler to let loose the biggest weapon in the German navy, the battleship *Bismarck*.

The *Bismarck* was laid down in 1936 at a time when Raeder had been ordered to build a navy able to crush the French fleet in battle. Although built for battle, the *Bismarck* was a fast, heavily armed ship suitable for mounting decisive long range raids on merchant ships. She could sink any British convoy protection ships with ease, and was vulnerable to only the largest British battleships. Raeder estimated that with the *Bismarck* at large in the Atlantic, the British would have to cancel all convoys. This was almost as good as sinking them, for it meant Britain would be starved of food.

the *Bismarck*. Fortunately for the British it turned out that the *Bismarck*'s steering control had been damaged. She was cornered by an overwhelmingly superior British force. After a bitter fight, the *Bismarck* was sunk.

This event had a profound effect on Hitler. Never very interested in the navy, Hitler now refused to allow the building of any new large ships. The battleship *Tirpitz*, a sister to the *Bismarck*, was the last capital ship the Germans built during the war. Nor would Hitler allow the few ships he did have to go out on extended raiding voyages. *Tirpitz* was kept in a succession of docks and fjords in Norway from which it occasionally put to sea to attack convoys between Britain and Russia.

On 29 December 1942 a powerful German fleet led by the pocket battleship *Lützow* and the heavy cruiser *Hipper* set out from Norway to attack the British convoy JW51B heading for Russia. They struck at dawn on December 31, but found the convoy protected by a stronger escort than expected. In a confused fight two British warships were sunk and others badly damaged, while the Germans lost one destroyer and sustained serious damage to the *Hipper*. Not a single merchant ship had been hit.

When he heard the news, Hitler was furious and gave vent to one of his towering rages. He summoned Raeder and gave him a direct order to decommission the large warships as they were a complete waste of money and manpower. Raeder objected, but Hitler's anger knew no limits and Raeder was subjected to a vicious stream of insults and abuse. He resigned and played no further part in the war, reappearing only at the Nuremberg trials, where he was sentenced to life imprisonment. Hitler refused to hear his name spoken again.

HMS Hood fires on Bismarck before she is sunk by the German

On 21 May the *Bismarck* put to sea with the cruiser *Prinz Eugen* and headed for the North Atlantic. The two ships were spotted and shadowed by a pair of British cruisers, which called in the battleship *Prince of Wales* and heavy battlecruiser *Hood* to confront the Germans. With eight 15-inch guns on the *Hood* and ten 14-inch guns on the *Prince of Wales*, the British had a clear advantage over the Germans, with eight 15-inch guns on the *Bismarck* and only eight 8-inch guns on the *Prinz Eugen*. But when battle commenced at dawn on May 24, the *Prince of Wales* was badly damaged and the *Hood* blew up, sinking in seconds.

Raeder proudly passed the news on to Hitler. The Führer was delighted at the sinking of Britain's largest and most famous warship and sent a personal message of congratulations to the *Bismarck* crew. In panic the British rerouted or canceled all convoys and called in almost their entire fleet to track down

OPEN TO ATTACK

The new head of the Kriegsmarine was the head of U-boats, Karl Dönitz. Ironically, Dönitz's first achievement was to persuade Hitler to keep the big warships in commission. They were to be kept in heavily defended ports and not to be sent to sea. In this role they tied down large numbers of British warships, which were therefore not escorting the convoys, leaving them open to attack by U-boats.

Hitler told Dönitz to concentrate on the U-boat campaign and finally agreed to increase the production of submarines. The output of U-boats was increased to 40 per month and a new, long range model was authorized for service. It was, however, already too late. By 1943 the British had long range air cover over most of the Atlantic together with greatly improved location devices and depth charges. By May Dönitz had lost 87 U-boats, so he pulled his fleet out of the main convoy routes. In July Hitler took a break from concentrating on Russia to realize what had happened and ordered Dönitz back to the attack. In the first 30 days of the renewed U-boat war 64 German submarines were sunk. Dönitz pulled them out of action once again.

Finally, Britain was safe. Victory in the Battle of Britain had meant she could not be invaded. Now the defeat of the U-boats meant she could not be starved. There can be no doubt that Hitler himself was primarily responsible for these failures of the Wehrmacht. He had not believed Britain would refuse to make peace and so had made no plans for either a quick invasion or for a long naval war.

Just as conventional armed units were being built up in the 1930s, so was the murkier world of the spy and intelligence services. The infamous secret police organization, the Gestapo, is well known for its brutal suppression of political dissidence, but was then quite well known to

be a spy organization. That task was left largely with the Abwehr, or military intelligence, which was based in an anonymous office block in the Tirpitz Ufer side street of Berlin. The office was known as the Fuchsbau, or Fox Lair, to those who worked there and their task was dubbed the Game of Foxes.

Abwehr chief Admiral Wilhelm Canaris opposed Hitler

The chief of the foxes was Admiral Wilhelm Canaris, who had an exemplary record as a fighting seaman in the First World War. After the war ended, Canaris continued in the navy as a key player in the secret moves to gain modern weapons and training contrary to the Versailles Treaty. When Hitler came to power in 1933, Canaris welcomed the move, for he had forged contacts with several key Nazis. On January 1, 1935 Canaris became the head of the Abwehr.

Prior to the arrival of Canaris, the Abwehr had been a small and not terribly successful organization. It had largely contented itself with gathering information about the armed forces of other countries, rarely doing more than collating what was publicly available in newspapers. Canaris changed everything—and to do it he had a vast supply of money and resources supplied to him at Hitler's direct orders. Canaris began by installing an agent in each German Embassy with specific instructions to recruit agents in that nation's armed forces or armaments industry. He then established a new division devoted to planning sabotage and to producing the necessary equipment and recruiting agents able to fulfill the plans. Meanwhile, he forged close links with the Gestapo to trap foreign spies in Germany.

When he arrived at the Abwehr office block, Canaris found the organization already had an effective spy ring in the armaments industry of the USA. The ring had been begun in 1927 with the aim of bribing workers to hand over secret plans, and it was doing remarkably well. A string of top secret weapon plans flooded into Germany from the spy ring, known as Operation *Sexton* from the false name used by the man running the network. The greatest coup of this ring was to filch the plans of the superbly accurate Norden bombsight, with which the Luftwaffe was quickly equipped. This enormously successful spy ring went entirely unsuspected by the American FBI, whose task it was to track down enemy agents.

The American spy ring was the most outstanding, but the Abwehr had agents elsewhere. The military and political circles of France, Belgium, Poland, Czechoslovakia and Holland were riddled with Abwehr agents, who also had no scruples infiltrating the ranks of their own allies in Italy and Hungary.

Britain was, however, largely ignored by the Abwehr. Hitler was busy using German princes who were related to the British aristocracy and Royal Family to gain information and push the case for appeasement and peace. Although the recipients of such German flattery were friendly enough, the princes had to report there was little prospect of any British nobleman betraying his country, though some could be used to urge peace. The lavish attention poured on the Prince of Wales was effort wasted when he abdicated the throne he had taken as Edward VIII in 1936. The less glamorous but robustly patriotic George VI became the new king.

German attempts to infiltrate the British political system also came badly unstuck. The British Fascist Party, led by former government minister Sir Oswald Mosley, showed great support for Hitler and his ideas. But as soon as war looked likely, the Blackshirts, as they were known, declared total loyalty to Britain. As a result, it was not until war had actually broken out that the Abwehr made any serious efforts to infiltrate agents into Britain. Their activities were to be marked by failure, though this was not immediately obvious to the Germans.

Hitler's main problem with the Abwehr and with spying in general, was that Canaris and most of his men were officers of great deviousness, but also with an old school sense of honor. They served Germany, but were none too impressed by the Nazis, and unlike many regular army officers, the Abwehr was in a position to know exactly what was going on.

In September 1939, the Abwehr officers working in Poland reported back to Canaris that large scale executions of Jews, politicians, nobility and Catholics were taking place behind the advancing units of the regular army. Canaris and his men were appalled but, like so many other Germans, did not believe Hitler knew about the killings being carried out on the orders of Himmler, head of the SS and Gestapo. Canaris went to see Hitler to raise the subject, but was stopped by General Wilhelm Keitel, head of the Wehrmacht general staff. Keitel told Canaris that the mass killings were being carried out on the orders of the Führer. Hitler had originally ordered the army to carry out the killings, but after Keitel refused he had turned to Himmler and the SS.

Canaris was shocked, and soon afterward was staggered when Hitler went back on all his promises made before the invasion of Poland and declared that Britain had to be crushed. From his wide ranging contacts and spies, Canaris knew Britain would enjoy the support of the USA sooner or later. He also knew that if the USA declared war on Germany the war would be lost.

What happened next is unclear, for Canaris was notoriously secretive. It is clear, however, that from October 1939 onward the outstanding success of the Abwehr under Canaris began to go wrong. Mistakes were made, opportunities were missed and incompetence grew. For instance, the highly successful operation in the USA collapsed after a complete list of all German agents was sent to a radio operator in the ring who was known to be unreliable. Seeing a chance to get out of his double life, the agent, William Sebold, went to the police and turned over the names of the 37 top agents.

The impact of the many intelligence failures began to affect operations as the war progressed. Many believe that Canaris set out deliberately to undermine his own country and Hitler in particular. Certainly Hitler came to think so. In 1943 Canaris was removed as head of the Abwehr and in 1945 he was executed after being suspected of being involved in the July 1944 plot to kill Hitler.

By that time Hitler had long given up placing much faith in the intelligence reports he got from the Abwehr. Instead he preferred to place his trust in the SD, the *Sicherheitsdienst*. This was the intelligence wing of the SS, as the Gestapo was the secret police wing, and it came under the control of Heinrich Himmler. The original purpose of the SD, founded in 1931, was to gather political intelligence for the Nazi Party but once in power Hitler transformed it into his private secret service. By 1941 the SD had 3,000 staff in Germany and a vast number of agents abroad.

German intelligence had its greatest failures in Britain. In December 1939 the British cracked the secret codes used by Abwehr radio operators. As a result every single German agent in Britain was arrested, as were all agents which the Germans tried to infiltrate thereafter. Some were shot, others imprisoned but many agreed to work for the British in an operation that became known as Double-X. They continued to send reports back to Germany, but these were all written by the British with an eye to deceive the enemy. Some German agents claimed to have recruited entire rings of agents in the British military or munitions works, none of whom actually existed.

Only when the reports from these agents diverged too greatly from reality did the Germans suspect they might have a problem. But by that time Hitler was relying on the SD for information, and their reports tended to be colored both by Nazi ideology and by a desire to please Hitler.

As well as using espionage to undermine potential enemies, in the 1930s Hitler also aimed to use propaganda to gain advantage. The majority of Nazi propaganda was aimed at the Germans themselves, boosting their enthusiasm for the war and promising eventual victory. But propaganda was also directed outward to potential enemies, friends and neutrals. Hitler's use of propaganda was to be stepped up enormously once war was under way, but even in the 1930s it was a weapon of first resort.

It had been a central belief of Hitler and many other Germans that the German army had not, in fact, been defeated in 1918. Instead, it was believed, Germany had surrendered because the army had been stabbed in the back by traitors and defeatists in Germany. The blame for this was laid at the door of the communists and Jews who had, supposedly, been able to convince the civilian government to surrender. In *Mein Kampf*, Hitler also laid a large slice of the blame on British propaganda.

Directed through press reports in neutral countries, British propaganda had, indeed, reached large numbers of German civilians. Its effectiveness from 1914 to 1918 had been limited, but once the German war economy began to crack, the propaganda aimed at civilians began to be effective. Likewise, British leaflets dropped by aircraft onto German units in the trenches were largely ineffective until morale began to falter in the summer of 1918.

The British then came up with an effective message. It urged the Germans to surrender to enjoy a good supply of food for themselves and also to ensure that their families had a bread-winner after Germany's inevitable defeat. The message was made more effective by the fact that on occasion, when a German attack was expected, the front line trenches were stocked with large quantities of good quality food and the men given orders to abandon the trenches quickly. The Germans capturing the positions found the food and contrasted it with their own meager rations.

Hitler would have seen all this at first hand in the summer of 1918 before he was wounded, and it may well have played a part in his obsession with propaganda and his determination to use it on his own people to counter the expected British efforts. He was also to use it abroad, though with rather less success.

A prime target for propaganda was the effort to keep the USA neutral in any future conflict.

Ironically, the task for Hitler and his propaganda chief Josef Goebbels, was made much easier by the fact that the British had been so much better at propaganda than the Germans.

Propaganda chief Goebbels lent Hitler his formidable talents

In the First World War, British propaganda aimed at neutral states, especially the USA, had often concentrated on what became known as "atrocity propaganda," that is, spreading stories about the dreadful behavior of the German armed forces. In some instances, such as the sinking of the passenger liner *Lusitania* or the execution of the nurse Edith Cavell, the British simply embellished

Fritz Kuhn led the Bund until his arrest in 1941

WINNING THE PROPAGANDA WAR

Hitler was determined this would not happen again. Goebbels was given funds to set up organizations in the USA to win the propaganda war, even before the shooting had started. This drive took two main forms. The first was the establishment of an organization of Americans of German descent called The Bund, led by the German-American Fritz Kuhn. The aim was to ensure friendly relations between Germany and German-Americans. Mutual exchange trips were organized and determined efforts made to woo the American press and plant stories extolling the merits of Germany and Hitler.

Hitler also played a leading role in subverting any credence that might be given to news and views from France or, more particularly, Britain. As so often, Hitler used his heroic war record to good effect. During the 1920s the British had been forced to admit that many of the stories of German soldiers raping women or bayonetting babies had been fabricated. German diplomats and press men were instructed to lose no opportunity to ensure the Americans were made aware of these admissions.

the truth. On other occasions the British made up entirely false stories, faked evidence and misled their target audience. And it worked. By 1917 the USA had declared war on Germany, in part due to the urgings of British propaganda.

The German-American Bund parades through New York City in the late 1930s

Hitler himself made the point that front-line soldiers of both sides knew these atrocity stories were simply lies made up by clever, slick propagandists safe in an office miles from the shooting. Strenuous efforts were made to cultivate links between old soldier organizations in Germany and the USA. Whenever veterans from the USA visited Germany they were entertained by a high-profile Nazi who was likewise a veteran. Hitler and Göring themselves met many hundreds of such men, swapping jovial anecdotes about military service. Baldur von Schirach, the Youth Leader of the German Reich, also played a part in the Nazi propaganda offensive. Fresh-faced and charming, he had, like Churchill, an American mother, and counted two signatories of the Declaration of Independence among his forebears.

These propaganda efforts worked extremely well, but only as long as there was no war. When Germany invaded Poland in 1939 the British again began their stories of German aggression and atrocities. Germany responded by pointing out that Britain had declared war in 1939, not Germany, and anyway these were the same stories as in 1914, and those were now known to have been British lies.

Unfortunately for such German efforts, Hitler then took a hand. He demanded that the more subtle tactics be abandoned. Now that the shooting had started, the Bund organization was instructed to make open appeals to German-Americans to show solidarity with Germany. "Blood calls to Blood" was the slogan. It failed dismally. Messages that worked effectively on Germans in Germany were quite unsuitable for those of German parentage in the very different social scene of the USA. By the end of 1940, despite the efforts of certain US citizens, most notably the aviator Charles Lindbergh, American

Hitler waits to address a massed open-air meeting of the Nazi Party in Nuremberg

public opinion was hostile to Nazism and to Hitler.

A key problem for all the services outside the army was that Hitler did not really understand them and had little interest in doing so. Given the way the Nazi state worked, few resources were allocated to anything in which Hitler was not interested. Promotion and rewards came only to those who caught Hitler's eye, so the navy, the intelligence services and so many other vital parts of the modern military were starved of both funds and high quality recruits. Failing to appreciate the wider picture, a lack of interest in anything unfamiliar and a lack of flexibility in approach were all key weaknesses of Hitler as a military commander.

DOVER
BRUGGE
Ostende
POSTE
ITALIANE
Aire
Le Tréport
Bresle
Dieppe
AMIENS

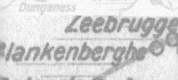

3

MILITARY ALLIANCES
ITALY—THE PACT OF STEEL

Hitler sought to make alliances with other countries that he thought might be favorable to German expansion, but he never had any illusions about the quality of the contribution they might make to the war

When Hitler came to power in 1933, Germany was still suffering the pains of defeat in the Great War. The new regime was determined to raise Germany to the status of a great power, despite the country's economic and financial weakness. Hitler knew that moving openly to secure his aims would attract unwelcome attention from those nations still wary of Germany. Rearmament of Germany was begun secretly, while economic reforms were pushed forward as if seeking a better standard of living for the German people.

Hitler knew he would need friends abroad, and that he would also need to woo potential enemies into neutrality or browbeat them into submission. In his search for friends, Hitler felt himself constrained. The Nazi movement was entirely homegrown within Germany so, unlike the Communists, there was no

Hitler with Italian dictator Benito Mussolini

pre-existing international network of which to take advantage. There were, however, plenty of regimes which had reason to fear the Communists, as did Hitler. And there was already one nationalist, right wing dictatorship in existence in Europe. It was only natural that Hitler would turn to Benito Mussolini, Fascist dictator of Italy, in his search for a foreign friend.

Unfortunately, the campaign to woo Mussolini got off to a bad start. In April 1933 Hitler announced a boycott of Jewish businesses. Mussolini sent the Italian ambassador in Berlin to Hitler with a message urging him to soften the anti-Semitic policies of Nazism. Eager as he was to make friends with Mussolini, Hitler was not to be put off. He told the Italian ambassador that there were very few Jews in Italy, so Mussolini did not understand the problem.

In October, Hitler upset Mussolini again when he took Germany out of the League of Nations. The Italian dictator had long viewed the League of Nations as a useful talking forum and shop window through which to present a reasonable face to the world. For a fellow right wing dictator to treat the world's largest international organization with contempt was, Mussolini felt, not merely a mistake but a blow to his own prestige.

Nevertheless, Mussolini was as eager to find an ally as was Hitler. In June 1934 he invited the German leader to Venice, tactfully including in the tour the Palazzo Vendramin where Hitler's favorite composer, Richard Wagner, had died. Hitler accepted, but must have regretted the decision the moment he arrived. Hitler landed in Venice dressed in a blue suit and an old raincoat. Mussolini met him in a glittering uniform of gold braid and mirror-polished jackboots and backed by an honor guard in the most gorgeous uniforms the fashion designers of Italy could produce. The

world's press was on hand to take photos which were, at best, unflattering to Hitler.

Hitler was furious and tried to regain dominance by subjecting Mussolini to a two hour speech the following day when they were supposed to be making complimentary statements to each other. Mussolini, in his turn, was now angry. Little progress was made on the main point of the meeting, which was to reach some form of agreement over the status of Austria.

Before the Great War, Austria had ruled substantial swathes of northern Italy, parts of which had sizeable German-speaking minorities. Hitler had made no secret of his ambition to absorb Austria into the Reich and to embrace all ethnically German peoples into the German state. Mussolini was understandably nervous about his northern borders, particularly the area around Bolzano and Trent, and wanted an agreement with Hitler. At Venice he got a vague promise from the Germans to respect Austrian independence, but it was far from being a firm pledge.

Austrian leader Engelbert Dollfuss (left) and Italian dictator Mussolini (2nd from left) formed an anti-German partnership in 1933

MURDEROUS DEALINGS

Almost as soon as Hitler got back to Germany he stepped up the financial aid he was sending the Nazi Party in Austria, further increasing the pressure by sanctioning a terrorist campaign of bombs and shootings in the hope of destabilising the Austrian state. In July 1934 the Austrian Nazis took matters to an extreme, murdering the Austrian Chancellor Engelbert Dollfuss and launching a coup.

Mussolini reacted swiftly. He rushed divisions of troops, backed by aircraft and tanks, to the Italian border with Austria and announced that he would intervene if any other power tried to invade Austria. "Hitler is the murderer of Dollfuss," declared Mussolini. "Hitler is the guilty man and a dangerous fool. It would mean the end of European civilization if his country of murderers and pederasts were to overrun Europe." Asked his opinion of the Nazi movement, Mussolini replied, "It is the revolution of the old Germanic tribes in the primeval forest against the Latin civilization of Rome."

But Mussolini was no fool. He told his colleagues in private that, "Hitler will arm the Germans and he will make war. We cannot stand up to him alone. We must do something and we must do something quickly." At first Mussolini tried to alert other nations to the German danger, but was met only with distrust. After the Italian invasion of Abyssinia, now Ethiopia, in 1935 the democratic powers gave Mussolini the cold shoulder. Like it or not, the Italian dictator realized his only potential powerful friend was Hitler. They would have to find a solution to the Austrian problem.

In October 1936 Mussolini's son-in-law and Foreign Minister, Count Galeazzo Ciano, travelled to Berlin to begin talks. He found Hitler in expansive and friendly mood. "Mussolini is the first statesman of the world with whom no one else has the right even remotely to compare himself," declared Hitler. Ciano was acquainted with Mussolini well enough to know this was not true, but accepted the flattery and signed a secret agreement with Hitler. The Germans could have Austria, but the current Italian border would be respected.

In September 1937 Mussolini himself travelled to Germany. The Italian had a new uniform designed by a top Milan fashion house for the occasion and not only wore the magnificent commander's uniform himself, but also dressed his hundred-strong entourage the same way. He even commissioned a special evening-wear uniform for the trip. Hitler, as usual, wore a more modest outfit, this time the Nazi Party brown uniform.

Italian foreign minister Count Ciano (center in black) visits a Luftwaffe base before the war

Mussolini and Hitler leaving talks during the Munich Crisis, 1938

There was nothing modest about the itinerary lined up for Mussolini, however. He was shown the new German army, including panzer troops, on maneuvers, then given a tour of the vast Krupp armaments factory before being whisked off to a mass meeting of the Nazi Party with 60,000 SS guards and a million people in attendance. Mussolini was impressed. It was then that Hitler made a promise that turned out to be far more rash than he had intended. He pledged firm and lasting friendship, then told Mussolini he could have a free hand in the Mediterranean if Hitler had a free hand north of the Alps.

It is likely that neither Hitler nor Mussolini realized the full importance of what they were agreeing. Mussolini seems to have thought he was agreeing to accept the union of Austria with Germany and to support Hitler in his diplomatic moves to gain control of the Sudetenland, that part of Czechoslovakia occupied by ethnic Germans. Hitler, in his turn, seems to have believed he was backing Mussolini's Ethiopian adventure and

Italian plans to tighten their hold on Libya and apply pressure on the French and British colonies.

At first the new agreement worked well. When Hitler marched into Austria, he had Italian approval. When Hitler took Britain and France to the brink of war over the Sudetenland in September 1938, he had Mussolini's forthright support. "Il Duce informs you that, whatever the Führer decides, Fascist Italy stands behind him," announced the Italian ambassador publicly, though he privately told Hitler that Mussolini thought the Germans should accept the compromise deal offered by Britain rather than go to war. Hitler did just that and Mussolini gained an inflated impression of his influence. It was Mussolini's suggestion that the final meeting of the premiers involved be held in Munich and it was Mussolini who basked in international acclaim as the peace-maker.

In October 1938, Hitler suggested to Mussolini that the successful friendship and agreements between their two nations should be converted into a firm military alliance. Hitler felt that he needed to be certain of Italian armed support before risking war with Britain and France. Such a war was, he was now convinced, bound to happen sooner or later. He wanted the Italian army to invade southern France and tie down the western Allies if German troops were busy in the east. At first Mussolini delayed and played for time. In January 1939, however, he came to believe that Britain and France intended to block his foreign policy aspirations. Mussolini authorized his diplomats to begin negotiations on the details of a military alliance with Hitler.

In March Hitler took over the rest of Czechoslovakia. He did not tell Mussolini of the plan in advance, and the Italian dictator was put out by this lack of trust. Partly in retaliation, and partly to show Hitler that the Italians also had military ability, Mussolini invaded Albania on April 7, 1939. The Italians had long been involved, both commercially and politically, in that impoverished country. Mussolini had been a staunch supporter of Albania's King Zog, but by 1939 the obvious corruption of Zog's regime and his delight in perpetuating internal tribal feuds had reached the point where Italy's business interests were at risk. The invasion was carried out by four divisions making an amphibious landing, supported by the Italian air force and navy. Armored divisions landed later the same day and the fighting was over within 48 hours.

Hitler was annoyed by Mussolini's adventure, but loyally supported the move because he still did not have Mussolini's signature on the formal alliance. In May 1939, Mussolini finally signed the alliance, the Pact of Steel. He even accepted Hitler's telling revision that the alliance would apply to all wars, not just those fought in defense. Hitler believed that he could plan the invasion of Poland secure in the knowledge that he would have Italian backing if Britain and France dared to intervene.

The German-speaking population of the Sudetenland welcomed the German annexation of 1938

HUNGARY

But Hitler was not going to invade Poland without having first assured himself of the support or neutrality of any country in a position to intervene. Sharing a border with both Germany and Poland was Hungary, a nation which would be able to cause Germany great problems if it took a hostile stance. In the 1930s Hungary had her own problems and these were of a nature to make her wide open to German influence and suggestions.

In the Treaty of Versailles which ended the Great War of 1914 to 1918, Hungary had been established as a country free of the centuries-long rule from Austria. Despite promises of self-determination for the nationalities of eastern Europe, however, millions of Magyars were left living in areas outside the boundaries of their nation state, Hungary. Not unnaturally, the Hungarian government and the Magyars outside the kingdom were dissatisfied. Like Hitler, they railed against the Versailles Treaty.

By the time Hitler began seriously to consider moves of aggression in the east, Hungary was under the control of a military dictator named Miklós Horthy de Nagybánya, an admiral in the Austrian navy during the Great War. Horthy supported the Hapsburg monarchy and wanted to restore the absent King Charles IV to the throne

of Hungary. Talk of such a move proved hugely unpopular, so Horthy had himself declared Regent instead and acquired almost dictatorial powers.

When Hitler came to power, Horthy was secure in government and had established reasonably friendly relations with the other states of eastern Europe, though relations with Russia were strained after an abortive Communist coup was put down with much bloodshed. When Hitler took over Austria, Horthy felt threatened. He had over half a million Germans living in western Hungary and feared his borders might be breached.

Hitler could not afford to have a hostile Hungary at his back, so he rushed to reassure Horthy with all the charm that he and his foreign minister, Joachim Ribbentrop, could muster. Charm alone was not enough to win over the wily Horthy. Instead, Hitler bought Hungarian friendship by allowing Horthy to take over those parts of southern Czechoslovakia that had a majority of ethnic Magyars. The Hungarian invasion came just two months after the Munich Agreement. Although Hitler fully supported Horthy in private, he could still tell Britain and France that the move was not his own. Indeed, Horthy's action allowed Hitler to claim that eastern Europe was in danger of falling into anarchy and needed a new settlement to replace that of Versailles.

When Hitler moved to occupy the rest of Czechoslovakia, he again encouraged Horthy to take action. This time Hungary annexed the far eastern tail of Czechoslovakia, an area known as Ruthenia. There were 175,000 Magyars in Ruthenia, but they formed only a minority of the population. For the first time, Horthy had embarked on a war of conquest without the figleaf of claiming to "liberate" a Magyar majority from oppressive rule. The price Hungary paid to Hitler

was to promise strict neutrality in the coming war against Poland. It was a price that Horthy was perfectly content to pay.

SLOVAKIA

By his invasion of the rump of Czechoslovakia in March 1939, Hitler created a new military ally in the shape of Slovakia. The agricultural Slovakia had never been an easy partner with the more populous and richer industrial Czech lands, but the two had been forced together by the Treaty of Versailles as neither was thought strong enough to survive for long on its own. There had been some agitation for Slovak independence in the early 1930s, but it was Nazi money and resources which boosted the demands from 1935 onward as Hitler sought to destablize Czechoslovakia. The leader of the separatist movement was a Catholic priest named Josef Tiso. When Hitler created Slovakia in March 1939, Tiso was installed as President.

As usual, Hitler extracted a price for such favors. He demanded that Slovakia join the war against Poland. Tiso was enthusiastic and ordered Slovakia's elite 1st Division to invade Poland over the Dukla Pass. The division was spearheaded by almost 100 of the latest tanks from the Skoda factories and was backed by thousands of infantry, all mounted on trucks. Ideally suited to a blitzkrieg campaign of fast movement, the Slovaks fought well as part of Rundstedt's southern army. When the short Polish campaign was over, Slovakia settled back to enjoy a privileged position in Hitler's New Order for Europe.

YUGOSLAVIA

When Hitler marched into Austria he not only opened up a border with Italy, but also with Yugoslavia. This strange, polyglot kingdom had been created by the Treaty of Versailles from the southern provinces of the old Austrian Empire. It was an area of desperately mixed ethnic populations. There were 4 million Croats, 1.3 million Slovenes, 1 million Macedonians, 400,000 Montenegrins and a sprinkling of German, Magyar, Italian, Albanian and Romanian minorities. But the largest ethnic component were the 7 million Serbs, who had lived under their own monarchy outside the Austrian Empire before Versailles.

Under the Versailles settlements, the realm of the Serb monarchy was expanded into the Kingdom of Yugoslavia. The various ethnic minorities were, however, protected not just by the most democratic constitution in eastern Europe, but also by the division of the kingdom into a number of semi-self-governing provinces. The Serbs had been allied to the British and French before and during the Great War, and remained friendly to the western powers throughout the 1920s. With their long coastline and excellent ports, the Yugoslavs believed that they were not as isolated as other countries in eastern Europe. The powerful fleets of Britain and France could reach Yugoslavia with ease, should the need ever arise.

In 1929 King Alexander I stepped forward to stamp on internal disorder and established himself with near dictatorial powers. After his death in 1934, the crown passed to his eleven year old son, Peter II, though power rested with a council of noblemen led by the boy-king's Uncle Paul. The council followed a foreign policy based on friendship with the western allies and a watchful neutrality towards Hungary and Romania, both of which could make out good claims to slices of Yugoslav territory.

When Hitler occupied Austria, the Yugoslav Council became alarmed. Several hundred thousand Germans lived in northern Yugoslavia and Prince Paul feared these were next on Hitler's list for incorporation into the Reich. Hitler managed to convince Paul that this was not the case. The Italian invasion of Albania rightly alarmed the Yugoslavs again, but Prince Paul concluded he had nothing to gain by antagonizing Hitler. When Germany invaded Poland, Prince Paul contented himself with neutrality, though he built up the Yugoslav army until it numbered about 350,000 men on permanent alert and many more in reserve.

King Boris of Bulgaria (center) tried to keep his nation neutral

BULGARIA

Beyond Hungary and Yugoslavia lay Bulgaria, Romania and Greece. The Bulgarians' traditional foreign policy was to be friendly with Russia to gain the support of that empire against the Turks and Austrians. Since the Communists had taken power, however, King Boris of Bulgaria had grown cool towards the Soviet Union. Boris was keen to win back lands lost to his kingdom in the Treaty of Versailles, but he was wary of Hitler, viewing him as a dangerous fanatic who was taking risks and would ultimately come to grief. Unwilling to aid Hitler, he was nonetheless pragmatic enough to remain on good terms with Germany. In any case, any problems Germany might cause were far away from Boris's southern kingdom and he felt able to ignore them.

GREECE

Greece, likewise, felt it was so far from Germany that it did not need to become unduly alarmed by Hitler's growing power and aggressive nature. In any case, Greece was in a state of armed and belligerent peace with her eastern neighbor Turkey. The two nations had been at war, off and on, for over a century with the most recent conflict in the 1920s. The Greek dictator, General Metaxas, maintained friendly enough relations with Hitler, but the two did not meet and diplomatic contact was minimal.

ROMANIA

Romania was quite different. The country had existed as a small kingdom before the Great War, but was hugely expanded by the Versailles Treaty to include Transylvania, Bessarabia and Dobruja. Although the overall population was overwhelmingly Romanian, some 13 million out of 17 million, the new areas contained sizeable populations of Bulgars, Magyars, Germans and Russians and many towns had large Jewish ghettos. King Carol of Romania naturally looked with some suspicion at Hitler and his policy of overthrowing the Versailles Treaty, from which Romania had done so well.

King Carol of Romania with his mother and son

Hitler responded by funding a Romanian extremist right-wing party. In the elections of 1937, this quasi-Nazi party won nearly a third of the popular vote and demanded posts in government. King Carol's reaction was swift. He dismissed Parliament and took emergency powers for himself. These powers were used to crack down on the extremists and sever their links to Germany. Nevertheless, Carol remained neutral during the Munich crisis of 1938. He pledged his support to Britain and France, but when they did nothing there was little he could do. As Germany moved towards the invasion of Poland, Romania could be counted upon to remain neutral.

This web of relationships with the countries of eastern Europe meant that by 1939, Hitler was assured of support or neutrality from all the small states which might previously have wanted to intervene in a German–Polish war. There was still one remaining problem and it was a big one: Russia.

THE SOVIET UNION

Ever since he joined the Nazi Party in the early 1920s, Hitler had been telling anyone who would listen that the three greatest enemies of the German people were Communism, Jews and Asia. Since all three were epitomized in Hitler's

mind by Russia it was only natural that he would see that vast Asian country as his natural enemy. At one time, Hitler had toyed with the idea of allying Germany to Poland to attack Russia, but soon dismissed the idea of an alliance with a Slavic nation.

By late in 1938, Hitler had his eyes set on invading Poland and he knew he would need Soviet neutrality to be confident of victory. Hitler was helped in his task of reaching an accommodation with the Soviet dictator, Josef Stalin, by the actions of his predecessors in control of Germany. They had co-operated with the Soviets on secret military experiments in tank design and air strike tactics. Although these were cut after Hitler came to power, the idea of Germany and Russia being linked because of mutual ostracism by the outside world persisted.

In March 1939 the Soviets took the first step when they invited Peter Kleist, a minor official at the German foreign office, to tea at the Russian Embassy. He was met by an equally minor Soviet official, Georgi Astakhov, who talked at length about the benefits of economic co-operation between the two states. In April the Soviet ambassador himself, Alexei Merekalov, dropped open hints that Stalin wanted friendship with Hitler. The Germans responded favorably, but took no active steps.

Then, in May, Stalin sacked his anti-German foreign minister and replaced him with Vyacheslav Molotov. The move was seen by Hitler as marking a distinct change in attitude by Stalin, but he was still wary of being trapped by false promises of friendship. Hitler was, in any case, in talks with Japan which in turn was fighting a bitter frontier dispute with the Soviet Union in Manchuria. Japan was unwilling to join the Germany–Italy pact, but had not ruled the idea out completely. Talks with

Stalin were, therefore, fraught with difficulties.

On August 15, with the planned date for an attack on Poland just weeks away, Hitler ordered Ribbentrop to reach an understanding with Molotov, whatever the cost. The Soviets responded by signing an economic treaty, which was generous to the Soviets, but asked for a week to consider the implications of a non-aggression pact. On the 20th Hitler sent a personal telegram to Stalin stating that there was a need for speed as German relations with Poland were deteriorating rapidly. In response Stalin sent back a Soviet draft of a ten-year non-aggression treaty. The draft contained articles highly favorable to the Soviet Union, but Hitler had little time to debate the issue. He needed to be certain of Russian neutrality within nine days. Ribbentrop was sent to Moscow to finalize the deal.

Almost as soon as Ribbentrop's aircraft landed in Moscow, he was whisked off to see Stalin. The Soviet dictator announced that he wanted secret additions to the non-aggression treaty. He wanted the Germans to accept that the Russians could occupy and annex Estonia, Latvia, Lithuania and a large slice of eastern Poland. He also wanted Bessarabia, then part of Romania. Ribbentrop hurried back to the German embassy and put through a call to Hitler on a secure line. An hour later came the reply. Hitler agreed to everything, except Bessarabia, which would have to wait for a favorable moment. Ribbentrop hastened back to the Kremlin to sign the deal.

On August 24 the Molotov–Ribbentrop treaty was announced to the world, though the proposed carving up of eastern Europe was kept secret. At the very last minute, Hitler had finally put in place the network of alliances, friendships and neutralities that he needed in eastern Europe. He could go to war with confidence.

Soviet Foreign Minister Molotov meets Hitler in 1940 to discuss British actions in the Mediterranean and Black Sea

The very next day it all seemed to go horribly wrong.

Although Mussolini had kept the news very much to himself, the Italian attack on Albania had not gone as well as the Italians had made out. The Italian navy had operated superbly and the air force had flown with skill and daring, but the army had proved a grave disappointment. The tanks had broken down, ammunition jammed or misfired and the supply system collapsed with embarrassing speed. The soldiers, perfectly understandably, had proved reluctant to risk their lives in battle when carrying equipment which was so obviously faulty. The main problem was rumored corruption in the army's purchasing department where bribes had been taken to accept less than perfect equipment.

Mussolini was trying to solve these problems, though without much success, when he received news of the Nazi–Soviet pact. Mussolini rejoiced at the diplomatic coup, until Ciano made it clear to him that the move meant an attack on Poland was imminent. Realizing this would involve Italy in war, Mussolini sent a desperate message to Hitler. Rather than admit his army was not up to scratch, Mussolini claimed that the campaigns in

Ethiopia and Albania had cost a lot of equipment. Italy, Mussolini told Hitler, could not possibly go to war against France and Britain without new supplies of military hardware, which he proceeded to list at length.

When Hitler received the letter he was furious. He sent the Italian ambassador packing, then raged at his aides at Italian treachery and the fact that they could never be relied upon in a war. But time was precious and for once Hitler calmed down quickly. He summoned the Italian ambassador back again and asked him that, if Mussolini would not actually go to war, at least to mobilize his forces along the French frontier. This, Hitler hoped, would tie down French forces and weaken any French attack into Germany. Mussolini agreed.

The Italian let-down aside, Hitler's network of alliances and agreements worked well when he invaded Poland. The Slovaks sent troops to help the invasion and, once Polish defeat was assured, the Soviets attacked from the East. Four countries ceased to exist: Poland, Latvia, Estonia and Lithuania. Hitler was the sole arbiter of events in eastern Europe.

Later in June 1940, having conquered Luxembourg, Denmark, Norway, Holland, Belgium and France, Hitler became temporarily concerned with his relations in western Europe.

NEUTRAL COUNTRIES

Sweden was providing Germany with the bulk of her iron ore, though French supplies were now available. With German troops in Norway, Sweden was in no real position to defy Hitler, but the Germans wanted more. They wanted Sweden to transport the iron ore in Swedish ships and for Swedish fighter aircraft to attack any Allied bombers which strayed over Swedish air space.

The Swedes readily agreed.

Next Hitler turned his attention to Spain, now in the hands of the right wing dictator General Francisco Franco. Hitler had sent German panzers, aircraft and men to help Franco win the Spanish Civil War of 1936 to 1938. Now Hitler wanted to extract the price for that help. He asked Franco to join the war against Britain on Germany's side, promising to give him Gibraltar as soon as the British were defeated.

Franco knew that Spain was exhausted after the civil war and needed all her energies to rebuild the economy and heal the internal divisions. On the other hand, Hitler seemed to be winning the war and German troops were stationed on the Spanish border with occupied France. Franco decided to opt for friendship with Germany, but not to join the war. He changed Spain's official position from neutrality to "nonbelligerence," promising to do what he could to help Germany.

By October 1940, Hitler was losing his patience. He wanted permission for German troops to go through Spain to attack Gibraltar, but Franco was refusing. He wanted German warships to have access to Spanish naval facilities, again Franco refused. On 23 October the two dictators met at the Franco-Spanish border to discuss their differences. The talks dragged on for nine hours as Hitler alternately expounded his world views, or asked for practical help from Spain. Franco was charm itself, but insisted on outrageous concessions if Spain were to enter the war, which entry, he added, must be some months away at least. The meeting ended with virtually nothing having been agreed, leading Hitler later angrily to remark that he would "rather have several teeth pulled than go through that again." That was the last time he and Franco met.

After the abortive meeting with Franco, Hitler travelled to meet Marshal Pétain, the new leader of defeated France. Installed in the small town of Vichy, the French government knew that German troops were to occupy much of northern and western France, but waited anxiously to learn what else Hitler wanted. What he wanted, they learned, was for France to join the war against Britain. Pétain demurred. He could not, he said, declare war on anyone without summoning the French parliament and that would open a whole can of worms about the German occupation and the ways in which Pétain was already supplying

In October 1940 Hitler met Spanish dictator Francisco Franco in a vain effort to get Spain to join the war

raw materials to Hitler. Pétain could, however, promise to keep the powerful French Navy neutral and block British access to the many ports and airfields in the French colonies. Again, Hitler had to be satisfied with less than he wanted.

Meanwhile, Mussolini was again causing Hitler problems. In June 1940, with the war apparently won by Germany, Mussolini had finally declared war on France and Britain. His troops marched into southern France, as French resistance was collapsing, and invaded British-occupied Egypt from Italian Libya. The attack in North Africa came to a halt, though Italian troops were deep within Egypt and were fortifying their positions.

Then, on 28 October as Hitler travelled back from his meeting with Pétain, Mussolini started a war all of his own. He invaded Greece from Albania. Hitler was annoyed and predicted that the Italian attack would soon get bogged down in the autumn rains and winter snows, which it did. At first Hitler seemed content to let his ally suffer humiliation and losses, but in January the Italians lost Bardia, Tobruk and 130,000 prisoners to the British in North Africa. This sudden British success worried Hitler deeply. If the Italians were defeated in North Africa, Hitler believed, then the British forces in Egypt would be free to repeat their strategic coup of 1918 and invade the Balkans via Greece. In 1918 this move had knocked Austria out of the war: in 1941, it might capture the vital Romanian oilfields.

In February Hitler took the decisive step of agreeing to help Italy. He sent Rommel and the

The victory parade before Field Marshal List in Athens

Afrika Korps to North Africa and ordered Field Marshal List to take the Twelfth Army through Hungary, Romania and Bulgaria to conquer Greece. This move not only delayed the attack on Russia by a fatal six weeks, but it also upset Hitler's delicate balance of alliances in eastern Europe.

In 1940, Hitler had redrawn the map of eastern Europe by forcing Romania to give up some of the extensive territories given to her by the Versailles Treaty. Transylvania with its 1.5 million Magyars was given to Hungary, Dobruja with its 300,000 Bulgars was handed to Bulgaria and Bessarabia with 750,000 Russians was given to Stalin.

In the spring of 1941, Hitler began building up a network of alliances in the new eastern Europe for his war against Russia. The Slovaks agreed readily, the entire existence of their state depending on Hitler. Further north, the Finns were also willing allies. They had lost territory to Russia in the war of 1939 and were eager to regain it. They agreed to send their entire army, small though it was, to attack Leningrad from the north.

Admiral Horthy, grateful for the large expansion of Hungary, agreed to lend Hitler two mechanized brigades and one brigade of cavalry. This commitment was to be enlarged in 1942 to include eleven divisions. Hitler hoped that Bulgaria would be similarly grateful, and so was amazed when King Boris flatly refused to declare war on Russia. He did, however, declare war on Britain.

In Romania King Carol had been forced to abdicate after accepting the dismemberment of his country and was replaced by his young son, King Michael. Power was, however, in the hands of the army council, led by General Ion Antonescu. Antonescu's first move was to ban the pro-Nazi political party, the Iron Guard, and throw its leaders into prison. But when Hitler asked for Romanian support in the war on Russia, Antonescu agreed readily. He demanded the return of Bessarabia, to which Hitler agreed. Romania sent two entire Armies north to join the Germans.

That left only Yugoslavia, the most pro-western of all the eastern European states. Prince Paul had been devastated by the collapse of France and the apparent defeat of Britain, but he was not yet ready to join his country to Germany. After much cajolery by Hitler and smooth offers from Ribbentrop, Prince Paul finally agreed to sign a treaty with Germany. He specified, however, that Yugoslavia would not go to war with any other country, nor would German troops be stationed in Yugoslavia. It was less than Hitler wanted, but it was enough.

On March 25, Prince Paul signed the treaty. Next day a quarter of his government resigned in protest and there were massive public demonstrations. At dawn on 27 March the military launched a coup which ousted Prince Paul, repudiated the treaty with Germany and put King Peter, now aged 17, in power.

Hitler was furious and ordered that the invasion of Greece, scheduled for 6 April, be expanded to include Yugoslavia. The hurriedly revised plans were put into effect and the panzers rolled forwards as planned. Yugoslavia capitulated on April 17, Greece on April 23.

There has been much discussion as to why Hitler diverted his forces into the Balkans and North Africa when preparing for Operation *Barbarossa*, the invasion of Russia. The move is widely believed to have delayed the invasion of Russia by six weeks, thus shortening the time available to the Germans to crush the Soviets before winter set in.

Some have suggested Hitler made the move to support his ally Mussolini. Certainly Hitler and Ribbentrop gave the Italians this impression, emphasising the importance of the Pact of Steel to the Führer. But Hitler had made no move to help the Italians when they first got into difficulties. It is more likely that it was hard military realities that brought the panzers to the Balkans. Hitler was terrified that a British landing would take his invasion forces in the flank and rear as they drove into Russia. Such a move could be confounded only by securing the Balkans and strengthening the Italian effort in North Africa.

In any case, Hitler's original plans for the Balkan campaign timetabled the panzers to be back on the Soviet frontier in time for *Barbarossa* to begin at the end of May. It was the diversion into Yugoslavia that caused extra wear and tear on the panzers, requiring them to undergo an overhaul before being thrown into battle again. It was this that made the delay and for that Hitler's temper was solely to blame. While the invasion of Yugoslavia may have been politically desirable, from a purely military point of view, given the realities of a Russian war, it was a mistake.

So long as the war in Russia went well for Germany, Hitler's military allies remained loyal. But after Stalingrad things changed rapidly. By February 1943 the Hungarians had lost over 60,000 dead and many more injured. Horthy withdrew his men from the front line, informing Hitler that the Hungarians could be used only to guard supply lines and rear area bases. He did, however, allow SS recruiting officers to contact ethnic Germans in Hungary, and over 30,000 joined up. Later in 1943 Horthy came under increasing pressure to move his men back into the front line, but again he refused. To calm Hitler's anger he agreed to arrest Hungary's Jewish population and send them off to "slave labor camps." Horthy probably knew by this date that

the Jews were being murdered at death camps, but coldly calculated it was better to lose Jews to the Nazis than Hungarians to the Soviets.

THE TURNING TIDE

The Finns made peace with Russia in September 1944, when they could gain good terms. They had to hand over their military hardware and some slices of territory, but the country remained intact.

The Italians had sent some troops to help the Germans in Russia, but most of their military

effort went into the Mediterranean area. Their army occupied Greece and Yugoslavia, as well as fighting in North Africa, while the navy and air force battled the British Royal Navy in the Mediterranean. By May 1943 the Italians, along with the Afrika Korps, had evacuated North Africa and in July the Allies landed in Sicily. A few days later Mussolini was ousted from power by his own Fascist Party, acting with the agreement of King Victor Emmanuel III. In August, Italy surrendered to the Allies, although German troops in Italy ensured the Allies could not capture the country without months of hard fighting.

Romania, in contrast, kept her men in the front line. By the summer of 1943, the Romanians had lost over 200,000 men, having been hit particularly badly at Stalingrad. Throughout the following winter the Romanians continued to fight, but when the end came it came very quickly. On August 22, 1944, King Michael made a radio broadcast in which he announced that he was asking Stalin for peace terms and ordered all Germans to leave Romania. A week later, Romania declared war on Germany and entered the fight again as allies of Russia.

Bulgaria, which had never declared war on Russia, helped Germany occupy parts of Greece and Yugoslavia but otherwise stayed out of the fighting. In 1943 King Boris had died and the government passed into civilian hands. When Soviet troops reached the Bulgarian border in August 1944, the Bulgarians declared war on Germany. This was not good enough for Stalin, who declared war on Bulgaria and only agreed to peace when a new Communist regime took power in Sofia.

In contrast the Hungarian army went back into the front line when the Soviets reached the Hungarian border in September 1944. The battle for Budapest that winter was long and hard, but in March 1945 the Hungarian army simply collapsed.

In the end Hitler's Germany was battling alone. All the allies that Hitler had courted so assiduously before and during the war, the majority of whom had had little choice but to enter into alliance with him in the face of the Nazi military machine, abandoned him as the remorseless might of the Allied war effort ground the Germans down to defeat.

American troops prepare to land on Sicily, 1943. The landings forced Italy out of the war

4

CORPORAL HITLER

Hitler spent the First World War fighting in the trenches, where he proved to be a first class infantryman. He was in hospital when the war ended and never accepted that the German army had been defeated

The Great War was a defining experience for Hitler. He later said of this period that it was "the greatest and most unforgettable time of my earthly existence." His experiences as a soldier shaped his political views, his abilities and ultimately propelled him into the political arena. His undoubted bravery and exemplary war record gave him the status of a war hero that was to be so useful when seeking votes.

The years in the trenches were Hitler's only real experience of soldiering before he became commander of the armed forces of the Third Reich. As such, these experiences had a decisive impact on his later career as a military commander. Although fighting conditions changed greatly between 1918 and 1939, Hitler frequently justified the decisions he took in the Second World War by referring back to his experiences of fighting in the trenches. Nor was this mere bluster.

Fritz Wiedemann was a junior officer in Hitler's regiment during much of the first war and then served for four years on Hitler's staff when he became

A remarkable photograph taken in Munich on the day war was declared in 1914 shows Hitler (circled) celebrating the news

Führer. "His memory of the war was excellent," recorded Wiedemann later. "I never heard him lying or exaggerating when he told of his war experiences." If anyone is to understand Hitler as a commander, they must look to Hitler as the commanded.

When war broke out in August 1914 Hitler was enthusiastic. He had recovered from some years of destitution in his native Austria and was earning a living as a freelance artist in Munich. He was already holding forth on political subjects at meetings, but had no burning interests beyond keeping up to date with current affairs. Hitler, at this time, had no intention of becoming a politician, though he was deeply interested in politics, rather he aimed to be an artist or architect.

The declaration of war overwhelmed Hitler. "I fell down on my knees and thanked Heaven from an overflowing heart for granting me the good fortune of being permitted to live at this time," he wrote later. On August 5 Hitler sat down and wrote to the Bavarian King Ludwig III asking permission to serve in the regiment of his adopted city, Munich, rather than the forces of his own nation, Austria. This request was never actually answered, but Hitler was summoned to report to the Bavarian 16th Infantry Regiment on August 16.

HITLER'S WEAKNESS

One of the most important, but often overlooked, features of Hitler's service in the First World War is that he joined up in Bavaria. In 1914 the German Empire, ruled by the Kaiser, was composed of a number of smaller kingdoms and states, each with its own government and powers. The Kingdom of Bavaria, ruled by King Ludwig III, had its own army but, lacking a coastline, no navy.

As a result, Hitler's enthusiasm for the war and desire to play a part in it was channelled into the army. One long term result of this on Hitler's future career as a military commander was that he was totally ignorant of naval affairs until he became Führer and was forced to take account of them. Even then, Hitler's interest in naval matters was restricted largely to a knowledge of facts and figures. He knew, for instance, the range and weight of the guns on the major ships of the Kriegsmarine, the German navy, and of those on many British ships as well.

But Hitler never really understood naval strategy. Like Napoleon before him, Hitler looked on the navy as being able to support the actions of the army, but as having no real independent value of its own. Nor did he care about the crucial importance of the naval war in the task of defeating Britain. Once it became clear in the late summer of 1940 that the army would not be able to land in Britain and that attempts to weaken her would be relegated to a naval affair in the Atlantic, Hitler lost interest in the project. The task of defeating Britain was, to a large extent, dismissed from Hitler's mind. There were other reasons for this, but Hitler's four years in the trenches undoubtedly helped to concentrate his mind on the army at the expense of the navy.

When he reported for duty in 1914, Hitler found himself in a regiment with the ranks composed almost entirely of new recruits, though the officers and many NCOs had seen previous service. The men were drilled relentlessly for two months, then told they were to board train on October 21 for active service. Hitler wrote to his landlady in Munich that he was looking forward to seeing action and, ironically given what was to happen later, that he and his comrades were anticipating a landing in England.

Gheluvelt where the Germans were halted by the British

In the event, the 16th Bavarians were sent into battle on the infamous Menin Road near Ypres. Hitler encountered his first fighting on October 29 as the German army attempted to break the British control of Flanders and so secure the Channel coast. Hastily-dug field trenches marked the front lines, but the elaborate trench systems were still in the future. The 16th Bavarians attacked at 5:30am towards the town of Gheluvelt. The author's Great Uncle George was in the Worcestershire Regiment which defended the town against the German attack and testified to the ferocity with which it was pushed home.

The German attack failed and Hitler's regiment took 349 casualties out of a strength of 3,600. Hitler himself was unhurt and was promoted to lance-corporal to replace a casualty. The 16th Bavarians remained in the front line and on November 5 they attacked again, near the village of Wytschaete. This time Hitler won promotion to full corporal.

In the fighting at Wytschaete, Hitler saw his colonel lying wounded in an open field and went to fetch a first aid medical assistant. The medic would not brave the British rifle fire sweeping the field, so Hitler went out and dragged the helpless officer into cover. Hitler received a British bullet through his sleeve, but was unhurt. He was awarded the Iron Cross, 2nd Class, for this action. No other German soldier has ever won this major award so quickly after joining the army.

By the time the regiment was pulled out of the fighting on November 8 some 700 men were dead and over 2,000 had been wounded. Only 611 were fully fit for duty. One of these was Corporal Hitler.

In the reorganization of the regiment that followed the bloody fighting around Ypres, Hitler was confirmed in his battlefield promotion to corporal. He was also transferred away from his company to the regimental staff. His new duties were to be those of a dispatch runner, or *Meldegänger*. The 16th Bavarians had eight such men, tasked with carrying the orders received at regimental HQ by telephone to the company commanders in the front line.

Much was made during the 1920s of Hitler's duties as a dispatch runner, both by his supporters and his opponents. Those wishing to belittle Hitler's war record pointed out that dispatch runners spent much of their time loafing about at regimental HQ waiting for something to do. Those wanting to talk up Hitler's war heroism countered by pointing out that dispatch runners traditionally took heavier casualties than other men for their duties involved them scampering across open ground and between safe havens.

NEAR MISS

In fact, Hitler's war was a blend of both styles of activity. He found time to continue with his painting and to read books, but he also found himself exposed to extreme danger. On November 15 just days after taking up his new job, Hitler delivered an order to a forward command post. Given a reply, Hitler had covered only about 15 yards of his return journey when an artillery shell landed on the post and wiped it out.

By the middle of 1915 the 16th Bavarians were settled into the deadly trench warfare of the Western Front. They had a section of trench just over a mile in length to defend, taking turns with another regiment to serve in the front or rear lines. Hitler became a master of the art of delivering messages. His fellow dispatch runners admired him for his detailed knowledge of the country, of where to hide, of how to slip past snipers and which dangerous sections to avoid. The officers reckoned Hitler the most reliable of men. When, on 25 September, the regiment was cut off by a British advance it was Hitler who was sent to get messages to the rear.

It was during this time that Hitler formed his opinion of the duties of a soldier. He believed a soldier should be ready to obey an order instantly and without question. This involved being continually ready with well-maintained equipment, a fit body and a thorough knowledge of what was going on. And while a soldier might devise his own way of achieving his objective, there could be no excuses or arguing with direct orders or questioning of the objective to be gained. Efficiency and obedience were, Hitler believed, paramount virtues in a soldier. It was a theme to which he would continually return when he became supreme warlord of Germany. He might discuss with the army high command how an objective was to be achieved, but he felt the army officers had no right to debate which objective should be achieved.

During his time in the trenches, Hitler lived up to his own ideals superbly. He cared for his equipment better than any man in his regiment and when the alarm sounded was always first to be ready for action. Nor did he shirk any duty, no matter how dangerous. Indeed, some of Hitler's fellow soldiers thought he was brave to the point almost of insanity. His belief in eventual German victory was absolute and if anyone voiced doubts, Hitler would launch into a long tirade to convince them otherwise.

In June 1916 the 16th Bavarians moved south to take up a position near the Somme. There they came under heavy attack during the British advance that is now known as the Battle of the Somme. Hitler's regiment took heavy casualties and on October 7 a shell sent a shard of shrapnel into Hitler's leg. Although he begged to stay with the regiment, Hitler was evacuated to a hospital near Berlin. As he recovered, Hitler spent several days in the capital. He was disgusted by the profiteering going on and by the left wing politicians calling for peace. The comparison between such people and his heroic comrades in the front line struck Hitler deeply—and the fact that many of the profiteers and defeatists were Jews reinforced the latent anti-Semitic views he had gained as a teenager in Vienna. More enjoyably for Hitler, he also found time to paint seriously. The watercolors he completed at this period are generally considered to be his best.

In December Hitler left hospital, but was sent to the training camp of his regiment. Not until March 1917 was Hitler pronounced fit for front line duty and returned to his regiment. There was talk that Hitler should be promoted to sergeant. His long experience in the front line would make him a valuable instructor to the raw recruits coming into the regiment. But the promotion was never made. One of Hitler's officers later alleged that this was because Hitler lacked leadership qualities, and implied that Hitler did not salute properly, rarely polished his boots and was inclined to slouch about in a most unofficer-like way, which is rather different from the other accounts we have of him.

It might have been that Hitler did not want to be promoted. He enjoyed his role as a dispatch runner and was widely recognized as the best in the regiment. But as a sergeant he would have had to give up this duty for work in a regular company. Hitler, long a despised itinerant artist, loved the respect his dispatch-carrying skills brought him and would have been reluctant to give that up for the dubious delights of a sergeant's role. He remained a corporal.

As Hitler returned to the front line the German army was carrying out one of the more impressive defensive strategies of the war. On February 4 the Kaiser had ordered a massive withdrawal to a series of prepared defenses known as the Hindenburg Line. By pulling back from the land fought over during 1915 and 1916, the Germans managed not only to establish themselves in more robust defenses, but also to abandon a series of salients and kinks. The move made the front line 25 miles shorter than it had been and thus easier to defend.

In the trenches, however, Hitler saw a very different effect. All the German soldiers knew that they were to fall back in a series of phased withdrawals. They knew that engineers were laying waste the ground to be abandoned and were constructing massive fortifications along the new line of defense. Why, they asked themselves, risk being killed for a stretch of trench which was soon to be abandoned in any case? The soldiers became less willing to fight and lacked determination. In some areas the withdrawal had to take place earlier than planned, in others it became a disorderly bolt for the new positions.

Supreme German commanders General Paul von Hindenburg, Kaiser Wilhelm II and General Ludendorff

NO GOING BACK

Hitler observed well and drew the lesson that if soldiers know they are to retreat, they give up the will to fight. Not only did this apply to soldiers, Hitler thought, but to generals as well. He was to put the policy of avoiding retreat whenever possible into strict practice when he got into a position to start issuing orders.

In the spring of 1918, the 16th Bavarians were involved in the great attacks of the Ludendorff Offensives, which drove the British and French back for miles from the front line, but which failed to achieve a war-winning breakthrough. If Hitler learned anything from these sweeping advances, it was that capturing territory without decisively beating the enemy army was useless. It was during these attacks, however, that Hitler himself achieved a personal triumph of his own.

As well as winning his Iron Cross, 2nd class, in 1914, Hitler had also won the Military Cross with swords, the Service Medal 3rd Class and been mentioned in dispatches for bravery. One morning during the great advances, the story went later, Hitler was taking a message to a forward unit when he saw what he took to be a discarded French helmet a short distance off. Slipping across the field to retrieve the souvenir, Hitler found himself looking down into a shellhole occupied by a number of French soldiers. He whipped out his pistol and began shouting orders over his shoulder as if he were backed up by a number of other Germans. The Frenchmen surrendered, and were shepherded to the rear by the jubilant Hitler.

It is not entirely clear how many French soldiers Hitler captured that day. Nazi propaganda later claimed the figure to be 15, but men in the front line that day thought it may have been six, or perhaps four, while they also disagreed on whether the captured soldiers were French or

English. The event was enough to prompt his officers to recommend him for another medal in recognition of this and many other instances of initiative and bravery. On August 4, Hitler was awarded the Iron Cross, 1st Class. For a mere corporal to be awarded such a prestigious decoration was almost unheard of, particularly as the medal was specifically for leadership skills as well as for bravery and initiative.

Ironically the officer who signed Hitler's citation was Hugo Gutmann, a Jew.

In October the 16th Bavarians were back on the defensive, and they were back at Ypres. On 14 October, Hitler was blinded by mustard gas during a British dawn attack. The attack was beaten off and Hitler was, once again, sent back to Germany to recover from wounds. For days Hitler was prostrate with pain and shock. Slowly he recovered both his sight and his health.

Then, on November 10, a clergyman came into Hitler's ward and announced to the wounded soldiers that Germany had surrendered. He went on to announce the abdication of the Kaiser and the founding of a republic.

Exactly what happened next has been the subject of perhaps more speculation and debate about Hitler's life than any other period. According to Hitler's account written later in *Mein Kampf*, he suffered a severe relapse which left him again blind and prostrate. While lying helpless, Hitler claimed, he received a quasi-mystical vision in which he was instructed to save Germany from the traitors and Jews who had stabbed the heroic armed forces in the back and brought about defeat.

That Hitler suffered a relapse is certain, but it was not severe enough to stop his discharge from hospital on November 20—though he could read only newspaper headlines, not the articles themselves. Whether he received a vision or not is impossible to know, but he was certainly a changed man.

Throughout the war, Hitler had found a home in the army and in his regiment. After years of drifting from one rented room to another, Hitler had found stability and friendship as well as a clear sense of purpose and the ability to carry that purpose out. The defeat of Germany swept all that away and Hitler was devastated.

Like many others, Hitler could not bring himself to accept that the magnificent German army and its heroic soldiers had been defeated on the field of battle. Instead, Hitler looked for another cause of the defeat and he found it easily enough.

By October 1918, Germany was staggering. In the previous four months the German army had taken its heaviest battlefield casualties ever, added to which were over 1.6 million soldiers sick with disease and another million or so unavailable for duty for a variety of reasons, some of them fabricated. At home, food was running out and the economy was in turmoil. The actual catalyst for the collapse of Germany had been a series of demonstrations, uprisings and mutinies that swept German cities and military bases in early November 1918. The lead role in many areas was taken by communists or socialists, some of them Jews, and the ordinary citizens or soldiers took no action to stop them. In Munich, Hitler's home town, the collapse of the monarchy was swiftly followed by an attempt to set up a communist government, though this was quickly overthrown in a brief but bitter civil war.

For Hitler and millions of other ex-servicemen the peace was a devastating experience. From being highly valued members of society bonded together by shared dangers into strong units, the men were suddenly adrift and alone. Even worse, many found themselves being treated as failed representatives of the old military elite of the Hohenzollern monarchy. They were unemployed, alone and poor.

Among these men there began to form the idea that later became known as *Dolchstoss*, or "stab in the back." It was said that the German army had been holding its own at the Front and was undefeated on the field for battle, but that it had been undermined by the agitation of communists eager to foster revolution and by Jews eager to return to the money-making conditions of peace.

The legend was encouraged by the words and actions of the leading generals. On August 8, 1918 the British and Empire troops attacked on the Western Front and drove the Germans back seven miles, capturing thousands of prisoners. The German second in command, General Erich von Ludendorff, called it "the Black Day of the German Army." He contacted the supreme commander Paul von Hindenburg and the two men decided that Germany could no longer win the war. The task they set themselves was to avoid losing it.

Hindenburg, Ludendorff and others argued that the politicians should seek an armistice immediately. If peace could be agreed while the army still projected to the Allies a semblance of might and strength then the peace treaty might be fairly lenient on Germany. The government, led by Prince Max of Baden, refused to take responsibility for defeat. If the army was beaten, Prince Max said, it was up to the army to hoist a white flag over the trenches.

By early October, Ludendorff and Hindenburg were telling Prince Max that an immediate armistice was essential if the army was not to collapse. Worried by incipient signs of communist revolution, Prince Max was convinced. He decided he would need the army intact to put down a red revolution. He contacted the Allies to ask for terms for an armistice.

Allied commanders during the surrender at Compiègne

The generals, meanwhile, had changed their minds. On October 17 Ludendorff met with the Kaiser to review the state of the German army, its supplies, ammunition, equipment and potential reinforcements as well as to inspect the latest intelligence reports on the Allies. Ludendorff left the meeting convinced that the Allies were incapable of mounting a major offensive within the next four weeks, by which time the winter rains would have set in. Mud had favored the defense throughout the war and so, Ludendorff reasoned, the German army would be able to hold out until the spring of 1919. He now advised Prince Max not to ask for an armistice. Max refused, so on October 25 Ludendorff resigned. Hindenburg also sent in his resignation, but the Kaiser refused to accept it.

On October 30 Germany's ally the Turkish Empire surrendered, followed on November 3 by the second ally, Austria–Hungary. In Germany riots, demonstrations and communist seizures of town halls were taking place. On November 7 the official German peace negotiators crossed the front line into France. The fighting continued and in some areas German resistance was so effective that the Allied troops had to retreat. On the morning of November 11 the Germans signed the Armistice.

The army generals could therefore state, quite correctly, that they had advised against surrender and that the German army had been holding the Western Front and even advancing in some areas. They could also point out that the politicians were forced to surrender because of unrest at home in Germany. It was a distortion of the truth, of course. The German army was exhausted and fast running out of morale, ammunition and recruits. It might have been able to hold off the Allies for a few weeks, perhaps months, but the end result was not in doubt. Germany had been defeated on the battlefield.

Men such as Hitler, however, preferred to believe that the great German army had been betrayed, that it had been stabbed in the back by communists and Jews. From his self-imposed exile in Sweden, Ludendorff poured out a stream of memoirs and diatribes which supported this view. As the humiliating terms of the final peace treaty became known in Germany in 1919 the servicemen felt even more betrayed. Their views spread rapidly and before long many citizens of Germany at least half believed the *Dolchstoss* legend.

For Hitler, it was a major campaigning tool. As a highly decorated ex-serviceman who, literally, bore the scars of battle, Hitler was in a position to appeal to his fellow former soldiers. When he was joined by the heroic flying ace Hermann Göring, Hitler's appeal broadened to include all those who respected the men who had fought for Germany.

It was his war record that made Hitler acceptable to many voters who might otherwise have dismissed him. And it was the views Hitler formed during his time as a soldier, and immediately afterwards, which won him and the nascent Nazi Party its early support. It is not within the scope of this book to detail the rise to power of Hitler and the Nazi party, but it is important to realize the importance, at least in the early years, of the influence of the war and Hitler's war service on the German public and the fortunes of the Nazis.

It was Hitler's war record that enabled him to conjure up what was to become known as the Hitler Myth, though the propaganda chief Josef Goebbels later developed it more fully. Essentially the Hitler Myth held that Hitler was a common man of the people who had fought an exemplary war of great heroism and as such personified the Germany of the hard-working, decent citizen. As the Nazi Party grew in the early 1920s, the image was refined slightly to put Hitler as the champion of the little family man against big business. For this he drew on his rank of corporal to show he did not have ideas or ambitions other than to support the ordinary German. When the Nazis engaged in brutal street fights or other violent action, the Hitler Myth had it that a corporal could lead his men, but could not be held responsible for their every action.

This myth would be reworked under the hand of Goebbels so that by the time Germany again went to war, Hitler was being hailed as the greatest military strategist of history. Such grand claims were far removed from reality. But the underlying myth was rooted in Hitler's battlefield heroism and exemplary service. Without the man who was Corporal Hitler, there could have been no Führer.

By the time Hitler became Chancellor of the German Republic in 1933, he had left his war record far behind him—at least as far as the German public was concerned. He was, however, about to bring his military views and opinions to work on the full armed might of the German nation and, significantly, on the proud aristocratic officer corps which dominated it.

Hitler in a formal portrait designed to show steely determination

DOVER
Ostende
BRUGGE
DOVER
Le Tréport
Bresle
Dieppe
AMIENS

RE-ARMING THE REICH

The Treaty of Versailles that ended the First World War reduced Germany's armed forces to a tiny rump. On coming to power Hitler was determined to re-arm his Reich to make it a military superpower

In his rise to power inside Germany, Hitler had used luck, skill, propaganda and violence—or the very real threat of it—to achieve his ends. It soon became clear that he was to use very much the same tactics in achieving his aims now that he was the Führer of the German people. For the luck and skill he would rely on his own talents and for the propaganda he could rely on the dark genius of Josef Goebbels. For the violence he turned to the armed forces of Germany, the Reichswehr, and at once realized that this instrument of war was quite simply not up to the job.

The Treaty of Versailles, which ended the First World War, was dictated to Germany by the victorious Allies. The numerous provisions were prompted by the unshakeable belief that it had been Germany and her aristocratic, military elite which had started the war. If war were to be avoided in future, the authors of the treaty believed, Germany had to be stripped of any offensive power. Under the terms of Versailles, the German armed forces were to number no more than 100,000 men, none of whom could be conscripts, and were allowed

Panzerjäger I or "tank-hunter", a Panzer I chassis mounted with a 47mm anti-tank gun, France 1940'

The German army on maneuvers in 1925

neither tanks nor aircraft. The famously efficient Army General Staff was disbanded.

The new Reichswehr was composed of the Reichsheer, or army, and the Reichsmarine, or navy. The majority of the manpower was in the Reichsheer, which consisted of 2 Group Commands, 7 Infantry Divisions and 3 Cavalry Divisions. The Reichsmarine was so reduced in size that it was little more than a fisheries protection and coastguard service. The aim of Versailles was, simply, to stop Germany from having sufficient armed forces to be tempted into starting a war. The effect was to drive the German governments and military establishment towards finding new and imaginative ways of creating effective military power.

The rearmament of Germany after the catastrophic defeat of the Great War began before Hitler became Führer, but it was to gather pace and urgency once the Nazis were in power. Crucially, it was Hitler's ambition for an aggressive foreign policy that not only gave the rearmament a timescale, but also pointed the direction which it took. This ambition and the restrictive military terms of the Treaty were to have a direct bearing on the form of the new German war machine which Hitler was to create.

Less well-known clauses in the Versailles Treaty committed the victorious Allies to reducing their own armed forces. These reductions were not on anything like the drastic scale imposed on Germany, but would have been significant if they had ever been carried out. However the idealistic euphoria for peace and the perceived benefits of the influence of the League of Nations which dominated thinking in 1919 soon wilted in the face of belligerent communism radiating from Soviet Russia and the practical needs of Britain and France to police their empires and colonies. In the event, the planned disarmament of the victorious nations never took place. This, of course, gave Hitler the ready-made excuse he needed for rearming Germany.

BREAKING THE RULES

In 1935 Hitler openly renounced the Treaty of Versailles when he put before the Reichstag the Law for the Reconstruction of the National Defense Forces. The Reichswehr became the Wehrmacht. The newly formed Wehrmacht would still consist of an army and a navy—the renamed Heer and Kriegsmarine, but a new air force was born as well—the Luftwaffe. Although an efficient and effective armed fist was vital to Hitler's foreign policy, he preferred to leave most of the detailed work of rearmament to his subordinates. Hitler spent most of his time in these years securing his grip on power at home and engaging in diplomacy abroad. Only when a weapon or idea caught his imagination did he become personally involved in re-arming his nation.

The re-arming of Germany had, in fact, already begun before Hitler came to power. In 1920 the task of establishing a Reichsheer, or land army, was given to General Hans von Seeckt. Allowed less than 100,000 men with no tanks or aircraft and only light artillery, Seeckt set out to get around the restrictions of Versailles without actually breaking the letter of the Treaty.

He began by deciding that the men would all be trained as officers or NCOs, no matter what their nominal rank. In this way, Seeckt planned to be able to expand the army massively by the drafting in of large numbers of recruits to be commanded by the existing professionals, who would all be upgraded in rank. To ensure the prospective recruits had some training, Seeckt not only tolerated the existence of private paramilitary units, such as Hitler's brownshirts, but in some cases provided cash and training. Likewise, schools and universities were given help in training their students along military lines.

Other provisions of the Versailles Treaty were evaded by the misuse of language. Forbidden to have a General Staff to plan campaigns in detail, von Seeckt established an Administrative Office, which did much the same thing. Instructed not to have tanks, von Seeckt ordered the construction of "tractors" which were light tanks in all but name. In 1926 von Seeckt was caught on the fringes of a political scandal and resigned, but his basic ideas continued to be implemented.

Guderian formulated the concept that became blitzkrieg

It was in the later 1920s that a new school of thought grew up in the army. A leading proponent of the new theory was Heinz Guderian. Supported by a number of other able young officers, Guderian believed that the close integration in the tactical use of modern weapons could break the trench stalemate which had dominated the First World War. In particular, Guderian believed that a force of mixed tanks, linked by radio to each other and to mobile command posts could punch a hole through any defense. If supported by motorized artillery and motorized infantry, the tanks could then speed on to exploit a breakthrough over a massive area of the enemy rear. It was a nascent form of blitzkrieg.

Guderian's ideas had two main problems in the early 1930s. The first was that the senior generals did not trust the tanks to be mechanically reliable in actual battlefield conditions of mud and dust. The second was that Versailles banned Germany from having tanks. While calling the vehicles "tractors" or even "command vehicles" was a successful ploy in covering the construction of a few prototypes, mass production of service vehicles could not be hidden.

Then, in 1933, the new Chancellor Adolf Hitler was shown a regiment of armored cars and light tanks cooperating with anti-tank guns and motorized infantry at an army maneuver. "They are what I need," declared Hitler. After his experiences in the trenches, Hitler would have appreciated the importance of armor and the benefits of mobile warfare. Likewise, his political ambitions for Germany would demand a series of swift, successful strikes on other countries. The slow, merciless grind of conventional warfare with its artillery barrages and infantry advances would not deliver the sort of fast victory Hitler needed. But panzer attacks might. He sought out Guderian

A squad of Panzer Mk I tanks at a pre-war Nuremberg rally

and made him Chief of Panzer Troops. Hitler told Guderian to develop the hardware, tactics and strategy needed to crush enemy armies in short, brutal campaigns. With Hitler's open support and in flagrant disregard for Versailles, the rearmament of the German army could begin.

Although Guderian concentrated largely on the design and production of his tanks, the panzer units were organized to be an elite. About 40 per cent of the men came from the old cavalry regiments, who believed themselves to be the best

soldiers in the army, and the new recruits were selected on merit, with many men being turned down. The successful elite were given a smart black uniform designed by top fashion designers and a distinctive black beret.

The men were trained harder and more thoroughly than recruits to other units. Each man in a tank crew, be he driver, gunner or radio operator, was expected to be able to perform the duty of at least one other crew member. In this way a battlefield casualty would not incapacitate the tank. The panzer crews were drilled relentlessly in mobile warfare tactics. When ordered to take part

in the occupation of Austria and Czechoslovakia, they treated the assignments as full scale war drills. The panzer troops believed they were the shock elite of the new German armed forces.

In April 1934 Guderian proudly presented Hitler with the first 15 panzers off the production line, the Panzer Is. The name is short for *Panzerkampfwagen*, meaning "armored war car." The Panzer I was a light tank equipped with twin machine guns or a single 20mm gun. When Germany openly breached the Versailles Treaty in 1935, it was the Panzer I which appeared at parades, rallies and on maneuvers, often in large numbers. They impressed the German public, but did not unduly worry military observers from Britain or France. The Panzer I was never intended to be anything more than a training or scout vehicle. The British and French had much larger and better tanks already in service. Even the Poles had better tanks.

The Panzer II, ordered from Daimler-Benz in 1934, was a real fighting tank. The first ten came off the production lines in January 1936, then manufacture was held up while modifications were made to the design. Finally, in March 1937 full scale production began. Almost 1,900 Panzer IIs were completed that year, though production dipped to 1,000 in 1938 as newer models took over in the factories. Production of the Panzer II was to continue until late in 1943, though by then it was being used as a training tank or as the base for mobile bridging equipment or as an armored ammunition cart to support other panzer models and other specialist uses.

LONE WOLF

The Panzer II that entered service in 1937 was a light tank of 10 metric tons which could travel at 30mph and was armed with a 20mm automatic cannon as well as a heavy machine gun. It also had a two-way radio fitted as standard and later models had smoke canisters. When it was ordered, the Panzer II was envisaged as a fast-moving tank able to keep up with cavalry units and to be used to crack strongpoints which the cavalry could not reduce. In the invasion of Poland in 1939 some of the Panzer IIs were used in this way, though the tank commanders sometimes found themselves moving on alone without cavalry support.

A pair of Panzer Mk II tanks on maneuvers

The key weakness of the Panzer II proved to be its armor, which was easily pierced by enemy artillery and cannon. During the invasion of France in 1940, swarms of the Panzer IIs moved ahead and on the flanks of the rapidly advancing panzer columns. Their task was to act as scout vehicles able to deal with enemy infantry or cavalry units and other soft targets, but with instructions to stop and wait for the larger panzers if any serious opposition was encountered.

In the event the vast swarms of these small panzers sweeping across the countryside spread panic and fear so effectively that many enemy units simply fled without bothering to find out if these were the light Panzer II or heavier and more formidable tanks. The reports sent back by the retreating units to their HQ inevitably reported the tanks from which they fled to be heavy panzers, creating the impression that vast numbers of unstoppable heavy tanks were moving forward. It was not an effect that Guderian had counted on, but it made the battlefield success of the panzers all the more impressive.

By 1935 Heinz Guderian had worked out the main features of the tactical system to be known as blitzkrieg, or "lightning war." He wanted to see massed assault units made up of panzers, supported by mechanized and non-mechanized infantry and artillery. The assaults would be closely supported by targeted bombing from the skies, especially dive bombing. All units were to be linked by radio. These armored assaults would smash holes in the enemy line, then drive deep into the enemy rear to destroy supply and communication routes, wipe out reserves and generally disrupt the ability of the enemy to fight any sort of co-ordinated form of defense. The remainder of the German infantry and cavalry would advance on foot to mop up the scattered remnants of the enemy army. In terms of numbers, the units on foot composed the bulk of the army and were expected to encounter heavy fighting as they reduced strongpoints bypassed by the panzers.

Guderian envisaged the main fighting elements of the armored assault columns to be made up of two types of tank, which were produced as the Panzer III and the Panzer IV. The Panzer III was the center of some controversy. Guderian saw it as an anti-tank weapon equipped with a 50mm cannon and twin machine guns. The section of the army responsible for ordering equipment wanted to arm the Panzer III with the standard 37mm anti-tank gun of the German artillery to save costs and to ensure that ammunition would be compatible between the two. In the event the tank was produced with the 37mm gun, but with a turret capable of taking the 50mm gun, which later models did actually carry.

The design of the Panzer III included very heavy frontal armor as the vehicle was intended as an attack weapon. More crucially all members of the tank crew were linked to each other by an intercom system. This ensured that communication in battle was not hindered by the noise of gunfire or engines and proved to be a key advantage in the tank vs tank battles of 1940 and 1941. Soon all tanks had such a system.

After a series of prototypes were field tested, the Panzer III entered production in December 1938. About 100 had been produced by the outbreak of war, but over 500 were with the Wehrmacht by the time of the invasion of France in 1940. With the sister tank, the Panzer IV, being produced on a similar timescale it can be seen that the rearmament of the Wehrmacht for blitzkrieg was barely complete by the time Hitler threw the army into action.

A German sniper armed with a 98k rifle and telescopic sight

The Panzer IV was envisaged by Guderian as being the main assault weapon of the armored columns. It was to have a heavy gun able to attack strongpoints and fortifications as well as to overrun infantry or artillery positions. It was to be defended against enemy tanks by the Panzer III. Hitler took a very close interest in the development and production of the Panzer IV, more so than the other panzers produced before the outbreak of war. Hitler approved the prototype specification of an 18 metric ton tank with a speed of 25mph and a 75mm cannon combined with frontal armor able to withstand most French artillery.

Various companies were approached to produce prototypes, but it was Krupp which won the contract for mass production of the Panzer IV in 1936. The first 35 tanks were produced in 1937, but design changes after the tanks entered service meant that only 100 or so were in service with the army when war began. The Panzer IV went on to be produced in large numbers throughout the war and to be adapted for a wide range of battlefield purposes. The chassis of the Panzer IV were used as mobile bases for anti-aircraft gun platforms, assault guns, anti-tank guns, siege howitzers, rocket launchers, bridges, tank-recovery cranes and as ammunition carriers. After the surrender of Germany in 1945 large numbers of the Panzer IV were taken into service by the Red Army or sold to friendly nations by the British and Americans. The Panzer IV last saw action in the desert tank battles of the Arab–Israeli War of 1967 and can lay claim to being the most successful tank design in history.

While the panzer production program was getting under way, other methods of supporting rearmament were being driven forward by Hitler. In 1933 he ordered a massive increase in steel production and the stockpiling of oil and gasoline. Then, in 1935, Hitler ordered the resumption of conscription. At the age of 20, men were called up to serve in the army, to learn how to handle weapons and to refine the habits of discipline and order which they had already been learning in the Hitler Youth movement, to which all children were recruited at the age of 14. By 1937 the Wehrmacht was 5 million strong, with 8 million trained reserves.

This was the mass mobilization that Seeckt had envisaged in the 1920s. True to Seeckt's plan the permanent soldiers were all immediately promoted to being officers and sergeants, ensuring the recruits had well-trained commanders. The plan worked smoothly, and Seeckt lived just long enough to see it happen. Having left the German army after a scandal, the 70 year old Seeckt was in China advising Chiang Kai-Shek on his resistance to the Japanese invasion. A year later, he died.

These vast numbers of men now in the German army were equipped with a surprisingly traditional array of weapons, the panzers aside. The basic German infantry weapon remained the Mauser rifle, the Karabiner 98k. This was the same rifle Hitler had used in the trenches during the First World War. It had a five shot magazine and a robust bolt-action as well as a shorter than average barrel.

Sub-machine guns were, at first, a weapon used only by a minority of troops. However as the new war experience showed that rate of fire was more crucial on the battlefield than long range accuracy, these machine guns became more common. The first sub-machine gun to enter service was the MP40, though some troops preferred a version of the British Sten gun. During the 1930s, the Germans settled on two light machine gun designs and used these guns, the MG34 and MG42, throughout the war. The latter design was so successful that it was copied by the USA after the war and, in the slightly modified form of the M60, remains in use.

The new theory of offensive blitzkrieg had little room in it for the use of purely defensive weapons, though it was recognized that they would be needed around static installations. However many senior generals did not really believe Guderian's blitzkrieg ideas would work and so insisted that defensive weapons were also developed and manufactured. By the outbreak of war, the Germans had developed a wide variety of mines.

The "pot mine" was a basic, upwardly exploding charge for use against infantry. The "shrapnel-mine" was more sophisticated. When triggered, a small charge launched the main canister into the air. When this exploded it spread a deadly rain of metal fragments across a large area. The "Tellermine" contained one pound of TNT in a large flattened circular plate. It could be set off by pulling on a long trigger wire, or left to explode when a vehicle weighing over 350 pounds pressed down on it. It would disable a tank with ease.

Many German criminals joined up and were given weapons

German infantry with a 3.7cm anti-tank gun in Belgium

In the fields of artillery, the Germans were continually seeking new designs, and developments continued right up to the end of the war. The standard anti-tank gun of 1935 was a 37mm caliber gun firing heavy projectiles at very high velocity. At the other end of the scale, the Germans also had a number of huge artillery pieces mounted on railway carriages. The 800mm Dora had a range of 29 miles, a crew of 250 men and could fire a 10,500 pound shell that measured 25 feet long at a rate of two rounds per hour. Even the most formidable defenses would be reduced to dust by such weapons. In the field they proved of limited use because the rail lines to get them into action were usually destroyed during the swift advance of the panzers. Such guns would have been more suited to the static defense systems of the First World War.

The greatest of all the German artillery was the versatile 88mm. This gun fired a high velocity shell which could penetrate almost any tank armor in existence and its accuracy became legendary. It could also fire anti-aircraft ammunition. This gun was just 25 feet long and needed a crew of only six men to fire eight rounds per minute over a maximum range of 33,000 yards. The army was equipped with a variety of other artillery pieces, but few were as lethal or as respected as "The 88."

Far more than any other army in the 1930s, the Heer used motorcycles for communication and reconnaissance purposes. The BMWR/75746cc was the military motorcycle in most widespread use, especially in its sidecar guise. One of Guderian's key moves was to attach an infantry battalion mounted on motorcycles to each panzer division. This ensured that the panzers had infantry with them, no matter how far or how fast they advanced.

An essential element of the new methods of waging war being pioneered by Guderian was close air support. This was to be provided by the Luftwaffe, created by Hitler in 1935.

As with the other branches of the German armed forces, the air force had long been the subject of clandestine training and rearmament. The army had schools which officially trained glider pilots, but in reality taught general flying skills. During the 1920s, when Russia and Germany drew close as nations shunned by the victorious Allies, there was a secret training base in the Soviet Union, and various cover organizations for the initial forming of the new German air force.

ACE IN THE HOLE

The Luftwaffe was the beloved creation of Hermann Göring, who had ended the First World War in command of the Richthofen squadron and with an impressive reputation as an heroic ace fighter pilot. While working as a civilian pilot, Göring married the Baroness von Fock-

Göring, Raeder and Hitler in 1940

Kantzow before joining the small Nazi Party in 1922. Göring brought upper class grandeur and elegance to the working class Hitler and together the two war heroes led the Nazis to power. Hitler rewarded Göring with wealth and luxury, and also with the position of *Reichsluftminister*, (Reich Air Minister) in charge of rebuilding the Luftwaffe as a war machine.

Göring found that during the previous years, the leaders of Germany's civilian aircraft industry, Hugo Junkers, Ernst Heinkel and Willy Messerschmitt, had been secretly working toward re-arming Germany with military aircraft. They had used expertise gained in building passenger aircraft to prepare plans for up to date bombing aircraft while racing machines had served as a cover for the design of fighters.

One of Göring's first acts was to bring in Ernst Udet, another First World War fighter ace, to act as the Luftwaffe's director of supplies and equipment. Together the two men worked out what the Luftwaffe would be expected to do in time of conflict, and set about finding the right aircraft for the job.

The first aircraft to be ordered in large numbers was the twin-engined bomber, the Heinkel III. This aircraft was in production as a transport aircraft, but Heinkel had full plans for a bomber version ready and, with a few minor modifications, these were used to produce the workhorse of the Luftwaffe bomber service. The Heinkel III had a maximum speed of 252 mph and had a range of nearly 1,300 miles. Armed with 6 machine-guns, it could carry 5,501 pounds of bombs. The next aircraft to be approved was the versatile Junkers 88 which, in its various modifications, could be used as dive bomber, level bomber, night fighter, photo reconnaissance or tank destroyer.

To protect these bombers, and destroy those of the enemy, Göring ordered the construction of swarms of fighters from the Messerschmitt company. The first to enter production was the Messerschmitt 109, a single engined fighter which could out perform any other aircraft in the world and could carry a deadly armament of machine guns and cannon. The Messerschmitt 109 first flew in 1935 and saw extensive service in the Spanish Civil War, where a tendency to wobble when firing was recognized and the problem solved in time for the outbreak of war in 1939.

The following Messerschmitt 110 was less successful. It drew on the same technology as the 109, but was a heavier twin-engined machine. In the later 1930s, Göring had high hopes of the 110 as a long range fighter and light bomber. It was, indeed, superior to most fighters in Europe at that date, but by the time the war began Britain in particular had single-engined fighters able to outmaneuver the 110 in dogfights. Subsequently the Messerschmitt 110 was converted to perform a fast, light bomber role in support of battlefield troops, and also made a name for itself as a defensive fighter able to bring a heavy armament to bear on enemy bombers.

The aircraft in which Hitler himself took the closest interest, however, was the Junkers 87 Stuka. From the start this aircraft was intended to be used in close co-operation with the panzers that were coming to dominate German military thinking.

WINGS OF DEATH

The term Stuka is short for *Sturzkampfflugzeug*, a word used to describe all dive bombers. The concept of dive bombing allows for much greater accuracy in the aiming of bombs than the method of standard level flight bombing, but it puts enormous strains on the aircraft. As the bomb is released, the aircraft has to be pulled out of the dive at speed, which puts great stresses on the wings and fuselage. This means that a dive bomber needs to be heavy and robust, without reducing its performance in level flight to the point of making it too vulnerable to enemy attack.

It was Udet who first saw that the dive bomber could provide very close and devastating bomber support to rapidly advancing panzer units which might get outside the range of their own conventional artillery. In 1934 the Luftwaffe tested a prototype from Junkers, the K47. This was an all-

metal, low-wing monoplane designed as a two-seat fighter, but its failure to perform well in that category led to it being put through diving tests. The results of these trials led to the development of the specialist dive bomber, the Junkers 87.

The peculiar demands of dive bombing led the Junkers designers to develop the characteristic inverted gull wing equipped with a maze of slots and flaps on the trailing edge. The blunt nose of the aircraft had a deep radiator, and tapered upward to the cockpit to give the pilot a good view of his target as he dived. The bulky and ungainly undercarriage was necessary because the aircraft was expected to operate from a series of temporary air fields as the armored columns advanced, and the wheels would have to stand up to coping with slanting or bumpy surfaces that were far from ideal. On the wheel legs the Stuka was fitted with a siren which screamed out a loud, piercing shriek as the plane dived at high speed. The adverse effect of the Stuka scream on the morale of enemy troops on the ground was phenomenal and became a key element in blitzkrieg.

Hitler was delighted with the Stuka and

A force of early D-1 variants of the Messerschmitt Bf109 in 1939

A squadron of Junkers Ju87 Stuka dive bombers

warmly praised a propaganda film made by Goebbels which showed the dive bombers pounding a town to rubble. The film was sent to neutral countries in the late autumn of 1939 as news of the bombing of Warsaw reached Britain and France. The message was clear—make peace or the Stukas will get you!

Despite occasional slips in the preparations for war, however, Hitler and his subordinates had achieved marvels. For two years, from 1933 to 1935, they had kept their rearmament preparations secret. Then from 1935 onward they had openly flouted the Versailles Treaty, but without any adverse diplomatic impact.

The armed forces they built up were formidable and, arguably, the best in the world at that time. But they were not as good as the military men had wanted. When Hitler threw Germany into war in 1939 the navy was barely half built, while the army wanted at least two more years of panzer production to be ready.

When the shooting began, the rearmament situation was not perfect. It remained to be seen if it was good enough.

DOVER
BRUGGE
DOVER
Berck
Noyelles
Bresle
AMIENS
St Valéry-en Caux

6

TAKING CONTROL

The German army and navy had no intention of blindly obeying Hitler's orders, but if Hitler was to put his war plans into effect he would need complete control over the armed forces. He set out to subjugate the military to Nazi rule

Before the Nazis took power in Germany the armed forces had a definite and vital role in German society and government. It was not a role with which Hitler was comfortable. He wanted to have total control over all aspects of the German state and from 1933 onward set out to achieve dominance over the armed forces. By 1938 he had very largely succeeded.

The senior officers of the army and navy believed that they were the natural guardians of the German nation. Although they considered it improper for the armed forces to become involved in politics, they did believe the army had a right and a duty to preserve what they considered to be the best in German national spirit, pride and honor. It was a fine line to walk, but the officer corps had no doubt that it was one they were called upon to follow. In part, this was a duty inherited from the landed aristocracy who had made up the bulk of the army officers in the days of the Kaiser.

Hitler in Landsberg Prison with Hess (2nd from right): during his 264 days of imprisonment in 1924 he wrote Mein Kampf in which he set out his blueprint for Germany's future

SHARED VIEWPOINT

Many officers had resented the forced abdication of the Kaiser in 1918 and still wanted a return to monarchy in Germany. Some wanted a constitutional monarchy, such as that in Britain, others looked on this as an effete compromise and wanted a return to full absolutism. The one thing all officers could agree on, however, was that communism was bad for Germany and must be crushed. Hitler believed the same.

Before Hitler had come to power, the officer corps had been involved with the government and with maintaining the constitution for many years. It had also had close dealings with Hitler himself. In 1923 Hitler launched a Nazi coup in Bavaria. The aim was to replace the civilian government with one led by Hitler. The Nazi stormtroopers seized

Hitler bows to President von Hindenburg, 1933

key government buildings while Hitler announced his assumption of power in a meeting room in a beer cellar. A large march of over 2,000 armed stormtroopers was brought to a bloody halt by a hail of gunfire from police marksmen, while soldiers waited in support. Hitler was arrested and briefly imprisoned for the abortive coup.

The coup was crucial to Hitler's relationship with the army. He had on his side Erich Ludendorff, the highly respected First World War general, who had been second only to Hindenburg in the German High Command. Despite this, the serving army officers had preferred to support the constitutional republic rather than follow their old general. Hitler learned, and did not forget.

At his trial after the failed coup, Hitler declared, "We never thought to carry through a revolution against the Army. We believed we should succeed with the Army." Hitler subsequently made much of the fact that the 1923 march had been halted by armed police, not the army—though he conveniently forgot the army had been hostile and would have been on the scene soon enough if the police had failed. He thus began to build up a legend that he had always been friendly to his old colleagues in the army and wanted to gain power legally, allied to the officer corps.

Indeed, by 1926 Hitler was going much further in his wooing of the army by insisting that the Nazi Party was the only political party that promised to overthrow the Versailles Treaty and restore the German army to its rightful, glorious place. He declared that the Nazis were the natural allies of the army. In 1926 few senior officers listened to him. But in 1929 that changed.

The occasion for the change was the trial in September 1929 of three junior army officers who had been caught distributing Nazi propaganda. The dissemination of any party political material by officers was strictly forbidden, so the men went on trial. Hitler chose to give evidence at the trial as a means of talking directly to senior officers and, through the accounts of the trial in army publications, to all members of the officer corps.

Hitler's main point was to emphasize that the Nazi Party wanted only what was good for the German people and the German army. In particular he declared that the National Revolution, outlined in the leaflets the officers had been handing out, referred not to an illegal seizure of power like that in Russia in 1917 but to a mighty outpouring of Germanic spirit, channelled through legal and constitutional means with the glorification of the martial spirit and the armed forces as a key aim.

It was a good message to give to the officer corps, but Hitler skated over one fundamental problem. The army officers believed that they alone had the right to bear arms and control military power. They might choose to tolerate freelance quasi-military formations for various reasons, but it was up to them alone which ones were tolerated. Hitler, however, frequently declared his brownshirt stormtroopers to be a natural armed voice for the German people, or at least of those who voted Nazi. In his 1929 evidence, Hitler merely brushed this control problem aside, but it would return to haunt him.

In the elections of spring 1932, the Nazis became the largest party in the Reichstag, the German Parliament, but did not have an overall majority. The President at this time was Paul von Hindenburg, the great commander in chief of the Germany army in the First World War. Now aged 86, Hindenburg was a figure of immense prestige and respect, and fully aware of the political machinations going on around him. He famously referred to Hitler as "a jumped-up Bohemian Corporal," but was under no illusions as to Hitler's ambitions.

Hindenburg had the power to choose a government, as there was no majority in the Reichstag. He appointed the moderate right winger Heinrich Brüning to be Chancellor of Germany. Hindenburg then summoned Hitler and offered him the post of Vice Chancellor, making it very clear that he viewed Hitler as not fit to be head of government, though of some use as a minister under somebody more reliable. Hitler refused.

Heinrich Brüning was Chancellor of Germany 1932–33

The Nazis, communists and other extremists went back to the streets. They organized rival marches and public meetings, sent their tough paramilitary units to attack each other and unleashed bloodshed in the community. Hundreds of people were killed or maimed and the numbers of injured ran into thousands. In the Reichstag the militants combined to undermine Brüning and his moderate policies aimed at getting Germany out of the economic depression into which it was

Von Papen (right with arm raised) with his chief ministers, June 1932

Schleicher was ousted to make way for Hitler

falling. Brüning resigned and was replaced by another moderate, Franz von Papen, who resigned in turn and was replaced by the army officer Kurt von Schleicher.

Both Schleicher and Hitler believed that, as an army officer, Schleicher would have the support of the army. In reality he lacked the support of the aristocracy and upper middle classes from whose ranks the officer corps was recruited and so his hold on the armed forces was weak. The Nazis continued their street battles and subversive parliamentary tactics. Civil war appeared imminent.

Finally, in January 1933, Hitler made a deal with Papen and the two men went to see President Hindenburg. Essentially, the compromise saw Hitler as Chancellor, Papen as Vice Chancellor and the ministries divided up between the Nazis and a number of smaller moderate parties. The Communist Party was, of course, excluded.

Hindenburg was unimpressed for he still harboured concerns about Hitler and the Nazis. Papen, however, persuaded Hindenburg that he could handle the upstart corporal who, he said, knew only the provincial politics of Bavaria. Hindenburg insisted that the Minister of Defense had to be General Werner von Blomberg so that the army would be in safe political hands. Hitler agreed, so Hindenburg appointed him Chancellor.

Just four days after becoming Chancellor, Hitler called the elite officers of the armed forces to a dinner. He was determined to win over the officer corps to support Nazi power, if not Nazism itself. He had briefed himself well on what the distinguished audience wanted to hear, and he neatly wrapped up Nazi policy in the language of the generals, emphasizing the common ground between their positions. First he dealt with the disastrous state of the German economy. Communism was no answer, Hitler said, and should be destroyed. Nor could the economy be rescued by export drives or sales patter. German goods would not sell abroad unless Germany recovered first its self-respect and then the respect of the world. Then German goods would sell themselves. How was this to be achieved? Through the rearmament of the armed forces and the restoration of the German pride that had been destroyed by the stab in the back of 1919.

In this way, Hitler told the generals, the historic German pride and self-respect would be rebuilt. He nearly slipped when he went on to talk about the army playing a key role in "the Germanization of the East." The officer corps had no desire for a war to acquire Lebensraum. Hitler quickly read the mood of his audience, however, and in response to a question assured the officers that he was talking

Werner von Blomberg (right) was made Minister for War in 1933

about reacquiring the lands lost to Germany under the Versailles Treaty of 1919, not to wars of conquest. Then he turned to the main problem, the Nazi stormtroopers. Again he skated over the difficulty, stating that, "the Army will be the sole bearer of arms and its structure will be unchanged."

Reaction was mixed. Admiral Raeder was impressed, General Fritsch was nervous, General Leeb, who had been in command of troops in Munich in 1923 during Hitler's abortive coup, was dismissive. But it was the reaction of General Blomberg, the Defense Minister, which was to be crucial. Hitler not only trimmed policy to suit the views of the officer corps, he lavished attention on General Blomberg and went out of his way to pay him compliments. The general came to believe that, under Hitler, the new Germany would be supported by what he dubbed "the Twin Pillars." These pillars were the Nazi Party and the Armed Forces. In this he was to be mistaken, though in 1933 it seemed a not unreasonable view. Blomberg's support was to be crucial in winning the support of other officers. But even Blomberg made it clear to Hitler that something had to be done about the stormtroopers.

Known officially as the *Sturmabteilungen*, or SA, the stormtroopers had been formed in 1921 as a squad of large, intimidating doormen to keep troublemakers out of Nazi Party meetings. The SA grew rapidly in numbers and soon had their own para-military uniform dominated by the brown shirts which gave the SA another nickname. The SA became notorious for starting fights at the meetings of other political parties, or pouncing on known communists in the street. In many working class areas it was the dashing uniform and sense of belonging which they got in the SA that induced many young men to join the Nazis.

At first the SA had been led by Ernst Röhm, who created the organization and drill. He left in 1926 after becoming embroiled in a particularly sordid homosexual scandal. Röhm was forced to leave the country, spending some time in South America as a military adviser. Hitler called him back to Germany as soon as he was the leader of a large party in the Reichstag and Röhm again led the SA. By the end of 1932 the SA had 300,000 members, making it three times larger than the armed forces. In 1933 the added prestige of Hitler's being Chancellor brought a flood of recruits to the SA, which in May 1934 had 4 million members. Only a minority of the SA had guns, but all were trained in their use and in military-style drill and combat duties. Röhm and his chief supporters in the SA made no secret of their view that they and their men represented the true martial spirit of the German nation and that they should become the armed forces of Nazi Germany. It is easy to see why the generals were nervous of the SA and its possible future in a Nazi Germany.

FLY IN THE OINTMENT

At the same time, Hitler was beginning to have doubts about the SA and about Röhm in particular. Ernst Röhm was another war hero. He had been wounded in action three times and had joined the Nazis in Munich in the party's earliest days. Röhm was a fervent believer in the need to overthrow the decadent German democracy, as the Nazis saw it, which was undermining the country's greatness and he proved to be an inspirational leader for the SA. After his return in 1931, Röhm organized the rapid growth in numbers and power of his stormtroopers as they took over the streets.

It was just as the SA was achieving its greatest

A parade of the Sturmabteilung *(SA) in 1920s Munich*

Ernst Röhm (center below Hitler) led the SA 1924–25 and 1931-34

success that Hitler began to grow apart from the revolutionary fervor of Röhm. Hitler and the Nazis needed the support of the army officers and the wealthy industrialists if they were to hold on to power, and Röhm despised and was despised by both. He had also managed to make enemies within the Nazi Party.

While the SA were guarding early Nazi Party meetings, a second organization was guarding Nazi Party leaders. These were the *Schutzstaffeln*, the Protection Squads or SS, led from 1929 by Heinrich Himmler. Under Himmler, the SS took on the task of rooting out disloyalty or divergent views among Nazi Party members. Himmler was soon in command of some 50,000 men working full time or part time for the SS. As Hitler consolidated his power as Chancellor, the SS took on some of the duties of the state police, especially when it came to tracking down communist activists. Already the SS was earning the reputation for extreme violence and ruthless actions that would become its hallmark.

By early 1934 the intensely ambitious Himmler had come to see Röhm and the SA as rivals for power in the soon-to-be-established Nazi dictatorship of Germany. He decided to get rid of both, but Röhm was an old friend of Hitler's. Himmler cultivated the army officers, stirring up their unease about Röhm, knowing that they would make this clear to Hitler. Meanwhile, Göring joined Himmler in dislike of the SA.

Before long, reports were appearing on Hitler's desk alleging that key senior members of the SA were planning a coup. It was alleged that the SA felt Hitler had done a deal with the conservative establishment and so betrayed Nazism. Many of these reports came from Himmler's SS in their role of finding internal disquiet in the Nazi Party. While there is no doubt that many SA officers felt Hitler was betraying Nazism, there is no real evidence that Röhm himself was anything more than peeved. Certainly no coup was planned. Nevertheless, Himmler built up a case against Röhm based on half-truths, innuendo and smears. When in June 1934 Hitler was finally shown "evidence" implicating Röhm in a plot to overthrow him, Hitler was ready to believe it.

At this time the SA was enjoying its traditional June break from active duties and Röhm himself was at the spa town of Bad Wiessee enjoying a cultural holiday. On 28 June Himmler phoned Hitler while he was attending the wedding reception of a senior Nazi Party official and poured out a stream of accusations, allegations and "evidence." Göring was also at the wedding and added his own voice of warning to Hitler that the SA were about to move in revolt.

Hitler at once ordered all the senior SA officers to travel to Bad Wiessee to join Röhm for an emergency meeting with himself. The army, meanwhile, was put on alert and all troops ordered to report to barracks at once. The senior generals were told that Hitler had heard the SA were planning an armed coup and that the army might be needed to put it down. Most generals welcomed the chance to put the SA in their place, though some worried about taking on 4 million men, and others were convinced the SA were planning no such thing as a coup.

On 29 June, Hitler flew to Bad Wiessee to confront Röhm and the SA leadership. He did not wait for his armed SS guards, but stormed into Röhm's bedroom at dawn waving a revolver. Aided by a dozen other men, Hitler personally arrested the SA's most senior officers and locked them in a laundry. There was a nasty moment when 50 armed SA men arrived, but Hitler persuaded them to go back to the SA barracks, where he followed and delivered an hour long speech to the SA stormtroopers present who were wondering what was going on.

Meanwhile, the SS were in action across Germany. In Berlin, the former Chancellor of Germany Kurt von Schleicher and his wife were shot dead at their home. Other political rivals were shot, stabbed or simply vanished. Senior SA men everywhere were killed out of hand. Nazis from the the old days in Munich also died, if they had annoyed Himmler in some way. At least 180 men and women, perhaps as many as 800, died in the few hours of the SS action.

Back at Bad Wiessee, the Bavarian Minister of Justice, Hans Frank, arrived with a squad of police to take charge of what he thought was a straightforward arrest of political subversives. Hitler had, by now, left for the Nazi Party offices in Munich. Soon after Frank and his police took control of Röhm and the other prisoners, a force of armed SS men led by Sepp Dietrich, later to be a crucial SS figure, arrived and announced

Himmler (center), head of the SS, on a tour of Mauthausen prison camp, later to become a slave labor camp

they had come to execute the prisoners. Gallantly Frank refused to let them in and insisted that all prisoners should get a fair trial. Dietrich phoned Hitler, Hitler phoned Frank and told him to allow Dietrich to carry out the orders of the German Government "unless you are in league with those scum." Frank eyed the SS machine guns and gave way. Röhm's colleagues died in a hail of bullets; Röhm himself was given the option of suicide, "due to his former close relationship with the Führer." He chose not to take it, and was shot by SS-Standartenführer Michael Lippert.

Hearing of the purge of the SA leadership, President Hindenburg put into a telegram to Hitler the views of most of the army officer corps. "You have saved the German Nation from serious danger," he wrote. "For this I express to you my most profound thanks and sincere appreciation." But then he heard of the deaths of Schleicher and his wife, and began to have second thoughts. When he learned that the musician Wilhelm Schmid had been shot dead in mistake for the

SA officer Wilhelm Schmid, Hindenburg was even move disturbed by the violent action, taken outside the normal course of legality.

Other army officers were having a similar reaction. Their initial satisfaction at the elimination of the SA turned to disquiet at the methods used and the innocents killed. Hitler moved quickly to assuage military alarm. The widows and orphans of the dead were given generous pensions, though some refused them, and the propaganda machine of Josef Goebbels went into overdrive.

On July 13 Hitler appeared before the Reichstag, the first time since the killings that he had been seen in public, to justify what had happened. The building and all routes to it were under heavy guard by the army and the SS. Hitler reiterated the "evidence" against Röhm and other SA men, then claimed that only 74 people had been killed, including three SS men who had shot an innocent man during a bungled arrest. None of it was true, nor was Hitler's claim that he had taken "the bitterest decisions of my life" in order to "preserve the most precious treasure of the German people, internal peace and order." The Reichstag then voted to approve the executions in retrospect.

It was Blomberg who won over the army officers. He convinced them that the SA had, indeed, been planning a coup which would have spelled the end of the German army and established the armed SA as the sole political and military power in Germany. Some officers were convinced and wholeheartedly embraced Hitler's view. Others, such as the future submarine admiral Karl Dönitz, merely went along with it. Only a few voiced opposition, and those were mainly older officers who were near or past retirement. Hitler could afford to ignore them.

The importance of the so called "Night of the Long Knives" to Hitler's relationship to the army cannot be overlooked for it was immense. In April of 1934, Hitler had met with Blomberg together with Raeder, head of the navy, and with Werner von Fritsch, head of the army while watching a series of naval maneuvers. Although no notes of that meeting have survived, if any were made, it is clear that the four men had made an agreement. Hitler had promised to break the power of the SA, while the three military men had agreed that after Hindenburg ceased to be President the Chancellor, Hitler, would become the symbolic head of the armed forces, not the President.

In the event, things moved faster than anyone could have imagined. Hitler destroyed the SA in June and at the end of July Hindenburg fell dangerously ill. He took to the old iron camp bed he had always used on campaign and refused the offer of a soft, fur cloak. "Soldiers do not wear robes," he said contemptuously. When it became clear the old warrior was dying, Hitler rushed to the deathbed, but Hindenburg refused to talk to him. On August 2, Hindenburg died.

Later that day the German government announced that the offices of President and Chancellor had been merged into one. Hitler was not merely head of government, he was now head of state as well.

He was the Führer.

Above: Hitler speaks from the window of the Chancellery, Berlin

A NEW OATH OF LOYALTY

The same day, Hitler summoned Blomberg, Raeder and Fritsch to his office. It was traditional for the heads of the armed forces to be the first to recognize a new head of state, be he Kaiser or President. They came to swear an oath of loyalty to the Fatherland and the President. But when Hitler read out the oath for them to repeat they had a surprise.

"I swear before God this holy oath: to give my unconditional obedience to the Führer of the Reich and people, to Adolf Hitler, the Supreme Commander of the Armed Forces, and I pledge my word as a brave soldier to observe this oath always even at the risk of my life."

It was an unprecedented oath. Even in the days

The military high command attend a Nazi Party rally at Nuremberg

of the Kaiser the oath had been to the Fatherland as much as to the monarch, and since then the oath had been to the office of President not to the individual holding that office. But now the senior commanders were asked to swear a sacred oath to Adolf Hitler by name. To a German army officer an oath such as this was a very serious thing—it was not called a holy oath for nothing. The sanctity of a promise, and even more so of an oath, was a fundamental truth for army officers brought up in the proud Prussian tradition.

Despite this, none of the senior commanders murmured a word of disquiet that day in Hitler's office. They swore the oath, then left to pass the wording of the oath on to the men under their command. By midnight on August 2, 1934 every serving officer and man in the German armed forces had taken the exact same oath of loyalty to Adolf Hitler. Thereafter everyone joining the services made an identical promise.

On August 6 the funeral service for Hindenburg took place in Berlin amid great solemnity and ceremony. The streets were lined with the soldiers of the army, but there were also on parade units from the SS and even the SA. The service over, Hitler led the funeral march to the strains of Wagner's *Götterdämmerung*, the Twilight of the Gods. The coffin was then taken to the scene of Hindenburg's greatest military triumph, the Battle of Tannenberg, and buried beneath the vast memorial to the German dead.

Hitler then hurried back to Berlin and asked Hindenburg's son if the President had left any papers. There was a sealed envelope addressed to Hitler. The new Führer opened the envelope and his face darkened with rage. He shoved the paper in his pocket and stormed out. On August 15 the contents of the letter were published. The letter applauded the army, its officers and men and then went on to praise Hitler and his government. There were widespread rumors that the letter had been altered.

Nevertheless, on August 19 a referendum was held in Germany to seek changes to the constitution that allowed Hitler to merge the powers and duties of his two offices into one. The proposal was carried by an overwhelming "Yes" vote of 90 per cent.

Despite the rise to the position of Führer and the extraction of the personal oath of loyalty, Hitler was still not master of the military. Many senior officers viewed Hitler as a superb politician but, as far as military matters were concerned, merely a very brave corporal. They had an inbuilt belief in the powers and duties of the generals and high command to control the army. Like Blomberg, they saw the armed forces as a pillar supporting the German nation, a pillar which was entirely separate from government, from politics and, in particular, from the Nazi Party. Hitler saw the armed forces as just one more cog in the machinery of state. He now set out to make it so.

In 1935 Hitler announced that he was renouncing the Versailles Treaty and its stipulations limiting the size of Germany's armed forces. He also announced a reorganization of the Reichswehr, which now became known as the Wehrmacht. This reorganization affected only the very highest personnel, but was crucial. Each of the three services—the army, navy and air force—was to have its own Commander in Chief who was directly answerable to Blomberg. Blomberg was made not only Defense Minister in the government, but also Commander in Chief of the Wehrmacht as an active military commander.

As President, Hitler was Supreme Commander of the Wehrmacht. Unlike earlier Presidents,

Hitler provided himself with his own staff officers. This allowed Hitler to produce detailed plans of his own and to test whether his senior officers were right when they told him a particular plan was possible or not.

Hitler conferring with Minister of War Blomberg and Chief of Staff Keitel in 1938

Hitler also had the power to appoint officers right down the hierarchy. He used this power to appoint General Wilhelm Keitel as Blomberg's chief of staff. Keitel was from the old landed gentry and had been serving as an army officer since 1901. He had risen rapidly through the echelons of the officer corps and by the late 1920s was a senior member of the planning staff. Throughout his military service, he had remained scrupulously outside politics, and actually seemed bored by them. He was, therefore, eminently acceptable to the more traditional officers.

But, as so often, Hitler knew his man. He had met Keitel in 1933 and it was clear from the start that the general had fallen victim to the charm that Hitler's personality could work on so many people. Keitel was completely won over, believing Hitler to be a genius sent to save the German nation. Over the next few months, Keitel seemed almost to lose his own personality and to be absorbed into that of Hitler. Some of his colleagues jokingly called him *Lakeitel*, meaning "toady" or "lickspittle," but such puns soon became dangerous. With Keitel in place as Blomberg's chief of staff, Hitler had a man totally loyal to himself at the heart of the war machine.

But for Hitler, the control this gave him was not enough. He knew the military was a powerful force in German society and politics. By 1935 it was probably the only force able to remove him from power. Hitler wanted total obedience from such a dangerous organization.

In part, this was coming slowly of its own accord. The massive increase in the size of the armed forces was bringing in large numbers of new, younger officers. By 1936 these men outnumbered the older professional officers by a large margin. They were drawn from a broader cross section of society than the officer intakes of the 1920s and had grown up during the years that the Nazi Party was gathering strength. They were more open to Nazi ideology and, in particular, to the magical charm of Hitler. Slowly the army was changing its character. But not the senior ranks and the high command. To get instant and total obedience from them, Hitler would have to make more effort.

Again the situation Hitler desired was slowly evolving. Throughout the later 1930s, the generals continually urged caution on Hitler in his forays into foreign policy. The military professionals were very aware that Germany was ringed by countries with more powerful armed forces. They knew that in a direct confrontation in 1934 Germany would undoubtedly lose. Even with rearmament taking a firm hold, as late as 1938 the senior staff officers doubted Germany's ability to win a war and some still had doubts in 1939.

Hitler, however, was playing a very different game. Although aware of the military strength of his opponents, he was paying more attention to their moral strength. He calculated that the British and French were so terrified of another bloodbath in the trenches that they would do almost anything to avoid a major European war. Hitler also believed that the smaller states of eastern Europe would do nothing so long as he kept them divided diplomatically and so long as the major powers did not move. After one meeting with Lord Halifax, the British Foreign Secretary, Hitler turned to Göring and said, "We can do what we like in the East. They won't do anything."

BEGINNER'S LUCK?

Throughout the course of the early, bloodless victories Hitler was proved right time and again. While the generals fretted about the dire consequences of a military confrontation, Hitler pressed on and got what he wanted without war. After cautioning Hitler several times, and being proved wrong, even the most determined of the senior officers were beginning to wonder if, perhaps, the Führer was after all infallible. Their doubts began to be expressed in increasingly muted tones.

Even this was not enough for Hitler. By 1938 he wanted a way to make his grip on the armed forces absolute. As with the crushing of the SA in 1934, it was Himmler who gave Hitler the weapon he needed.

In 1932 Blomberg had been widowed, but soon picked up a social life involving rather more women than was normal for a single army officer. In September 1935 he met a girl 35 years younger than himself named Margarethe Gruhn and fell helplessly in love with her. Blomberg's fellow officers were unimpressed with the working class typist, but Blomberg proposed and was accepted. As a senior general privy to state secrets, Blomberg needed the consent of the Führer for the marriage.

Hitler liked the girl and agreed, even offering to be an official witness at the wedding. Hitler was keen to emphasize that he did not approve of the snobbery prevalent in the officer corps, and attended the wedding on January 12, 1938.

On January 21 Göring was passed a file by a very worried Keitel. The file was from police records and gave a detailed and colorful account of the career of a pornographic model and prostitute named Margarethe Gruhn who had been active in Berlin in 1931. There was a photo of the woman attached, but Keitel had never met Blomberg's new wife. Göring had. Was this, Keitel asked, the new Frau Blomberg. Göring looked at the photo. It was.

Göring went to see Hitler on January 24. The Führer was stunned. What really shocked him was that the photographer with whom Margarethe Gruhn had run her porn business was a Jew. Assuming that Blomberg did not know of his wife's past, Hitler sent Göring to see the War Minister to show him the file and suggest a quiet divorce. To Hitler's astonishment, Blomberg had known all about the sordid past of his new wife and refused a divorce. Senior officers were consulted and were adamant that they would not serve a man who had married a whore. Blomberg had to go.

Hitler then looked for a successor as Minister of War and Commander of the Armed Services. The obvious candidate was Blomberg's deputy Werner von Fritsch. Although Fritsch had voiced some doubts about timing, he seemed to support Hitler's use of force to gain German foreign policy aims in Eastern Europe. Hitler decided to put Fritsch in Blomberg's place. At which point Himmler slipped a new file into Hitler's hands.

This file detailed accusations that had been hushed up in 1936. During the trial of a Berlin young male prostitute named Otto Schmidt for the blackmail of some of his clients, Schmidt had named "General of Artillery von Fritsch" as a client. A quick investigation by Himmler's SS had revealed Fritsch to be heterosexual with no hint of homosexual leanings and the matter had been hushed up. Now, Himmler chose to resurrect the accusations and even brought Schmidt from prison to be on hand if needed.

On 26 January, Hitler summoned Fritsch and confronted him with the file. Fritsch denied everything. When Schmidt was brought in to repeat his allegations, Fritsch insisted he had never even met the man. Then Fritsch made a mistake. He went on to say that any meetings he may have had with young boys had been purely in his role of enthusing the Hitler Youth with tales of army life.

For Hitler, already suspicious and egged on by a ruthlessly ambitious Himmler, intent on building his SS empire, the comment was enough. Fritsch had to go as well.

The sudden dismissal of the two most senior officers in the armed forces gave Hitler the chance to bring forward a change he had been planning to implement at some undecided point in the future. He would, once again, reconstruct the organization of the armed forces. To make it look as if this was a well-planned decision and not a hurried move, Hitler delayed the resignations of Blomberg and Fritsch for a few days. When they were finally allowed to leave in February, the two men followed very different paths. Blomberg went to Switzerland to live a comfortable life with his new wife while Fritsch returned to his artillery regiment to serve Germany loyally until he was killed in action during the war.

On 4 February 1938 the new face of the Wehrmacht was announced. Twelve generals were removed from active service, along with 50 other senior officers and members of the staff. The

Foreign Minister was also sacked and replaced by the loyal Nazi Joachim von Ribbentrop. Much was made of the personalities of those leaving and of their replacements. But the real changes were organizational.

Himmler had hoped to take over from Blomberg, but instead Hitler announced that he would himself now be the new Minister for War and the new Commander of the Wehrmacht. The staffs of Hitler and Blomberg were combined to form a new organization known as the High Command of the Armed Forces, the *Oberkommando der Wehrmacht* or OKW. This was the top level staff group which oversaw the strategic planning of all three services. It was directly responsible to Hitler. The man in charge, under Hitler, of this formidable new organization which combined the powers and roles of government, army and president was the ever-loyal Keitel.

Beneath OKW were the High Commands of the three services. *Oberkommando der Luftwaffe* (OKL), the High Command of the Luftwaffe, was handed to Göring who was promoted to

Von Ribbentrop, Hitler's Foreign Minister 1938–45, fell into disfavor for his pro-Russian sympathies after 1941

Field Marshal. *Oberkommando der Kriegsmarine* (OKK), the High Command of the Kriegsmarine, was given to Admiral Raeder. For Hitler the most important appointment was to *Oberkommando des Heeres* (OKH), the High Command of the Army. This post went to Walther von Brauchitsch.

Like Keitel, Brauchitsch was outwardly acceptable to the officer corps and to conservative opinion, but was in reality Hitler's man. He had been born into the Prussian aristocracy in 1881 and followed his family tradition by entering the army as a career. He served with distinction throughout the First World War and, like Hitler, won the Iron Cross 1st Class. After the war he saw steady promotion and by the time of the crisis of 1938 was a member of the general staff with a solid reputation for top class organizational abilities.

He had, however, divorced his first wife in 1932 and the financial settlement had crippled him. Although in love with a new woman, a dedicated member of the Nazi Party named Charlotte Schmidt, Brauchitsch could not afford to marry her. Hoping to win a key ally among the officer corps, Hitler secretly siphoned state funds to Fraulein Schmidt and the wedding went ahead. Brauchitsch was therefore under a serious and very personal obligation to Hitler. As the new head of OKH, he could be relied upon to be loyal to Hitler.

The organizational and personnel changes which were precipitated by the Blomberg–Fritsch crisis made Hitler the undisputed master of the military. Through OKW he had supreme strategic control and with pliant commanders such as Brauchitsch and Keitel he could count on the obedience of his subordinates.

With the armed forces rearmed and under Hitler's control it was time to put them to the test. The serious business of bullying Germany's eastern neighbors could begin in earnest.

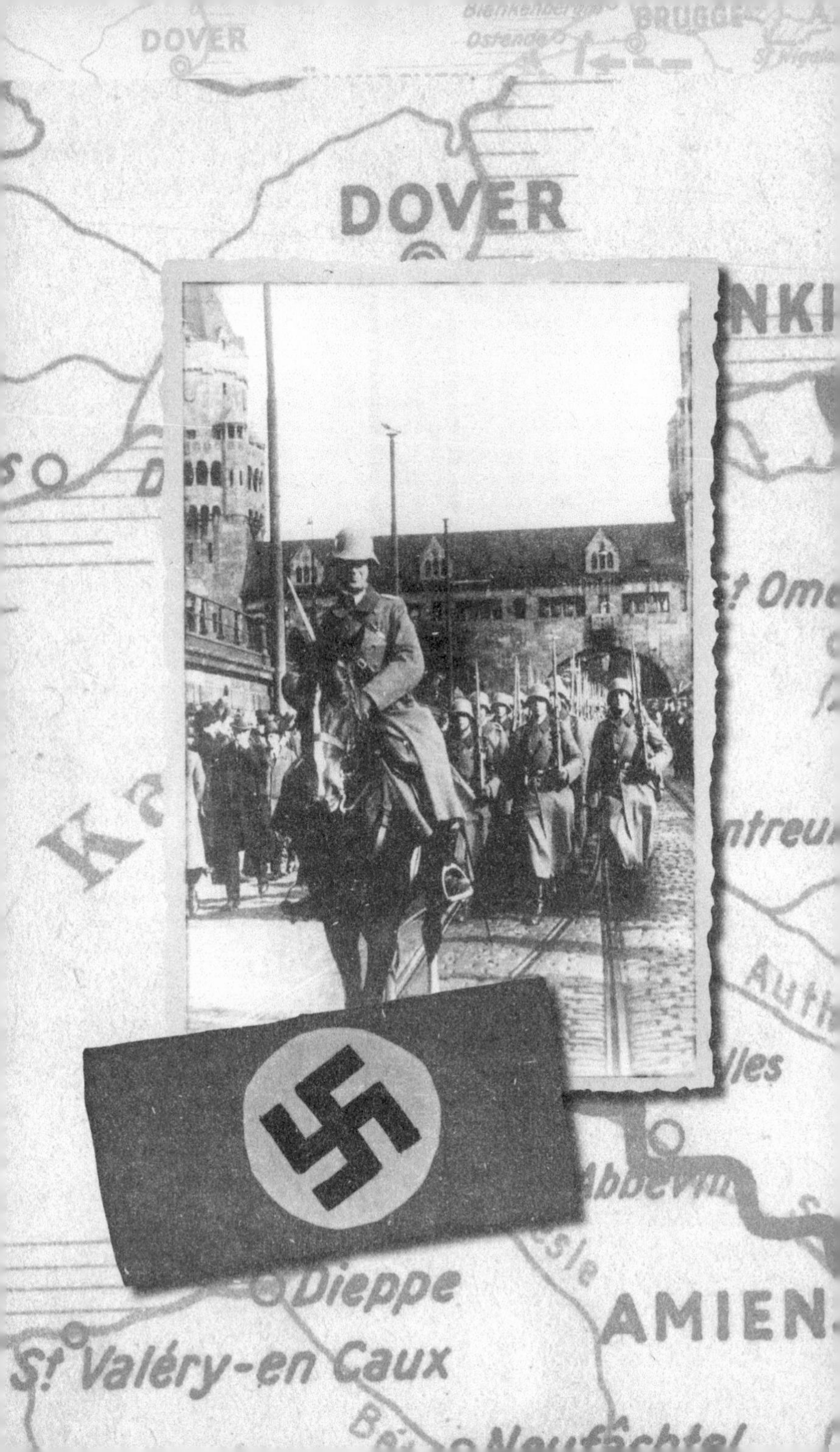
DOVER
BRUGGE
Ostende
DOVER
Dieppe
St Valéry-en Caux

EARLY VICTORIES
THE RHINELAND 1936

Hitler's stunning successes were won by a combination of an acute appreciation of the weaknesses of others and the ability to use daring and surprise to stun opponents into submission even before the real action had begun

Having become Führer of Germany, Hitler soon found himself in the position of needing a foreign policy triumph to divert attention from the continuing economic problems in Germany itself. He turned to the army to secure the success he needed, but the army was not at all sure it wanted to cooperate.

By January 1936 Hitler had decided exactly what he wanted to do. As ever, he needed a realistic excuse for action, but there was none available. Then the French played into his hands. The Versailles Treaty of 1919, which had ended the First World War, had imposed many onerous restraints on Germany. The resentment many Germans had felt toward the Versailles Treaty had been behind much of the support given to the Nazi Party, the only party in Germany openly stating it would repudiate the hated Treaty.

German soldiers march into the Rhineland, a part of Germany from which they had been banned under the Versailles Treaty

One of the most resented clauses in Versailles was the stipulation that a large swathe of Germany near the border with France was to be closed to Germany's armed forces. No German troops were allowed on the west bank of the Rhine or within 30 miles of the east bank, an area known as the Rhineland. France had insisted on the clause for the purely defensive military reason that it would take the Germans so long to get an invasion army over the Rhine and into position that should they do so the French would have plenty of time to call up their reserves and form a strong defense. The Germans, however, resented the fact that their entire western border was wide open to attack.

In January 1936 Hitler heard that the French were preparing to sign a treaty with Russia. Hitler believed that this move put France in breach of the mutual non-aggression treaty signed by France, Germany and Belgium in 1925 and known as the Locarno Pact. He decided to use this alleged breach of the Locarno Pact as justification for marching troops into the Rhineland and over the Rhine.

On 12 February 1936, Hitler told his War Minister, Werner von Blomberg of his plans, then summoned General Walther von Fritsch, head of the army, to his office. He asked the general how long it would take to move a few battalions of infantry and a battery of artillery into the Rhineland. Fritsch told him it could be organized in three days, but warned Hitler that the army was in no condition for a war with France. If the French sent their forces into the Rhineland to drive out the German troops, Fritsch warned, there would be a catastrophe. He advised it would be better to negotiate.

Hitler refused to consider a debate with France, both because it would take too long and because it would be a sign of weakness. He did, however, promise Fritsch that he would not order the remilitarization of the Rhineland unless he was certain France would not react. He also pledged that the German force involved would be merely a token one and that they would have orders to retreat at once if the French did intervene. Mollified, Fritsch left to make the necessary arrangements.

Hitler had already made tentative diplomatic moves. He had sounded out the new British king, Edward VIII, on the grievances of Germany over Versailles. Edward had declared himself most sympathetic. Although Hitler knew the British government did not take orders from the king, he did think it unlikely that Britain would move if the king disagreed. Moreover, Hitler's diplomats in Britain informed him that the British public were in no mood for war, especially not over something fairly trivial. And Britain had never been very enthusiastic about the Rhineland clauses of Versailles in any case.

It was France that was the real worry. Hitler set March 7 as the day for the army to march into the Rhineland, an operation codenamed Winter Exercise. It was a Saturday and Hitler hoped the key men in the French government would not be in their offices that day. "They'll get back on Monday' he said. "By then it will all be over."

However Hitler was not as confident as he seemed. He knew that Fritsch and Blomberg were right when they warned the German armed forces were not ready for a confrontation with France. The night before the army marched, Hitler did not sleep at all.

On March 7, just after dawn, 19 infantry battalions marched into the Rhineland, with a handful of aircraft circling overhead. By 11am they had reached the Rhine and three battalions marched over to the west bank. Hitler was already on his feet at a special meeting of the Reichstag. He began his speech by rehearsing the complaints against the Versailles Treaty and, in particular, those clauses relating to the Rhineland. He paused, then said, "At this very moment, German soldiers are marching into . . ." He got no further for the audience erupted into sustained cheers.

In Britain, Prime Minister Stanley Baldwin took the news calmly, then sent a message to Paris asking what the French government intended doing. While waiting for the reply, he turned to his Foreign Secretary, Anthony Eden and remarked. "Now we know we cannot trust him."

In Paris, the French government asked their Commander in Chief, General Maurice Gamelin, to take "energetic action," but they did not say exactly what he should do. Gamelin was naturally cautious and refused to march into Germany without first ordering a full mobilization of the French army and its reserves. He told the French government this, and then sent 13 divisions to the border to show he was doing something.

When Blomberg learned from his scouts that thousands of French troops were massing on the border, he rushed over to Hitler's office and begged for the order to retreat. Hitler asked if the French troops had crossed the border into Germany. On being told they had not, he stared at Blomberg and said, "Then we wait. We wait. We can always retreat tomorrow." They waited.

It was a crucial moment for Hitler. If the French had marched into Germany the weak Wehrmacht forces would have been forced to retreat. Given his crumbling support at home it is likely Hitler would have had severe difficulty holding on to power. But the French did not march.

Hitler was jubilant. He was even more firmly convinced that Britain and France were so terrified of involving themselves in another bloodbath that

they would always prefer to back down in the face of possible war. All Hitler had to do, he thought, was to come up with a passable pretext for what he was doing and give his opponents a seemingly honorable way out. With this in mind he moved on to his next foreign policy objective.

ANSCHLUSS WITH AUSTRIA 1938

A long term aim of Hitler as Führer had been to unite under German rule all the German peoples of Europe. The largest number of these not living in the Reich were in Austria, an almost exclusively German-speaking country. He had written in *Mein Kampf* back in 1923 that "One blood demands one Reich. Austria must return to the mother country."

The relationship between the two nations had been centuries long and very complex. At one time the Austrian monarchs exercised a very loose authority over the German princes in the Austrian monarchs' role as Holy Roman Emperors, but that authority had been destroyed by Napoleon in 1806. Thereafter the German princes, dukes, republics and states had gone their own ways until united under the Kaiser in 1871. After the First World War the mighty Austrian Empire, which had stretched from Germany to the Black Sea and from the Mediterranean to the Vistula, was broken up. This left the German-speaking part of the Empire as Austria, a tiny fragment of the once mighty empire.

There were many people in Austria who supported union with Germany, a concept known as Anschluss, or "joining on." There were, however, many more pressing issues facing Austria, such as economic stagnation, so Anschluss rarely featured in government debates. In 1934 a failed coup by the Austrian Nazi Party left the Chancellor Engelbert Dollfuss dead and the

Austrian government determined not to let their country fall into Hitler's control.

Hitler spent much of 1937 weaving the complex web of diplomatic maneuvers that was needed to ensure that Austria's neighbors would remain indifferent to Anschluss. Coincidentally late January 1938 saw the Blomberg–Fritsch crisis which ended with the German military's two most senior commanders resigning in disgrace and Hitler taking over as commander of the Wehrmacht in their place. Hitler's grip on the military was now secure. It may have been this which prompted Hitler to seek a military solution to the problem of taking over Austria.

BULLYBOY TACTICS

On 12 February the Austrian Chancellor, Kurt von Schusschnigg, travelled to Germany to meet Hitler. The Germans had arranged the meeting well. There were soldiers on hand to intimidate the small Austrian delegation and generals or high-ranking diplomats to be seen scurrying about to fulfil Hitler's every whim. Then Hitler told Schusschnigg that his patience was exhausted and that Austria had to do what he wanted or he would invade.

When Schusschnigg objected, Hitler went into a towering rage. By the end of the day, Schusschnigg had given in to Hitler's every demand. Three Austrian Nazis were appointed to the government, the Nazis still in prison after the 1934 coup were released and the Austrian economy and currency were merged with that of Germany.

It was only a first move. On 11 March the new Austrian interior minister, a Nazi named Seyss-Inquart, phoned Hitler to announce that his police forces could not cope with a series of riots, which had been carried out by the Nazis themselves. In response to this appeal for help, the German army

crossed the border. The ruse was transparent, but it served Hitler's purpose. He had a claim to legality for what he did, and Austria's neighbors had an excuse to avoid conflict.

All good army staffs have contingency plans for almost any eventuality. The German Army Staff, the OKH, had detailed plans, codenamed Otto, for the invasion of Austria. The plans laid down how many divisions and battalions were to be used, which roads they were to advance along and what objectives they should seize. The only open question was whether war would be declared and the Austrian army open fire, or if the move was to be peaceful. The new head of OKH, General Walther von Brauchitsch hurriedly updated the plan drawn up by his predecessors in the light of Hitler's orders issued on 11 March. These specified that, "the behavior of the troops must give the impression that we do not want to wage war against our Austrian brothers. There is to be no provocation. But if resistance is met, it must be broken ruthlessly." The orders also demanded that Hitler be consulted if circumstances demanded any change of plan: "The whole operation will be directed by myself."

The actual task of carrying out the forced Anschluss was given to General Heinz Guderian and his specially formed XVI Army Corps. He was to mass two columns of troops, one at Passau and the other at Traunstein. The first was to advance on Vienna by way of Linz and Krems, the second through Salzburg and Melk. Their tasks were to secure the main government buildings in the towns they passed through, disarm the Austrian army and occupy any military bases. The OKH had done their work well for Guderian had detailed maps of where to go and what to do.

The invasion was, again, planned for a Saturday in the hope of catching the world's diplomats and politicians out of the office. Late on the Friday night Seyss-Inquart phoned from Vienna to ask for the invasion to be called off. He thought he could take over the government without armed intervention. The head of OKH, Brauchitsch, added his voice to the call for delay, worried that the Wehrmacht would be crushed if France intervened. Hitler thought about it for a few minutes, then gave the order to continue and went to bed. Next morning he flew to Munich to await news of the invasion.

At 8am Guderian's troops crossed the border and headed east towards Vienna. At every town or village they reached, crowds flooded the streets to welcome them. The Austrian armed forces laid down their arms whenever they were encountered. The German troops occupied every building on their list without bloodshed. Guderian drove through Linz on the Saturday, but it then began to snow and he did not reach Vienna until Sunday morning. He found an Austrian military band waiting to play him into town.

Hitler announces the Anschluss in Vienna

On March 14 Hitler went to Vienna to be greeted by vast cheering crowds. On April 9 a referendum was held in Austria and Germany on whether or not to approve Anschluss. The result showed the Austrians were keener on the idea than the Germans, but not by much. The yes vote in Austria was 99.7 percent, in Germany it was 99.1 percent.

If Hitler was pleased with the political and diplomatic triumph, he was extremely unimpressed with the army. Guderian had to admit shamefacedly to his Führer that over two thirds of the panzers had broken down on the road to Vienna, and that was without anybody shooting at them. Moreover, several units had got lost trying to find the more remote Austrian army bases and several had found themselves without food, ammunition and sometimes both. A furious Hitler summoned Brauchitsch and ordered him to begin a thorough overhaul of German staff work. Then he ordered Guderian to make sure the panzers did better next time.

Both men went to work, painfully aware that Hitler would not tolerate failure a second time. Guderian embarked on a minute examination of what had gone wrong and found that the vast majority of panzers had been brought to a halt by relatively minor mechanical problems. The panzer crews were retrained to cope while several Panzer Is were converted into armored mobile workshops and attached to lead units.

Brauchitsch, meanwhile, found a key problem had been the confusion caused when two units tried to use the same road. Often the unit with the more senior commander went first, even if the other unit was more urgently needed by forward troops. A lack of gasoline had been particularly noticeable with fuel tankers driven by privates and corporals being made to give precedence to staff cars carrying colonels. A new system of road marshals was introduced to ensure that necessary supplies were given priority. Nobody, not even a high ranking officer, would be able to disobey the orders of a road marshal.

These were vital lessons which were being learned and would have good effect when the army moved next.

CZECHOSLOVAKIA 1938

Hitler's next target was Czechoslovakia. Several million Germans lived in the Sudetenland, that area of Czechoslovakia which bordered Germany. Again Hitler went to work on the diplomatic front while ordering the OKH, under Brauchitsch, to draw up invasion plans. This time the army did not expect anything other than a tough war. The Czechs had 35 divisions in their regular army and many more in reserve. Moreover the borders with Germany were mountainous and heavily fortified. The borders through from the newly occupied Austria were more open, but even here the country was not particularly suited to Guderian's tanks. Anyway, the Czechs had as many heavy guns as the Germans and their own modern tanks, manufactured at the famous Skoda works.

Brauchitsch reported that the defeat of Czechoslovakia would take some weeks and that this would give France, Britain or Russia ample time to intervene if they decided to do so. Hitler set his own staff at OKW, the supreme armed forces staff, to study the findings of OKH. They agreed.

It was therefore fortunate for the German army that Hitler managed to pull off the coup known as the Munich Agreement. Hitler spent the summer of 1938 playing up the human rights demands of the Germans living in Czechoslovakia and threatening war if they were not solved. On 29 September, Mussolini arranged a meeting in Munich between Hitler, the new British Prime Minister Neville Chamberlain and French premier Edouard Daladier. The Czechs were not invited, neither were the Russians. After an exhausting series of talks, with Hitler threatening instant war, the British and French agreed not to object to Germany taking over the border areas of Czechoslovakia where Germans were the majority population.

War had been averted, but Czechoslovakia was lost. Without the prospect of military aid from larger countries, the Czechs gave in. With the border areas they surrendered their mighty fortresses and gun emplacements. Hitler told Brauchitsch to draw up plans to occupy the rest of Czechoslovakia from start positions in the Sudetenland. Again, OKH began on the assumption that the Czech army would fight. Again, Hitler proved them wrong.

During February and March of 1939, Hitler courted the secessionists in Slovakia who wanted to be independent of Prague and those Czechs who were fascists. Riots and disorder spread rapidly and on March 13 Hitler met with President Hacha of Czechoslovakia, ostensibly to discuss various matters arising out of the earlier occupation of Czech territory. When Hacha arrived in Berlin it was almost midnight. He was treated to a guard of armed SS men, then subjected to an angry tirade of abuse, accusations and allegations from Hitler. If the Czechs did not surrender at once to Slovak independence and Nazi government, Hitler said, the German armed forces would invade at dawn. Prague would be bombed to rubble by the Luftwaffe at 6am. Hacha fainted. When he came to, Hitler offered to call off his armed forces if Hacha signed a surrender document.

At 3.55am Hacha signed.

At 6am the German army invaded. The Luftwaffe did not, as planned, fly in to secure the Czech air force bases because the entire country was covered by fog. The threat to bomb Prague had been a bluff.

This time the move went exactly as Brauchitsch and Guderian had planned. Mechanical breakdowns were kept to a minimum, road traffic ran in the correct order and virtually nobody got lost. There was one crucial difference to what had happened in Austria and the Sudetenland occupations. The detailed orders which were followed by the various units had been drawn up by OKW, not OKH. Hitler did not trust the older reactionary officers of Brauchitsch's staff, but instead preferred the staff work of his Nazi loyalists under Keitel. The reason Hitler had given to the military for this change was that close cooperation between the army and the Luftwaffe would be necessary. In the event, fog stopped that from happening.

POLAND 1939

The occupation of Czechoslovakia had one other military result of prime importance. The diplomatic reactions convinced Hitler that Britain was more likely to declare war if he invaded another country than was France. And Hitler was intending to invade another country with a German minority population: Poland.

In May 1939, Hitler announced to Keitel, Brauchitsch, Raeder and 11 other senior military men that Poland would be invaded. "We cannot expect a repetition of the Czech affair," Hitler warned them. "This time there will be a war." The invasion was to be codenamed Operation *White*. This time all three services were to be involved. Keitel at OKW, the supreme staff, issued instructions detailing the strategic objectives for each of the three services and called for detailed proposals on how these were to be achieved.

Throughout May and June the various branches of the armed services drew up plans, revised plans, replacement plans and alternative plans. At each stage, Hitler was consulted. He was taking a much closer interest in the arrangements for the attack on Poland than he had in any previous operation of the Wehrmacht. In July Hitler sat down with the plans that then existed and spent days going through them in great detail. He examined the role of each division, brigade and regiment, quizzing the generals as to what was suggested and why. If he did not like what he heard, Hitler altered the plans with firm marks of a black pencil.

In the case of the proposals for taking some crucial objectives, Hitler even discussed the roles of individual companies and called in the battalion commanders to discuss plans with them. A typical example was the operation to capture the half mile long bridge across the Vistula at Dirschau and hold it until the panzers could arrive to drive over it and on into northern Poland. The capture and defense of the bridge was organized by the navy. Staff at OKH thought it would take three days for the panzers to get there. Hitler said two days and changed OKH plans accordingly. In the event it took just a day and a half for the army to reach Dirschau.

It was late in July before Hitler was happy with the plans for Operation *White*. In their final form, the German invasion plans saw 53 divisions deployed for battle, of which 40 were conventional infantry and 13 new panzer divisions. These ground troops were backed up by the full might of the Luftwaffe which was to bomb Polish communications centers and have Stukas on standby to give close support to the army. The

navy, the Kriegsmarine, meanwhile was given the task of taking and holding coastal cities, including the disputed city of Danzig, now Gdansk, which had been in German territory until 1919 and was still populated mainly by Germans.

Operation *White* envisaged two main lines of attack. In the north the Fourth Army under General Hans von Kluge was to advance from Pomerania across the Polish Corridor towards the German enclave of East Prussia, taking Danzig and Dirschau as it went. Meanwhile the Third Army under Kuchler was to drive south from East Prussia to capture Brest-Litovsk and the Polish capital of Warsaw. The main attack was to come in the south. General Karl von Rundstedt was given three different armies to command, the Eighth, Tenth and Fourteenth. The Eighth Army was to take Lodz and the Fourteenth Cracow and Lvov. Between the two was placed the Tenth Army with the bulk of the panzers and close Stuka support. The Tenth was to drive fast and deep into Poland, surrounding Polish forces and breaking through to Warsaw.

The detailed plans called for the type of mobile, armored warfare that Guderian had been planning for years and Hitler had ordered the Wehrmacht to work toward since 1933. While the panzers punched through the defenses and then motored on at high speed to the enemy rear, the infantry and artillery were to move through the gaps created to outflank and crush the remaining front line defenses. The Luftwaffe was to penetrate deep behind enemy lines to bomb bridges, rail yards and roads to hamper the ability of the enemy to bring up reserves. The Stuka dive bombers of the Luftwaffe were to operate in close action with the panzers, bombing to rubble any strong point which threatened to hold up the

A German SdKfz232 armored car goes into action at Danzig during the invasion of Poland 1939

panzers. Everything depended on movement, speed and bringing overwhelming fire power to bear at specific points of tactical or strategic importance. All units were linked to their commanders, and to each other, by radio to ensure swift communications to bring up reserves, direct the Stukas or call for changes of direction.

While the military staff planned the campaign, Hitler again went to work on the diplomatic front and soon had Russia as an ally (see Chapter Three). Russia and Germany would carve up Poland between them, though Hitler would choose the time and the excuse for an attack. Hungary was already an ally. That left Britain and France. Hitler resigned himself to the fact that both nations would declare war on Germany as soon as he invaded Poland. But he calculated it would take at least three weeks for the Allies to be ready to invade Germany in the West, and he thought that by then Poland would be on its last legs. Hitler

hoped France would make peace rather than go to war for an already defeated Poland. He was less sure what Britain would do, but he discounted the risk by arguing that Britain had no land border with Germany and would probably follow the French lead.

By late August everything was ready. Only an excuse was needed.

The excuse was provided by Reinhard Heydrich, head of the party security service (*Sicherheitsdienst*—the SD) and Himmler's deputy at the SS. He dressed several squads of SS men in Polish uniforms, together with some political criminals dragged from the concentration camps. A little after midnight on 1 September, the men attacked a number of German customs offices and border posts. The guards fled, and the occupying SS men, still masquerading as Poles, used the radios to broadcast anti-German slogans in Polish. The prisoners from the concentration

camps were then shot dead to provide some "Polish" bodies. Hitler declared this proof positive of Polish aggression. The invasion began.

DAYS OF THUNDER

Two days earlier, on August 31, Hitler had issued his War Directive No.1 which set the time for the attack as 4:45am on September 1 and instructed all units to proceed exactly as laid out in Plan White.

The Poles, of course, had long known that a German invasion was a possibility. They had 40 divisions of infantry, 16 brigades of cavalry, 500 tanks, 400 aircraft. More than enough, it was thought, to give Hitler the bloody nose he deserved.

There were two schools of thought in the Polish army as to the form the German aggression would take. Some thought Hitler was after the disputed parts of Poland that had been German until 1919. They envisaged Hitler launching massive strikes to invade, conquer and occupy areas within two or three days and so present the world with an accomplished blow. It would be best, these people argued, to defend these areas in depth to slow the Germans and give Poland's allies time to intervene. Another group of Poles believed Hitler aimed instead to destroy the Polish army and then dictate surrender terms from a position of strength. If this were the case it would be better to lure the Germans into the forest and swamps of central Poland where they could be ambushed and defeated.

In the event, the Polish Commander in Chief, Field Marshal Edward Smigly-Rydz, chose neither plan. He put a third of his forces in the Polish Corridor and around Danzig, then spread the remainder of his men out along the long border with Germany. He kept only a small reserve under his own command near Warsaw. His plan was to bog down any attack around Danzig while holding the borders and using his reserve to counterattack any German breakthrough.

The war began as planned by the Germans, and it was the Kriegsmarine which was given the honor of firing the opening shot. The cruiser *Schleswig-Holstein* steamed into Danzig harbor and opened fire on the Polish military depot there. Just minutes later the panzers lurched forward, followed by the infantry and cavalry, while overhead the Luftwaffe began their bombing raids.

Later that day Hitler went to the Reichstag to announce that the invasion had begun following Polish attacks on border posts the night before. This was the first day of war and Hitler had dressed for the occasion. Gone were the civilian clothes and familiar brown shirt for Hitler had dressed himself in a field grey uniform. It was not an army uniform, for Hitler had no army rank, but a Nazi Party uniform made out of army material. Hitler waited in Berlin long enough to receive the responses of Britain and France to the invasion.

Once he was certain that war was declared, Hitler boarded his newly constructed command train and set off for the battlefront. The train was armor plated and equipped with a conference room, sleeping quarters, living room, toilets and guard rooms as well as a host of radio equipment and maps to keep Hitler up to date with the campaign. The train headed for Pomerania, near the Polish border west of Danzig, where the heaviest fighting was expected.

In fact the invasion was going better than even the optimistic Hitler had expected. On the day Hitler arrived at the front, Danzig fell and East Prussia was reconnected to the rest of Germany by the columns of Kluge's Fourth Army. The next day two Polish armies in western Poland were cut off by the panzers and motorized troops. The Poles, on foot or horseback, simply could not move fast enough to get out of the way of the encircling panzer columns. The Poles continued fighting, however, forcing the Germans to keep their own foot and cavalry in the region to contain the Poles.

On September 8 the first German scouting vehicles came within sight of the suburbs of Warsaw. Hitler was jubilant. He left his train in an open-topped Mercedes and drove off to visit the army units in the area. He drove around standing up in full view of the troops, just as he had done during parades in peace time. His staff tried to persuade him this was too dangerous, but to no avail. The task of protecting Hitler on these drives to the front, which became increasingly common as the campaign progressed, fell to the head of his HQ staff guard, a previously obscure middle-aged officer named Erwin Rommel.

On the same day, a serious disagreement blew up between von Rundstedt, the commander in the field, and Brauchitsch at OKH. Working from the reports of Luftwaffe scout aircraft, the OKH thought the bulk of the Polish army had retreated across the Vistula and issued orders to Rundstedt to pursue them eastwards. However, Rundstedt's forward panzer commanders were reporting that the Poles were retreating north towards Warsaw. He wanted to follow them. A series of increasingly blunt telegrams and radio messages flashed back and forth. Finally Rundstedt won his case and continued the drive north.

By the morning of September 9 the Poles had managed to mobilize their reserves east of Warsaw and linked them to the retreating Pomorze Army. Together the two forces launched a counterattack against the Germans advancing on Warsaw from the north. The Battle of Bzura which developed threw the German columns back in confusion, then spread to the south where the Poles stopped Rundstedt's armies at Lowicz.

Hitler was furious at the delay. He moved his train to Silesia and sent out a stream of messages demanding to know the current situation and what was being done. He still did not issue any direct orders to his military commanders. Having prepared the plans in great detail, Hitler was content to leave battlefield decisions to his generals, though he continually pestered them for action.

On September 15 the Polish forces involved in the Battle of Bzura began to run out of ammunition. The disruption in the rear caused by Luftwaffe raids and deep penetration by the panzers meant that Polish supply lines had been cut. General Tadeusz Kutrzeba ordered his southernmost units to try to break out toward the southeast to join Marshal Smigly-Rydz, then fell back with the rest of his men for a last ditch defense of Warsaw. German attacks began almost at once, with the Luftwaffe pounding Polish defenses from the air.

Marshal Edward Smigly-Rydz, commander of the Polish forces

Smigly-Rydz, meanwhile, had stopped the main German attack at Lvov and was busy gathering in reserves and retreating units. He drew up a strong defensive position, backed by artillery, and prepared to hold out until the French and British could intervene. He knew that over half the Polish army was already lost to him, though many isolated and surrounded units continued fighting in western and central Poland. The Polish government had already decided to order the Polish navy to steam for Britain. Some ships fell victim to the German Kriegsmarine in the Baltic, but most ships reached safety.

CARVE-UP

On 17 September, the Russians invaded Poland from the east. They gave as an excuse their desire to protect the ethnically Russian and Ukrainian citizens of eastern Poland from the fighting. In fact, the move was part of the deal Stalin had agreed with Hitler to carve up Poland between them. The Russian invasion force consisted of 1.5 million men, 6,000 tanks, 1,600 aircraft and 9,000 guns. The Poles in both north and south fought back, but now facing an enemy on both fronts there was little they could achieve.

In the south Smigly-Rydz ordered his men to march into Romania and throw down their weapons. The few pilots still with aircraft were told to fly to the nearest neutral country. Most of these men were in France or Britain by the end of the year and were rapidly formed into new Polish units to fight the Germans. The pilots were drafted into Britain's RAF and fought with distinction in the Battle of Britain. The majority of the 120,000 Polish soldiers who escaped preferred to join the French army, and were captured during the German invasion of that country in 1940. Only about 30,000 Poles who had gone to Britain remained as the Free Polish Army by the end of 1940.

The Poles in Warsaw were too isolated to escape to anywhere. They fought on until 28 September, then surrendered to the Germans. The last Polish troops to surrender were those in fortified areas of western Poland who fought on until October 5.

The German armed forces had lost 16,000

Polish cavalry galloping into action, 1939

killed and 32,000 wounded, nearly all of them in the army. The Poles had lost over 66,000 men killed, over 100,000 wounded and some 600,000 taken prisoner, with some 30,000 civilians being killed in air raids or cross fire.

The Germans divided Poland into three sections. The eastern provinces went to Russia while those parts which had been German before 1919 were returned to Germany. The rest was put under a German governor who ruled with autocratic powers. The SS went to work. Their first move in Warsaw was to arrest everyone who had a telephone at home, this being a rarity limited to the more prosperous families.

The Germans welcome a Soviet officer (center) to their map table

They then systematically stripped Poland of its political, religious and business leaders, who were put into concentration camps. German-speakers were made into German citizens and moved to that part of Poland which was, post invasion, now part of Germany. Non-German speakers in the newly created German part of Poland were expelled to the Polish areas. Jews were shot out of hand, thousands of civilians murdered and the rest brutalized. In the years of occupation that followed millions of Polish citizens, most of them Jews, were murdered.

Exactly how much the regular Wehrmacht knew of what was going on in the wake of their conquests is unclear. After the eventual German defeat, the soldiers had a strong motive for denying all knowledge of what went on. That the high command knew of the activities of the SS and other death squads is beyond doubt. They protested to Hitler on more than one occasion abut what was going on, but their protests got nowhere. Most generals probably guessed what was afoot, but found it convenient to believe the SS lies that the Jews and others who disappeared were being taken to slave labor camps. For the ordinary soldiers, however, there was little reason to suspect what was happening. By the time the murder squads arrived, most soldiers were far away.

In the aftermath of victory, the German army went about the business of regrouping itself and installing garrisons in key strategic locations. The army commander Brauchitsch ordered the planning staff at OKH, led by Franz Halder, to undertake a thorough appraisal of how the army had performed, with the Luftwaffe and Kriegsmarine undertaking similar studies. The main lessons the OKH drew related to the use of panzers.

The Panzer I, it was decided, was not fit for front line service. Although the German army had hundreds of them, they were taken out of the front line and turned over for use as ammunition carts, armored ambulances, training vehicles and the like.

The Panzer II had also shown itself to be highly vulnerable to artillery. It was decided to replace them as soon as possible with Panzer IIIs

and Panzer IVs, a process which was estimated would take a year or so.

Hitler at the joint German–Soviet Victory parade at Brest-Litovsk

The tactical deployment of the panzers was also studied. The majority of tank losses had taken place during street fighting in urban areas, when the enemy were able to get close to the tanks with mines, anti-tank guns and other weapons. It was decided that, whenever possible, the clearing of towns would be left to infantry and artillery. The fighting at Bzura had also shown the panzers to be vulnerable to anti-tank guns if the latter were well entrenched and the tanks in the open. This problem had been solved by the attacks of Stukas. It was decided to give forward tank commanders the authority to call up Luftwaffe attacks without the delay caused by routing such requests thorough divisional headquarters.

The Luftwaffe learned that bombers, and particularly Stukas, were highly vulnerable to enemy fighters. The Polish air force had been destroyed within a few days, after which the bombers had been able to operate almost at will. Priority would therefore be given to the destruction of enemy airbases and aircraft on the ground. Only then would the bombers be released for close support of the army.

The conflict between army demands for close Stuka support, and the Luftwaffe's desire to use their bombers to destroy the enemy air force first would come to be a key dispute in the planning of the attack on France. It would be crucial when the time came to fight Britain.

This complex process of studying the military lessons had barely begun when Hitler called the commanders of the armed services to a conference at OKW in Berlin. He announced the invasion of France would begin on November 12. Brauchitsch and Halder were aghast. The plans that OKH had for invading France were contingency plans some years old. With all the effort that had gone into preparing for the operations in Austria, Czechoslovakia and Poland there had been no time to update the arrangements for France with new information about roads, bridges and railways. Nor had there been any time to incorporate the lessons of the fighting in Poland into the plans. They begged Hitler for more time to prepare and to get their forces into position.

Hitler said he would think about it, but that the attack in the West must take place as soon as possible.

SCANDINAVIA 1940

In the event, Hitler decided on another move before invading France. Again, Hitler was displaying a grip on strategy that most of his generals lacked. It was to precipitate the first clash between the Wehrmacht and truly modern armed forces. The bold thrust was the German invasion of Denmark and Norway.

Hitler did not originally intend to invade these Scandinavian countries. When, in October

1939, Admiral Raeder had asked the Führer to "pressure" the Norwegians into allowing German warships to use the repair facilities at Trondheim, Hitler had refused. In December he told his staff he wanted Norway to remain neutral. But in January the OKK, the high staff of the Kriegsmarine, began to think that the British Admiralty, under Winston Churchill, was planning to occupy key naval bases in Norway.

Churchill was, in fact, planning exactly this sort of move, but had been overruled by Prime Minister Chamberlain who did not want to see the war extending any further than it already had. On 27 January, Hitler gave in to the pestering from Raeder to the extent that he asked the OKW to draw up plans for an invasion of Norway, but stressed this was only to occur "if the Führer deems it necessary to the war aims of the Reich."

The hands of both sides were forced by circumstances. A German freighter, the *Altmark*, was bringing the crews of British merchant ships sunk at sea back to Germany as prisoners. On 16 February it was sighted by British destroyers and sought the safety of Norwegian neutral waters. The British ships gave chase, capturing the German ship inside Norwegian waters. The Norwegian government protested, but Churchill ignored the message.

To Hitler this incident showed that the British would violate Norwegian neutrality, at least on a limited scale, if they felt the need was strong enough. Hitler's main cause for worry was the iron ore which came from northern Sweden. Huge supplies of this ore were supplied to Germany and were absolutely vital to the German war effort. During the summer they were shipped down the Baltic, but in winter, when the Baltic froze, they were taken by rail to the Norwegian coast and then shipped along the coast by sea. Egged on by Raeder, Hitler believed

the British would breach Norwegian neutrality to cut this essential supply.

Vidkun Quisling (left) meets Himmler, Reichskommissar Josef Terboven and General von Falkenhorst in Norway, May 1940

On February 20, Hitler summoned General von Falkenhorst. The 58 year old general had been given an infantry corps to command in the invasion of Poland where he had performed well, but not spectacularly. With the growth of blitzkrieg and panzer warfare, the old-style infantry soldier had been expecting a staff posting or even to be put on the reserve list. So he was surprised when Hitler told him he was in charge of invading Norway and Denmark. The reason, Hitler said, was that Falkenhorst was the only German general who had lived for some years in Scandinavia. Falkenhorst was even more taken aback when told to come back that evening with outline plans.

Falkenhorst dashed to the nearest bookshop where he bought a Baedeker guide to Scandinavia. Then he found an empty table at a nearby café and sat down to prepare his plans. He was back by 6pm with a draft outline, which Hitler approved. The invasion was codenamed Operation *Weser* and scheduled for April 9.

Although old-fashioned in the terms of the Wehrmacht in 1940, Falkenhorst was ideal for this task. Not only did he know Scandinavia, but the operation was to be an old fashioned army landing not a panzer–Stuka blitzkrieg. Working frantically with the OKH and OKK, Falkenhorst had detailed plans ready by April 1. They were put before Hitler, who made rather fewer changes than was normal before approving them. This may have been because the plans were largely dominated by use of the Kriegsmarine and Hitler had never been very familiar with naval matters.

On April 8 British ships, acting under orders from Churchill, began laying mines off the Norwegian coast along the route taken by the German iron ore ships. Although the German invasion fleet was already at sea, the move was used by Hitler as a pretext for invasion.

ALL HELL LET LOOSE

At dawn on April 9 German warships and transports sailed into Narvik, Trondheim, Bergen, Kristiansand, Oslo and Copenhagen while army units swarmed over the Danish border. In most places the Norwegian defenses were not fully manned—mobilization had been ordered only the day before. Only at Oslo was there serious resistance. The German cruiser *Blücher* was sunk by guns and torpedoes from the Oscarsborg Fortress and the landing force was halted. Within a few hours, however, the Luftwaffe had pounded the fortress to rubble and the invasion went ahead.

The main British war fleet was actually at sea, off Bergen, when the German invasion began. The commander, Admiral Forbes, wanted to attack the German transports in Bergen and Trondheim, but was ordered to wait until he had located and attacked the German battlecruisers and pocket battleship which were known to be at sea. In the event he failed to find the main German war fleet before it got back to harbor. In some minor skirmishes, the British did sink the cruisers *Karlsruhe* and *Königsberg* and damaged the pocket battleship *Lützow*. A spirited action between rival destroyers on 10 April ended with the sinking of two German and three British destroyers. Finally, on 8 June the British aircraft carrier *Glorious* and two destroyers were surprised and sunk by the battle cruisers *Scharnhorst* and *Gneisenau*.

The Germans could afford such losses less than the British, who had far more ships in reserve, but the few days of naval fighting gave the Royal Navy cause to look on their German adversaries with respect. Hitler, meanwhile, was satisfied that his strategic aims had been secured. He congratulated Falkenhorst and appointed him military governor of Norway with orders to govern with a light hand, leaving administration to the Norwegian civilian government whenever possible. Then Hitler turned to his next and much larger project: the invasion of France.

In the First World War, the German cruiser SMS Blücher capsized at the Battle of the Dogger Bank, 1915. On April 9, 1940 her namesake fared no better, being sunk in Drøbak Sound

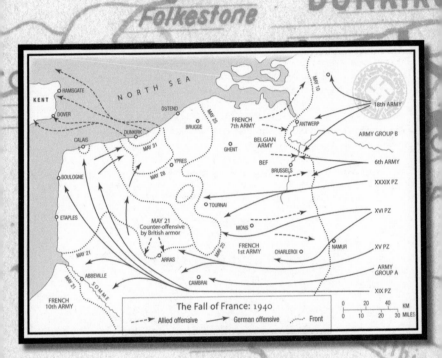

The Fall of France: 1940

- - -> Allied offensive → German offensive .... Front

KM 0 20 40

MILES 0 10 20 30

8

FRANCE 1940

It was the swift victory in France in 1940 that established Hitler's military reputation in Germany. At least some credit was due. It was he who chose the plan to use and he who supervised its implementation

With the conquest of Poland complete, Hitler could turn to deal with the unwanted war in the West. The declarations of war by Britain and France had provoked the Führer to one of his rages and, for once, he was in complete agreement with his generals about the dangers of a war on two fronts. The speed of victory in Poland and the slow rate of French mobilization had saved Hitler from such a prospect. The war in the East was over before that in the West got under way.

Hitler now hoped that the fait accompli in Poland would lead to peace with Britain and France, for the Reich was not yet ready for this war. OKH, Army High Command, was wary of attacking France, convinced that even if victory were gained it would only be at enormous cost in bloodshed and material. The navy was even more dubious of gaining victory in the autumn of 1939.

There were only 39 U-boats fit for sea and many of the larger warships, including *Bismarck*, were incomplete. Navy chief Grand Admiral Erich Raeder

The German advance into the Low Countries and France in 1940

believed the Kriegsmarine would not be ready for war until 1943, and would not be able to face the Royal Navy with any confidence until 1946.

Hitler, as usual, was more optimistic than his military professionals though this optimism was based more on political than military considerations. He held the French in utter contempt after they had failed to intervene when Germany had reoccupied the Rhineland in 1936. He believed that the Wehrmacht needed only to

achieve one swift victory for the entire French army to collapse. The invasion of France was given the code name Operation *Yellow*.

The British, he considered, were quite different. Hitler did not expect them to collapse like the French, but he did believe them to be a pragmatic people. His experience of the British government to date had been that it mouthed fine principles, but was willing to accept realities. If France could be crushed, thought Hitler, Britain would accept the generous and honorable peace he would then offer.

Hitler's Eagle's Nest HQ where he planned the invasion of France

Even so, it would be better for Hitler's long term aim of attacking Russia if war with Britain could be avoided. With this in mind Hitler sent his unofficial envoy Birger Dahlerus to Britain. "The British can have peace if they want it," Hitler briefed Dahlerus on September 26, "but they will have to hurry." On October 5 Hitler followed this clandestine approach with a very public one. At a speech in Berlin, Hitler portrayed himself as a reasonable man seeking only to reach a just and lasting settlement in Europe to replace the unfair and flawed arrangements of Versailles.

He went on to offer to meet Britain and France at the conference table "before millions of men are uselessly killed and billions of riches destroyed."

Three days later Hitler issued War Directive No.6 which outlined a plan for invading France and again set the date for implementation as November 12, 1939. The OKH was aghast by the imminent date and even Göring was taken aback. Hitler argued that peace in the East was only temporary and that Stalin remained unpredictable and dangerous. Moreover the French and British were rearming with modern weapons at

an alarming speed. Time was on the side of the enemy, said Hitler, so even if the Wehrmacht was not perfectly prepared it was better to strike now than to wait.

Although the timing of the attack caused consternation among the generals, the strategy laid out in War Directive No.6 was welcomed as being sensible and pragmatic.

"An offensive will be planned on the northern flank of the Western Front, through Luxembourg, Belgium and Holland," the Directive read. "The purpose of this offensive will be to defeat as much as possible of the French Army and of her allies, and at the same time to win as much territory as possible in Holland, Belgium and northern France to serve as a base for the successful prosecution of the air and sea war against England." This was sensible strategic thinking which made no undue demands on the abilities of the German war machine.

HITLER'S RAGE

By November 5 Walther von Brauchitsch, Commander in Chief of the army at OKH, was convinced the army could not possibly be ready for a major offensive in time. At that afternoon's regular meeting with the Führer, Brauchitsch outlined the army's concerns. The autumn rains in Flanders would bog down the tanks, he said, the mechanical problems with the Mark IV Panzer which had caused difficulty in Poland had not yet been solved, there was not enough ammunition stockpiled to take on France, some of the newly raised units had not fought as well as expected. All this meant, he told Hitler, that more time was needed to prepare for the attack.

Hitler was furious and let rip one of his terrible outbursts of temper. He accused the army in general and Brauchitsch in particular of cowardice, incompetence and much more. It was

an early example of the way Hitler was increasingly to treat opposition to his plans from the military professionals. In Hitler's eyes the generals were there to ensure the army was ready to carry out his plans and ideas. If they failed they were subjected to storms of rage and fury to cow them into submission. As yet, Hitler was not totally inflexible, but this interview was a disturbing sign of what was to come. When Brauchitsch returned to his offices he was gray-faced and his hands trembled.

Two days later heavy rains broke over the Western Front. Göring reported that the Luftwaffe could not fly, robbing the panzers of close bomber support. Hitler postponed the attack on France. The bad flying weather had settled in, however, and the attack was repeatedly postponed until mid-December, when Hitler granted the armed forces extensive Christmas leave and set a new date for his offensive: January 17, 1940.

The delay gave Hitler time to study the invasion plan drawn up by the General Staff at OKH in more detail—and he became increasingly unhappy as time passed. Operation *Yellow* was based on a draft plan drawn up by the OKH under Franz Halder in 1938, though it had been updated since to take account of the lessons learned in Poland. It was, effectively, an updated version of the Schlieffen Plan of 1914.

As in the earlier war, the main attack would be pushed through central Belgium around Liege, while holding actions were taking place along the Maginot Line to distract the French and small-scale attacks were launched in the center to tie down some of the French divisions. A key difference was the addition of a plan to race along the Channel coast and seize the ports to stop British supplies and reinforcements being sent to France.

Army Group B, which was to launch the main attack, was allocated all the panzer units and motorized infantry, together with most of the Luftwaffe's Stukas, to guarantee speed of movement in the anticipated blitzkrieg. Army Group A, to the south, was allocated only infantry and artillery as its role was essentially defensive.

STRATEGIC DIVIDE

As early as October Hitler had been expressing disquiet at this plan. He had, after all, marched into France in 1914 as a very small part of the original Schlieffen Plan and had seen its failure at first hand. He did not like repeating past mistakes and, in any case, usually preferred bold new plans to safe old ones. He asked Halder if it would not be possible to launch an armored attack in the south to outflank the French and British resisting the main assault in Belgium. Halder had replied it was not because the mountainous Ardennes region was unsuitable for tanks.

Halder was not alone in thinking this for the French generals believed the same thing and had drawn up their war plans accordingly. They firmly held the opinion that the Maginot Line of fortifications along the Franco-German border was invulnerable and that any German attack would therefore come further north. Knowing that the German military favored tank-led operations, the French Staff looked for favorable tank country. The Ardennes area was hilly and the only roads were narrow and twisting. While it would be possible to drive a tank through it, the French argued, the long supply convoys of petrol and ammunition would become hopelessly jammed. Looking further north still, the French Staff saw the open plains of Belgium and concluded the main German attack would, as in 1914, take place there.

To counter the expected attack, the French Staff envisaged the French and British forces racing forwards into neutral Belgium as soon as the German forces invaded from the east. Cooperating with the Belgian army, the allied armies would blow the bridges over the various water obstacles—such as the Albert Canal, the Meuse and the Scheldt—to form a series of gigantic tank traps. With the blitzkrieg advances thus slowed down, the French Staff believed, the Germans could be ground to a standstill by heavy artillery and massed infantry formations. The French believed that the Germans would not want to face another four years of bloodletting in the trenches. Once stalemate was achieved, somewhere between Namur and Amiens, it was hoped the Germans would sue for peace. If not, plans were in existence for massed mobilization of the French citizens to support a long war of attrition.

The French had good reasons for being confident. In almost every area of military comparison they had a clear superiority over the Germans. In terms of manpower the Germans could field 133 divisions, while the combined French and British forces had 112 and the Belgians and Dutch could add another 32. The French were particularly proud of their field artillery which was more accurate and easier to move than the German guns. Moreover the French had 11,000 guns compared to some 8,500 in the German army.

Nor were the French backward in using the more modern weaponry. They had 3,000 tanks to face the 2,600 German panzers, and each French design was at first glance superior to its German counterpart. The medium tanks were typical. The French S-35 had frontal armor 55mm thick, that of the Panzer III was 14.5mm. The S-35 carried a 47mm gun, the Panzer III a 37mm gun. The French tank could move at 25mph on roads, the German at only 20mph. Moreover the French could count on the 600 British tanks and those in the Belgian and Dutch armies as well as on its own.

Only in the air did the Germans enjoy a clear superiority. They outnumbered the French and British by about five to four in fighters, but by a massive 1,700 bombers to just 380. Although the paper strength of the opposing fighter aircraft was comparable, the German machines could reach 350mph with ease while the French aircraft had a top speed of 300mph. The superior British Hurricanes and Spitfires were present in such tiny numbers it was unlikely they would make much difference to the struggle in the air.

Given these figures, there were many generals on the German side who agreed with the French Staff. Most of these generals concluded that an assault in the West was doomed to end in stalemate and some tried to dissuade Hitler from making the attempt. But one man, the Chief of Staff in Army Group A, saw that while one plan would fail another might succeed. This was General Erich von Manstein and he was determined to get his ideas put in front of Hitler.

Von Manstein's plan to invade was adopted on February 17, 1940

Manstein based his alternative plan on two key factors. First the differences in the tactical use of tanks between the French and German armies and second the roads in the Ardennes.

French tactics envisaged a war fought in a tactical situation not too different from that of the Great War. They expected there to be long lines of field entrenchments forming a continuous front. Tanks could be used alongside artillery and infantry to create a local breakthrough. The lighter tanks might even advance with the cavalry to exploit such a breakthrough and to secure an objective, but it was expected that the defender's mobile reserves could be brought up before the attackers could advance more than a few miles. The defending tanks would then fight the attackers to a standstill and a new line of trenches and pill boxes would be established.

As a result of this tactical doctrine, the French spread most of their tanks among their infantry divisions to be used to support small scale attacks or defensive actions. The intended use of the tanks also affected their design. With limited, local objectives the French tanks in battle would have no need of a dedicated commander. Therefore they were not designed to cope with one, instead the tanks were equipped with small turrets with enough space for just one man, who directed the tank as well as operating the main gun.

The German tanks had much larger turrets with room for two men. One was the gunner while the other was the tank commander. This configuration allowed the tank commander to concentrate on keeping up to date with the changing battlefield and to keep in radio contact with his unit commander. Such an ability was essential to the more fluid, faster moving type of warfare envisaged by the Germans in blitzkrieg. Nor did the Germans tie their tanks to slow-moving infantry divisions, but formed them into dedicated panzer divisions able to operate on their own and supported by motorized infantry, the Panzergrenadier.

Manstein knew that these features would give the German tanks a marked superiority in fast-moving open warfare once a breakthrough had been achieved. The question he posed himself was how to achieve such a breakthrough. Manstein believed the existing Operation *Yellow* plan would lead the main German force head to head against the strongest enemy formations and result in a static battle of the type that would favor the French and British. To find a way around this, Manstein turned to another German officer known to be enthusiastic on mobile panzer warfare, Heinz Guderian.

Guderian was at this point the head of mobile field forces, charged with organizing the recruitment, equipping and supply of the panzer divisions. He was an expert on the practicalities and logistics of tank warfare, and knew exactly what the German panzers and their supply system were capable of achieving. In November 1939 Manstein consulted Guderian who later recorded "Manstein asked me if panzer movements would be possible through the Ardennes to capture Sedan. I knew the area from the Great War and, after studying the map of roads, confirmed that it was."

Manstein knew that once past Sedan and over the River Meuse an advancing panzer force would have wide open countryside ahead of it, ideal territory for German-style tank tactics. A fast advance would be possible, severely disrupting the enemy battle plan. Manstein took his idea to his superior, General Gerd von Rundstedt, the commander of Army Group A. Rundstedt was at first sceptical, but had his staff organize a series

Heinz Guderian in his command truck during the invasion of France, 1940. In the foreground is an Enigma coding device

of war games which showed the plan to offer dramatic possibilities. In December, Rundstedt passed Manstein's ideas on to OKH.

At OKH, Halder and Brauchitsch cast a cursory eye over the plans and dismissed them, largely on the grounds that they thought the roads in the Ardennes would be unable to support the large numbers of supply vehicles that would have to pass over them. Manstein would not give up, however. He sent the plans to General Alfred Jodl at Hitler's own OKW staff in the hope that the bold idea would appeal to the Führer. At this point fate took a hand.

On January 10 a parachute major was flying from Munster to Bonn to confer with the Luftwaffe over elements of the parachute landing planned to secure bridges in Belgium. He carried with him the complete OKH plans for the invasion, scheduled for January 17. The aircraft was hit by a snowstorm and made a forced landing on what the horrified major suddenly realized was a Belgian airfield. He hurriedly tried to set fire to his documents, but they failed to catch light. The delighted Belgians lost no time passing the plans on to the Dutch, French and British.

When news of the incident reached Hitler, he was predictably furious and ordered Brauchitsch to bring the attack forward to dawn the following day. A few hours later, after he had calmed down, Hitler countermanded the order and postponed the invasion of France indefinitely. Hitler ordered the OKH to come up with new plans and again put forward his own idea of a flank attack in the south. Jodl added Manstein's ideas to the mix of concepts on which the staff went to work.

In March 1940 a conference was held at the Chancellery in Berlin to discuss the different concepts being put forward and Manstein was given a slot to put forward his ideas. According to Manstein he explained his plans for a panzer assault through the Ardennes which would capture Sedan and cross the Meuse. He paused. "Hitler then asked me "and then what are you going to do?" Hitler was the first person who had thought to ask me this vital question. I replied that I would continue west. The supreme leadership had to decide if my aim was Paris or Amiens. I thought that I should go past Amiens to the English Channel."

Hitler merely nodded, but his question had shown once again that he was able to grasp the potential of a new idea faster than his generals. Within a few days of the conference he was

demanding that the OKH draw up detailed plans for the invasion of France based on Manstein's ideas. But Hitler added a significant touch of his own. He ordered that the attack should start in the north as originally envisaged, but that this should be merely a feint to draw the French and British deep into Belgium. Hitler also ordered the Ardennes column to be made even stronger than envisaged by Manstein. Hitler did not see this as merely a strong flank attack. He wanted to encircle the Allied armies to the north and destroy them.

ON THE ATTACK

Hitler was enthused by the idea, later dubbed *Sichelschnitt*, ("Sickle-stroke"), and threw himself into the detailed planning even more closely than he had done with the Polish campaign. It was at Hitler's insistence that the Panzer IVs were removed from other panzer divisions and concentrated in those which would make the main drive through Sedan. With his usual detailed grasp of technical detail he realized that the Panzer IVs would be needed in the south while the Panzer IIIs and other models would be quite capable of the less demanding tasks allocated to them in other areas.

Kurt Student, commander of the parachute corps, was summoned to see Hitler next. Student already knew that his tiny force of 4,500 parachute troops, backed by 12,000 infantry in transport aircraft, was to capture the bridges over the Rhine in Holland and he expected Hitler to quiz him over these plans. Student was in for a surprise. Almost as soon as he was through the door, Hitler had Student studying a map of the area around Maastricht. The problem, Hitler explained, was that once German troops crossed the Dutch border, the Belgian defenders on the Albert Canal would have plenty of time to blow the bridges. Even

Hitler with the paratroops who captured the Eben Emael fort in Belgium, just after he had awarded them medals for their feat

more fatal to a quick advance was the massively strong fortress of Eben Emael whose guns dominated the Maas and Albert Canals, making a forced crossing virtually impossible.

Hitler knew exactly how small a patch of ground was needed to land one of the new and top-secret transport gliders. He told Student that he wanted such a glider to land on top of Eben Emael. The troops would then use another top secret invention—a powerful form of plastic explosive—to blast open the casemates and gun emplacements. Student was taken aback and asked for time to think about the idea. Hitler gave him just 24 hours. Next day Student was back to express his full agreement with what he later called "the most original idea of the war."

By late March the plans were effectively complete. The staff at OKH had worked with their customary efficiency to draw up a scheme by which the assault troops could advance confident that they would be kept supplied and supported by a vast array of pontoon bridges, engineers, ammunition, food, tank recovery vehicles and even blacksmiths. Incredibly the bulk of the transport in 1940 was still horse-drawn. The invasion date was set for May 5.

As usual, Hitler was taking the full credit for himself. Talking of the attack through the Ardennes he said "When I spoke to the generals about this new plan for the West, the only one who really understood me was Manstein." The fact that Manstein had come up with the idea himself was conveniently forgotten.

As time went by Hitler became noticeably agitated. At the daily military conferences his fingers were rarely still as they fiddled with pens, papers and anything else at hand. At the conference on May 3 the Chief Meteorologist Diesing gave such an appalling weather forecast that the attack date was put back to the seventh. Next day the forecast was even worse, another 24 hour delay was ordered, then another. On May 6 the intelligence report gave alarming news. The Dutch army was being called up and road blocks were being erected. Hitler turned to Diesing and demanded to know the weather. "The conditions will be favorable on the tenth of May" came the reply. Göring wanted an assurance of at least five days good flying weather for the Luftwaffe, but Hitler interrupted before Diesing could answer. The attack would begin at dawn on May 10.

Hitler was determined to be as close to the front line as possible. Over the previous months he had ordered the construction of a forward command post near Euskirchen which he named Felsennest, the Eagle's Nest. Blasted out of the solid rock, the command post was linked directly to the headquarters of the various attacking armies. Hitler ordered that all news was to be passed directly to the Eagle's Nest and that any changes to the plan had to be approved by him personally.

On the evening of May 9 Hitler and his entourage boarded a train outside Berlin. The staff were told they were going to visit the troops on a morale-boosting mission which would be filmed to be shown in the cinemas. Not until they arrived at Euskirchen did Hitler reveal what was really afoot. He had little choice: as they got out of the train a vast formation of Luftwaffe bombers thundered overhead, flying west.

In Britain the attack prompted a change of government. Chamberlain resigned and was replaced by Churchill. This event had little immediate impact on the fighting, but that would soon change.

Hitler, meanwhile, was receiving the reports from his commanders. He was most thrilled when he heard that the Eben Emael attack had succeeded—Hitler literally hugged himself. The parachute forces held on for 24 hours, until the two panzer divisions earmarked to invade Belgium arrived, crossed the intact bridges and motored west. Further north the parachute troops had also captured the bridges in Holland and had secured a position in the heart of The Hague, paralyzing the Dutch government. These successes were vital to the plan. They convinced the French and British that the main German attack was coming in Belgium and caused them to march the bulk of their forces northwest to meet the threat.

German SS (left) and Luftwaffe (right) in The Hague, Netherlands

Hitler's eyes now turned south to where the massed panzer divisions were moving through the Ardennes. The main thrust was being made by Guderian's XIX Panzer Corps with Reinhardt's XLI Panzer Corps on his right flank, both formations under the command of von Kleist. To the north was the XV Panzer Corps under Hoth who, like Kleist, was responsible to Rundstedt, commander of Army Group A.

Guderian reached the Meuse at Sedan on May 12. As expected the bridges had been blown by the French, but the far bank was less defended than the Germans had feared. This was because the French had estimated it would take German infantry, marching and fighting on foot, at least nine days to reach the Meuse. French forces were, therefore, not by then in position. Guderian had identified a loop in the river near St Menges as being ideal for a forced crossing. The wooded hills on the German bank were ideal cover for massing his forces and allowed his artillery to dominate the far bank.

The 1st Panzer Regiment crosses the pontoon bridge over the Meuse at Sedan that proved crucial to the invasion's success

To make certain of success, Guderian called down a vast cloud of Stukas which pummelled the far bank on the afternoon of May 13. As soon as the Stukas had dropped their bombs, at about 4pm, Guderian sent his infantry across in rubber boats. By dusk a secure foothold on the far bank had been established and by midnight the engineers had built a bridge across which poured the panzers. By the afternoon of May 14 Guderian's entire corps was over the river and had crushed the French forces opposing them. There was now nothing between Guderian and the English Channel except open space.

The next day Guderian linked up with Reinhardt and then with Hoth. There was now a massive armored spearhead of seven panzer

divisions thundering west with some 40 divisions of infantry following as fast as they could march. By dusk on 16 May the panzers were approaching the headwaters of the Somme.

The French Prime Minister, Paul Reynaud, was one of the few Frenchmen to appreciate fully the possibilities of tank warfare. When he heard that so many German tanks were over the Meuse he phoned Churchill. "We have lost the battle" was Reynaud's grim message. Having put down the phone to London, Reynaud picked it up again and sacked the French commander, the elderly Maurice Gamelin, replacing him with the more aggressive Maxime Weygand. The move was understandable, but Weygand was in Syria and it took him three days to reach his new command. They were to be three days of hesitation and confusion in the French high command.

German troops in France, 1940. The tanks are Czech LTM38 tanks taken over by the Germans and redesignated Panzer 38(T)

ANXIOUS MOMENTS

Back at the Eagle's Nest, Hitler was not happy. The advance of the panzers had amazed him as much by its ease as its speed. The staff at OKH had been surprised as well, and their carefully laid plans were failing to cope. The supporting infantry, engineers and supplies were some 50 miles behind the panzers and would take 2 days to catch up. In Hitler's view, the precious panzers were becoming dangerously exposed. Vast reserves of French infantry and artillery were located to the south of the River Aisne, to the rear of the Maginot Line. In 1914 the French had used trains, trucks and even taxis to shift a similar reserve north to frustrate the German attack. Hitler was worried that they would do the same again. If the French mounted an attack north into the German left flank they could cut off the panzers from the rest of the army. At midnight on May 16 Hitler ordered the panzer spearhead to halt.

Guderian was aghast. In front of him were the rolling plains of northern France devoid of enemy forces, but he was being ordered to halt. He questioned the orders and was told by Kleist that he could not move forward until the infantry had come up and secured the south flank of his advance by digging in along the Aisne. Guderian resigned, Kleist contacted Rundstedt in dismay and Rundstedt turned to the Eagle's Nest. Messages flew back and forth throughout May 17. Eventually Guderian, his resignation refused, was given permission to carry out "reconnaissance in force."

Interpreting the phrase to mean what he wanted it to mean, Guderian sent his panzers forward once again. On May 18 the panzers reached St Quentin, on May 19 they were over the Somme, on May 20 they took Amiens and on May 21 they reached the sea at Abbeville.

On that same day Hitler's worries seemed to be coming true. The northernmost panzer division in the great drive west was commanded by Erwin Rommel, who had got the command at Hitler's instruction as thanks for his work in Poland. On the morning of May 21, Rommel's 7th Panzer Division was moving on the Aa River when its right flank was attacked by a force of British tanks at Arras.

The German commander on the ground signalled Rommel that he was being attacked by five divisions, and Rommel passed the message on to Rundstedt. Rommel then called down a massive Stuka strike as he redeployed his panzers to meet this new threat. At almost the same time a French assault was launched north across the Somme near Amiens. If the two attacks were to link up, the panzer spearhead would be cut off. Rundstedt passed the dire news on to the Eagle's Nest, where Hitler began to worry and rant at his staff.

Fairly quickly, Rommel realized he was faced by only two tank battalions and a couple of infantry regiments, which he quickly threw back. On the Somme, the French assault collapsed in confusion. Rundstedt later recorded that for a few hours the situation had "appeared to be a critical moment. We feared that our armored divisions would be cut off before the infantry could support them." In reality the threat was non-existent, but it had rattled the German high command and, in particular, Hitler.

The attack at Arras also had, unknown to Hitler, a profound effect on the Allies. Lord Gort, the commander of the British Expeditionary Force, was already frustrated by the impractical suggestions coming from the French under whose orders he was supposed to operate. He had already contacted Britain to ask that the Royal Navy be prepared to organize an evacuation of the British land forces. Now Gort began to lay his plans in

more detail, though the British government sternly forbade him to abandon their French allies. The main bulk of the British army was still deep in Belgium. The Dutch army to the north had already surrendered to the Germans and Gort realized the Belgians would not hold out much longer. Gort looked back to the Channel ports of Boulogne, Calais and Dunkirk for salvation.

The Channel ports were also being studied by Reinhardt and his XLI Panzer Corps. On May 22 Reinhardt surrounded Boulogne. On the next day he overran the country around Calais and reached the canal which runs inland from Gravelines to St Omer. The final Channel port of Dunkirk was less than 20 miles away. Reinhardt was confident he would reach it next day. In fact there was just one British battalion defending the 20 mile length of canal, and they could offer no resistance to the panzers. With Dunkirk in German hands, the British army would be cut off from the sea and from the Royal Navy and would be forced to surrender.

Reinhardt was staggered to receive an order from Kleist to halt at the canal. He complained. He pointed out that there were no enemy troops beyond the canal. He explained how important it was to capture Dunkirk. He told Guderian, who complained in his turn. But Kleist could do nothing, not even authorize a "reconnaissance in force." The order to halt had come direct and personally from the Führer.

The decision to halt the panzers in front of Dunkirk on May 24 is one of the most mystifying of Hitler's career as a military commander. By the time the panzers were allowed to advance again, the British had organized a defensive perimeter around the port. Gort's evacuation plans were being implemented and the British army was able to evacuate the Continent and prepare to defend Britain. Many historians have been baffled by

A German watches some of the thousands of British and French prisoners who were left behind at Dunkirk, early June 1940

Hitler's orders, but seen in the context of the day, the decision becomes more understandable.

Throughout the previous week, Hitler had been worried about the southern flank of his panzer advance. Despite approving Guderian's bold plans, Hitler still had the doubts of a Great War corporal. Above all he believed it imperative not to offer the French an open flank. It was this that had led to the halt order on May 16 and the worries had not been helped by the scare on May 21—especially as a general as close to Hitler as Rommel had been involved. Hitler clearly could barely believe his good luck and feared greatly that the enemy were better prepared than, in fact, they were.

On the morning of May 24 Hitler was met by Göring. The Luftwaffe chief slammed his hand down on a map of the campaign and declared "This is a job for the Luftwaffe." He promised Hitler that the bombers could smash the port of Dunkirk and cut the British off from the Royal Navy without the need to risk the precious panzers. The port of Dunkirk would undoubtedly be a bottleneck and dock facilities were highly vulnerable to aerial bombardment. There is no doubt Göring believed he could destroy the port of Dunkirk and there is little reason to suppose Hitler thought otherwise. Neither man had a naval background and Hitler most certainly did not consult Raeder at this crucial moment. It probably did not occur to Hitler or Göring that the Royal Navy could evacuate an army by any means other than a port.

Hitler then visited Rundstedt at his headquarters. Rundstedt was still in charge of Army Group A, the main force in the *Sichelschnitt*, but he had been informed by Brauchitsch that he would shortly be given command of the attack south to defeat the remaining French and British forces. Although we do not know what Rundstedt said to Hitler, it would be natural that he concentrated on the coming battle in the south. Hitler was already concerned about preserving his panzer forces. Rundstedt's assessment of the task still to be accomplished—and the Franco-British forces were still formidable—can only have confirmed Hitler's worries.

GROWING DOUBT

Back at the Eagle's Nest, Hitler would have been able to consult the maps and papers of the OKW. These told him what he already knew from his experiences in the trenches 25 years earlier—that Flanders was a wet and muddy place with soft, unstable ground. If it rained, Dunkirk would become a scrapyard for the tanks.

Such was the information available to Hitler when he made his fateful decision to stop the panzers. Alone it may have been enough to cause the Führer to give the order, but there might have been another reason as well. He dropped hints of this at Rundstedt's headquarters when he told the staff, "France is finished. I want to make peace with Britain on a basis that she would regard as compatible with her honor to accept." Hitler was later to insert provisions into the French surrender treaty deliberately aimed at conciliating Britain—for instance the French navy was specifically allotted to the Vichy regime not to the German Kriegsmarine.

It is possible that in halting the panzers, Hitler was offering Britain a way to achieve peace with honor. He knew the British would have to leave all their tanks and artillery in France, effectively making them defenseless to blitzkrieg, but without massive casualties British public opinion might favor stopping the war. Some months later Hitler complained to Bormann, "Churchill was quite unable to appreciate the way I refrained from creating an irreparable breach between the British and ourselves." A comment which may have been hindsight.

One other point needs mentioning. The official war diary of the Wehrmacht for May 24 records that the order to halt the panzers was given by Rundstedt. The diary makes no mention of Hitler's involvement with this order. On other occasions when corroborative evidence is available, the wording of the diary for May 24 would mean that Rundstedt initiated the order and that Hitler's only involvement was not to over-rule it. Perhaps it was not Hitler's decision at all.

Whatever the truth behind the orders of May 24, their meaning was clear. The army was to stop and the trapped British and French troops were to be finished off by the Luftwaffe. It was sheer bad luck, for Göring, that the main Luftwaffe bases were affected by fog, low cloud and poor visibility for the next few days.

The British government gave permission to Lord Gort to evacuate his army through Dunkirk on May 27. Gort had actually given his orders the day before and Admiral Ramsay had been organizing an evacuation fleet even earlier. At first the port was

filled with transport staff, engineers, cooks and the like, about 25,000 of whom were taken off by the night of May 28. The next day the Luftwaffe could launch its first major attack and, true to Göring's promise, the port of Dunkirk was smashed. "I hope the British are good swimmers," chortled the Luftwaffe boss over dinner that evening.

It was at this point that Ramsay's foresight came into play. He had been gathering almost any boat that could float around Dover and now sent them over the Channel to take men off the beaches of Dunkirk. There were not enough naval men to man the 900 ships, tugs and pleasure yachts which streamed over the Channel. Many were manned by their civilian crews or owners who braved the maelstrom of Luftwaffe violence to save the army. Some 200 of the vessels failed to return from their mission.

When it became clear how many troops were being taken off by the swarms of small ships—and that the port facilities were again in operation—the panzers were finally unleashed. It was too late. A firm defensive perimeter had been established and despite sustained and heavy attacks, the Germans could not break through. By dawn on June 4, 224,000 British and 116,000 French and Belgian troops had been rescued from Dunkirk and the rearguard holding off the Germans surrendered. Hitler left the Eagle's Nest that same day and gave orders that it was to be preserved unchanged as a museum to the glory of the German armed forces.

The battle was, however, only half fought.

To the south of the Somme and the Aisne remained the bulk of the French army and four divisions of British troops. Weygand, the new French commander, left 17 divisions in the Maginot Line and massed 49 divisions along the new front. He had few tanks and fewer aircraft, but was determined to stop the invader. Weygand had been on Foch's staff when the apparently unstoppable German advance was halted on the Marne in 1914. He now gave every impression of being confident that the miracle was about to be repeated.

VICTORY WITHIN SIGHT

Hitler was now ensconced in a new forward base at the village of Bruly-de-Pesche on the Belgian/French border. A large concrete bunker was hurriedly built and dubbed Wolfsschlucht—the Wolf's Gorge. From there Hitler issued an avalanche of orders for the conquest of France. The ten panzer divisions were brought back up to strength with repaired or replacement tanks. They were divided into five panzer corps massed in three columns. In Champagne, Guderian had two corps to drive east of Reims. At Laon, Kleist had two more to launch a pincer movement to link up with Guderian. On the coast, near Abbeville, Hoth had one corps to drive along the French coast. A further 130 infantry divisions were lined up to support the anticipated breakthrough.

The assault began on 5 June when Hoth attacked at Abbeville. For two days there was heavy fighting, then the French front collapsed and by June 9 Hoth was crossing the Seine at Rouen. Kleist attacked a day after Hoth and again hit determined French resistance. On June 9, Hitler decided to move Kleist's reserves to serve under Guderian whose attack was due to begin that day. The move was inspired for Guderian quickly achieved a breakthrough and swept around to outflank the French facing Kleist.

That same day Reynaud issued a statement declaring, "We shall fight in front of Paris. We shall fight behind Paris." But even as the statement was made, Reynaud and the French government were fleeing to Tours, later moving to Bordeaux. The next day Italy declared war on France, as Mussolini had promised Hitler he would do, and 32 divisions crossed the French border around Nice.

Weygand had already told Reynaud to sue for peace, but had been ignored. On June 11 Churchill flew to Tours to urge the French to continue the war from their colonies. The very next day a distraught Weygand spoke to the cabinet. He told them the war was lost and blamed the British, concluding, "I am obliged to say a cessation of hostilities is compulsory."

Stills from a movie showing Hitler's delighted reaction on being told of the Fall of France

Hitler was of much the same opinion. He announced he would not damage Paris if it was declared an open city and went on to deny he intended any harm to Britain. Indeed, the Führer emphasized, Britain had declared war on Germany, not the other way around. He was preparing the way, again, for peace moves.

Meanwhile the fighting had to go on. German troops entered Paris on June 14. The collapse of French armed resistance and the German advance had been so sudden that Paris was quite unprepared for what happened. Some German officers spent the afternoon shopping for French luxuries to send home to their wives.

On June 17 Reynaud resigned as Prime Minister and was replaced by Marshal Pétain. This hero of the Great War was enough of a military

man to know the war was hopelessly lost. He hurriedly contacted the Germans asking for an armistice. When Hitler heard the news at the Wolf's Gorge he slapped his knee in delight.

Now the French were beaten, Hitler knew exactly what he wanted to do. While his armies continued their armed tour through France, Hitler ordered the French envoys to Compiègne. On June 21 Hitler greeted the French while seated in the same railway carriage in which the German generals had surrendered in 1918. A companion noted that Hitler's face was blazing with revenge, anger and hate. Once the formal opening of negotiations was over, Hitler left. Keitel, his Chief of Staff, was to conclude the negotiations which were in reality little more than German dictation. At 6.50pm on June 22 France formally surrendered.

The superiority of German tactics in the defeat of France, Belgium and Holland was mirrored by the casualty figures for the fighting since May 10. The combined Allied losses were 90,000 dead, 200,000 wounded and something approaching 2 million captured or missing. By comparison the German losses were much lower at 30,000 dead and some 120,000 wounded. For a fraction of their casualties in the Great War, the Germans had achieved total victory over France.

Hitler clearly thought the war was as good as won. He went on a victory tour of Paris, viewing the grand buildings he had studied as plans during his time as an impoverished architectural student, then he returned to Germany. There Hitler gave extensive leave to the army and even ordered a partial demobilization. He began a charm offensive against Britain, confident that peace was soon to be secured. He was to be disappointed.

The actual situation was summed up by Winston Churchill: "The Battle of France is over. The Battle of Britain is about to begin."

On 22 June 1940 the French signed an armistice in the railway carriage in Compiègne where the Germans had surrendered in 1918

The Battle of Britain: July–October 1940

RAF Bases

⚡ Fighters
▽ Low level radar station
◇ High Level radar station

Luftwaffe Bases

✝ Bombers
⊥ Dive Bombers
✕ Fighters

9

OPERATION SEALION

Hitler had expected Britain to come to terms after the Fall of France, and was suddenly confronted with the need to launch an amphibious invasion. But first the Luftwaffe had to gain control of the air

As early as 1914, when a rumor swept his regiment that they were to land in England, Hitler had turned his mind to considering invading Britain. The rumor turned out to be false and Hitler spent the next four years in the trenches in France. But in 1940 he was faced with the prospect of fighting a war against Britain and was forced to try to find a way to defeat that country.

The main problem he confronted was that neither he nor anyone in the German military had expected to face a war against a Britain determined to resist. Hitler had never had any intention of attacking Britain nor any part of her empire; it simply was not part of his plan for conquest in the East. Although he had expected Britain to object to his aggression and, perhaps, even to declare war, Hitler had believed that Britain's essential interests were not threatened by his actions. He had reasoned, therefore, that Britain would make peace once his conquests were an established fact.

It was the first real strategic failure that Hitler had in his military career. He

RAF and Luftwaffe bases active during the Battle of Britain

had expected Britain to make peace. When she did not he had no pre-planned brilliant operation ready to knock her out of the war. The second, and much greater, strategic mistake was to follow the next year. With Britain still unsubdued, Hitler expanded the war by invading Russia. He had said before the conflict started that he would first have to ensure peace in the West before attacking the East. He did not do so. Arguably this cost him his victory; certainly it has been argued that this ranks as one of the greatest blunders in military history, superseded only by Hitler's 1941 declaration of war on the United States.

TAKING ON HITLER

The main reason why Britain did not make peace in the summer of 1940 was that it had chosen Winston Churchill as Prime Minister. Throughout the 1930s Britain had been run by honest, honorable men who simply did not understand Hitler. They did not trust him, nor like him, but they gave way time and again to avoid a war. Churchill understood Hitler perfectly well and realized very early on that he could not be bargained with nor controlled, only destroyed. Churchill believed that if Britain made peace she would ultimately end up as an offshore appendage of a United Europe run by the brutal dictatorship of the Nazis. That fate was unthinkable, so Churchill decided Britain had to fight. The people of Britain agreed.

Hitler, however, did not realize this. That was why he made the surrender terms for France more lenient than many of his advisers wanted, and why he specifically stated that the French Navy would remain under the control of the Vichy French government when he could easily have drafted the ships into the Kriegsmarine. He gave the armed forces extensive leave in June and led several senior military men, Commander of the Army

Walther von Brauchitsch among them, to believe that the war was over. Hitler even ordered that 35 divisions of infantry should be demobilized and put back into reserve.

Franz Halder at OKH was not convinced that Britain would come to a compromise peace. On 13 July he and Brauchitsch got out the provisional plans that OKH had prepared for an invasion of Britain and went to see Hitler. The Führer gave the plans a cursory glance and approved them, but told the army generals that they would not really be needed. "I am going to make them a very magnanimous peace offer," he declared. Ribbentrop, the Foreign Minister agreed: "They will fall on our necks in gratitude." Nevertheless, on July 16, Hitler ordered OKH to bring more detailed plans to a conference of the joint military chiefs on July 21, just in case.

On July 19, Hitler made his peace offer in the form of a speech broadcast by radio to Britain. Although lacking in details, the offer was effectively that Britain could keep her Empire and her navy and would be spared the horrors of invasion if she were prepared to let Hitler behave as he wanted in Europe. It was, he said, an appeal to reason. Less than an hour later the BBC broadcast a rejection. Britain would fight.

Hitler held his planned conference to discuss the defeat of Britain at the offices of the OKW, the general staff who planned and oversaw the general strategy of all three services. Brauchitsch was there for the army, Admiral Erich Raeder represented the navy and Göring spoke for the Luftwaffe. Hitler oversaw the conference, aided by Wilhelm Keitel the head of OKW, who had just been promoted to the rank of Field Marshal.

Of the men present, only Admiral Raeder had before 1940 given any serious thought to defeating Britain. He had discounted a military invasion and instead believed the answer was to starve Britain into submission by sinking the merchant ships which brought in her food. He had been building a fleet of submarines and fast, powerful surface ships for this task. He had estimated the fleet would be ready in about 1943 and that it would take a year, perhaps more, to starve Britain to surrender.

Raeder arrived at the Conference with all his files and data for a campaign against merchant ships with the forces he actually had in 1940, not those he planned to have in 1943. Instead he found that Hitler had decided to back the army plan for an invasion. Hitler subjected the Admiral to a barrage of questions about an invasion of Britain. How many invasion transports would be needed to carry the panzers? Where would they come from? How many warships would be needed to defend the transports against the Royal Navy? What about supplies for the army after it had landed? The surprised Raeder promised he would have the logistical questions sorted out in a few days' time, but that no invasion could succeed unless the RAF was first knocked out of action.

The conference turned to the Luftwaffe. Göring was confident. He was only waiting for the order to attack the RAF, he said. The job would be done in two weeks, three at the most. Raeder pointed out it would have to be done by mid-September or the weather in the Channel would make a large scale landing impossible. Hitler ordered his commanders to prepare detailed plans for their parts of the invasion project and to submit them to OKW for him to study and comment upon.

The invasion plan was to be called Operation *Sealion*. Until now German war plans had tended to be given meaningless names, such as colors, but now Hitler opted for a descriptive term for the operation. It was to be a weakness in later years when his enemies realized that a code name for an operation gave a clue as to what was intended.

A few days later Hitler sent for General Kurt Student, the leader of the small, but elite parachute force. Student had been impressed by Hitler's imagination and grasp of detail during the planning for the invasion of France, but this time he was to be disappointed. Hitler asked him if he could capture Plymouth docks with paratroopers to secure a port through which supplies could be imported to Britain. Student thought it unlikely as the docks would be heavily defended and there was nowhere near them to land large numbers of gliders. Hitler then waved a hand airily over the area around Bristol. "I suppose you could land here," he said. When Student suggested that it might be more feasible to capture a smaller port, he was dismissed.

At the headquarters of the Kriegsmarine, Raeder was in despair. After the naval operations of 1939 and early 1940 he had only one cruiser, four destroyers, three E-boats and 48 U-boats fit for immediate service, the rest of his fleet being docked for repairs and upgrades. He was convinced he could not defend an invasion fleet of vulnerable barges against the Royal Navy. The only chance, he concluded, was if the Luftwaffe first bombed every port in southern England to rubble, then attacked any British ship that moved during the invasion period.

Even then, Raeder estimated that he could assemble only enough barges to transport ten infantry divisions across the Channel for the initial assault. So few of the barges were large enough to carry tanks or artillery that not even a single panzer division could be transported. Yet the OKH had told him they needed to get about ten divisions of infantry and three divisions of panzers ashore in the first few days. And even if Raeder somehow achieved this, he had no idea how he would supply the troops and their equipment.

there. They decided to land on a broad front, from Ramsgate to Portland, concentrating on certain key beaches. The army was to establish itself in beachheads for the first three days, then break out with armor to seize the South Downs and link up the various landing grounds. This action was to be followed by a swift advance west of London, to outflank and capture the expected positions of most British defenders.

While OKH dreamed up these plans and the Kriegsmarine became frantic as it realized the difficulties of transporting the army, the Luftwaffe planned how to clear the RAF from the skies. They decided to bomb the radar stations first, for the Germans knew what a great advantage these would give the defending fighters, then move on to bombing every RAF base they could reach until they were out of service. Once the RAF was wiped out, a task Göring thought would take two weeks, the invasion could go ahead.

On July 31 Hitler called another meeting to discuss the various plans for Operation *Sealion*. The commanders outlined their views and their plans, while Hitler listened. It was clear that, unlike the build up to the invasions of Poland and France, these were matters in which Hitler had not been taking a great interest. He had not changed the plans much and hardly made any detailed comments. Finally, Hitler agreed that the RAF must be defeated before an invasion could be contemplated. He told Göring to unleash the Luftwaffe on August 5.

Then Hitler revealed why he was not terribly interested in the invasion of Britain. He told his military commanders that he was worried about Russia. He did not go into great detail, nor was he entirely honest with the commanders, but it was evident that his mind was already busy somewhere other than Britain.

A Panzer Mk III is hoisted aboard a ship for Operation Sealion

In the event, Raeder finally gathered 170 cargo ships, 1,277 barges and 471 tugs in ports and rivers around the mouth of the Rhine. These were quickly bombed by the RAF, which managed to sink about a tenth of the German invasion fleet. Raeder also needed men to operate the transport craft in the open sea, as most of their crews had experience only of river life. He drafted in 3,000 men from the army who had been seamen in civilian life, transferred 2,000 men from the Kriegsmarine and called up 9,000 reserves, but he was still 2,000 men short.

It is not surprising that Raeder concluded the invasion of Britain could not take place until more ships had been built and more men trained. He thought it would take until May 1941 to be ready.

Brauchitsch and the army staff at OKH were less troubled. They assumed that the Luftwaffe or Kriegsmarine would transport them safely to southern England and began their planning from

A Junkers Ju88 fast bomber gets ready to attack Britain

Because of bad weather the Luftwaffe did not go into action until August 13. Hitler's involvement with the subsequent Battle of Britain was minimal. While the RAF pilots fought against vast swarms of Luftwaffe aircraft, Hitler went to the opera. Then he turned his attention to various internal matters in the Reich that needed his input. The conduct of the war in the air over southern Britain was left to Göring.

TIT FOR TAT

On August 23 a few Luftwaffe aircraft missed their RAF targets and dropped bombs on London. The British retaliated by sending a few bombers to Berlin, though little damage was caused. Three nights later the RAF were back, and this time ten

people were killed. Hitler was furious. He was due to make a speech to an audience of women social workers, but went off his prepared script to declare "They increase the attacks on our cities. We will raze their cities to the ground." He ordered Göring to launch attacks on British towns.

German civilians clear bomb damage in Berlin, October 1940

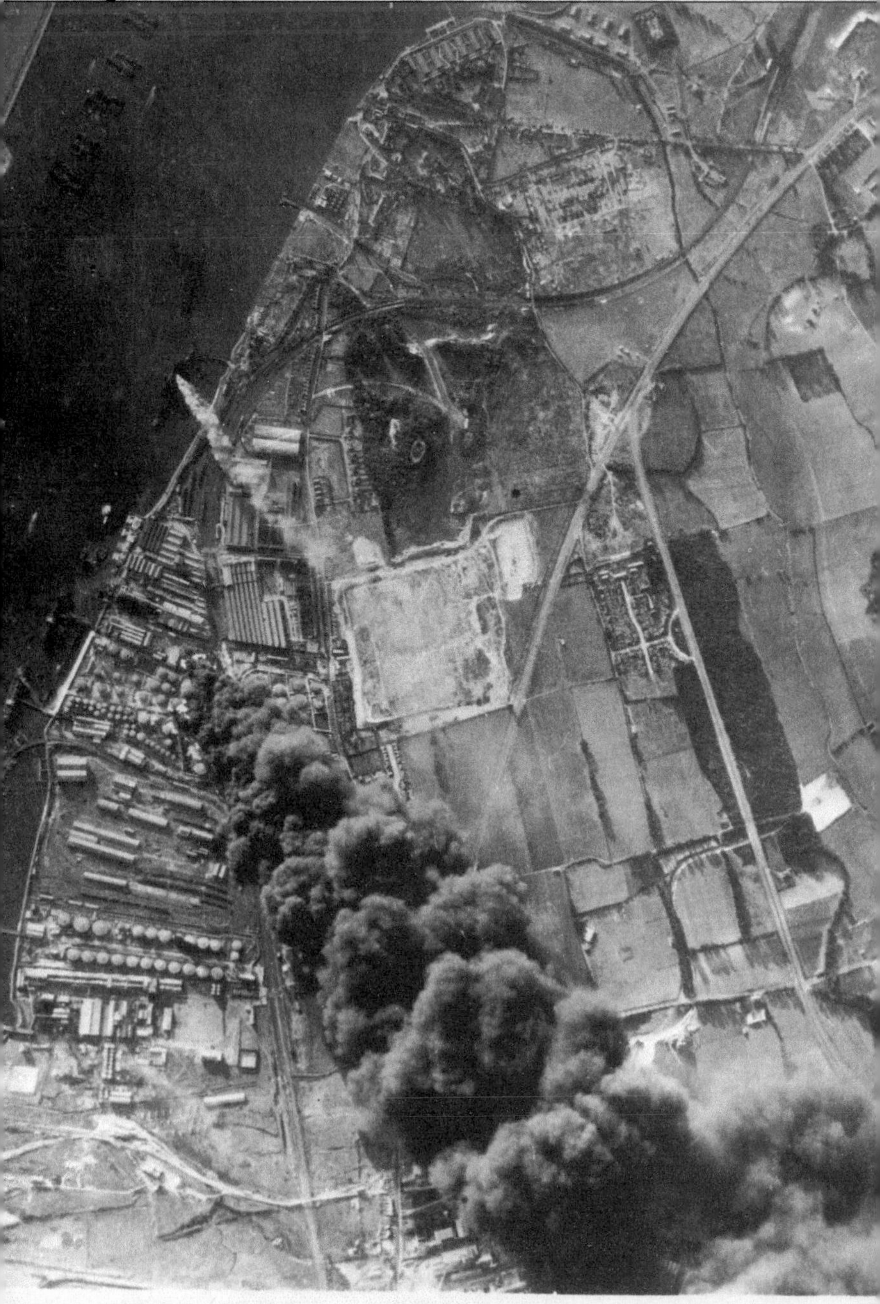

Bomb damage to Balham tube station: 66 people died

On September 7 Raeder went to see Hitler with the results of a mock invasion exercise mounted on beaches near Boulogne by the Kriegsmarine. The exercise had been a disaster as barges became unmanageable in the tide and surf. Raeder pushed his view that no invasion was possible until specialized landing craft had been built. Hitler nodded, but refused to make a firm decision.

On September 14, Hitler called a meeting of the various senior commanders to discuss reports. The only decision made was to postpone all decisions until another conference on September 17. At that conference, Göring admitted he had not gained air superiority and was unlikely to do so before the autumn weather set in. Raeder said

German photo of a bombing raid on factories in east London

he could not put his ships to sea to transport the army without air cover. The army said they could not land without Raeder's ships. Hitler called off Operation *Sealion.*

But if his plans for invading and crushing Britain were abandoned, Hitler did not give up hope of defeating Britain. His first decision was to instruct Göring to continue the bombing of British cities at night. This activity was to become known to the British as the Blitz. London was pounded every night for months and heavy and sustained attacks were made on other cities. Hitler took little interest in the planning of these raids, though he read the reports on damage caused with interest.

His next idea was to break the link between Britain and her Empire. In October he offered the Spanish the vitally strategic port-fortress of Gibraltar. All Hitler asked was for use of the bases and airfields near the Rock from which to launch the attack. Hitler knew that once the Royal Navy was driven from Gibraltar it would have to pull out of the Mediterranean, cutting the direct sea route from Britain to her African and Asian colonies. It was a tempting offer for the Spanish dictator General Francisco Franco, but he knew agreeing would take Spain into the war and he was not convinced that was a good idea. "The British are not beaten," he told his negotiating team. "They will fight and fight and go on fighting. Even if the Germans capture Britain itself, the British will continue the war from Canada. Hitler has not won this war.' In the most polite and diplomatic way possible, Franco refused to allow Hitler to use Spanish bases to capture Gibraltar.

Hitler's next idea was contained in his War Directive No.18, issued on November 12, 1940. Among other things, the Directive stated "One Panzer division will stand by for service in North Africa. German ships in Mediterranean ports will be converted to carry troops and supplies to Libya. The Luftwaffe will make plans for attacks on Alexandria and to close the Suez Canal." Although it was not entirely clear from the Directive, Hitler was planning to assist his Italian allies in their war against Britain in North Africa. If he could close the Suez Canal, Hitler would put Britain at an enormous disadvantage.

Hitler needed a talented and dependable commander for this project, but the command of such a small force was not very tempting for senior career officers. Hitler turned to the man who had commanded his personal guard during the invasion of Poland and who had commanded the 7th Panzer Division with great skill during the invasion of France. On February 6, 1941 Hitler summoned General Erwin Rommel to a meeting to brief him on his task.

THE DESERT FOX

Rommel was one of Hitler's favorite generals. Unlike most of the other senior officers, Rommel had not been born into the old aristocracy nor the landed gentry, but was the son of a schoolteacher. During the 1930s he had been a Nazi sympathizer, though he never joined the party, and had asked for command of the 7th Panzer Division as a reward for his personal services in the Polish campaign. During the invasion of France, Rommel handled his tanks with such skill and speed that his forces became legendary as "the Ghost Division."

The wide open spaces of North Africa were ideal for a panzer commander with the dash and imagination of Rommel. He accepted the posting with enthusiasm. In February 1941 Rommel arrived in Tripoli with the 15th Panzer Division and the 5th Infantry Division, which together were designated the Afrika Korps. The new Korps was given its own badge, a swastika imposed on a palm tree, and sent into action.

Hitler gave Rommel fairly broad orders. He was to co-operate with the Italian forces in North Africa and drive towards capturing Egypt and the Suez Canal from the British. Rommel's arrival with modern panzers and Stuka dive bombers was a nasty shock to the British, who had been accustomed to facing Italian troops with inferior equipment. In just two months, Rommel had driven the British out of Italian territory and was deep into Egypt. In Iraq a pro-German revolt broke out against the pro-British government. There were rumblings of revolt in Syria and even in Egypt itself.

But then Hitler lost interest again. Although he had correctly stated that cutting the Mediterranean link would be a serious strategic blow to Britain, Hitler refused to give Rommel the forces he needed to finish the job. In fact, Hitler was by this point so deeply involved in planning the coming attack on Russia that he did not have the time to devote to the complex situation in the Middle East. Nor was he willing to divert troops away from the attack on Russia to reinforce Rommel. So far as Hitler was concerned, Rommel had done his job by shoring up the Italian position and containing the British Mediterranean forces.

In retrospect this turned out to be a major strategic mistake by Hitler. If the British in Egypt had been finished off in the spring of 1941 then there would have been no need for any German troops to be kept in the Mediterranean. The task of occupying captured territory could have been safely left to the Italians. Instead, the Afrika Korps had to be kept in the field, causing a continual slow demand for men and supplies, thus diverting them from Russia. The strength of the Wehrmacht was being dissipated when it should have been concentrated in a single, powerful blow. In the long term the failure to capture the oilfields of the Middle East was to prove devastating to the German war effort.

Equally serious were the continued benefits the British gained from their position in Egypt. They put down the revolt in Iraq and continued to have access to the oilfields. They were also in a position to launch raids on the southern coastline of Europe. In 1941 these were paltry affairs, but when the German war machine began to falter the raids became more impressive and in 1943 culminated in the invasion of Italy. If they had been driven out of Egypt, the British would have had no launch pad for such an invasion.

But if the failure to subdue Britain was Hitler's first real mistake in strategic terms, he was about to make a second and even more serious one. He was to invade Russia before the Wehrmacht was ready for the task.

Erwin Rommel was selected to go to North Africa and eliminate British forces

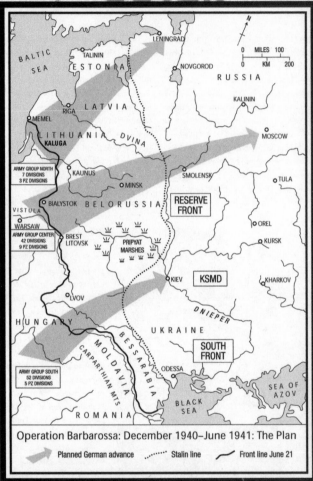

Operation Barbarossa: December 1940–June 1941: The Plan

Planned German advance ..... Stalin line ___ Front line June 21

10

OPERATION BARBAROSSA

The invasion of Russia in 1941 at first showed Hitler at his best, but soon reverses began that revealed Hitler's weaknesses as a commander. His failures here would ultimately doom the Third Reich to destruction

As early as the 1920s, Hitler had openly declared that the destruction of Soviet Bolshevism was his ultimate and overriding aim. The breaking of the Russian Empire would also open up vast tracts of land in the east for German expansion, providing Lebensraum for the agrarian Teutons. With Operation *Barbarossa*, Hitler was to make his attempt to put this ambition into practice. His plans were meticulous, clever and stood a fair chance of success. In the event it was Hitler himself who was to undermine them and cause ultimate defeat.

By the late summer of 1940 Hitler had decided to launch an attack on Russia in 1941. It is likely that he had always planned to mount a rolling war of successive campaigns. First Poland was to be crushed in the East, then Britain and France were to be defeated in the West, then he could turn east again to take on Russia. Driving this strategy was the traditional, and very rational, fear of a war on two fronts. If Hitler was to be certain of success he would need to concentrate the entire armed might of the Wehrmacht against one opponent at a time.

The initial German invasion plan envisaged three parallel thrusts reaching deep into Russia

This guiding strategy started to go wrong when Britain did not, as Hitler had expected, make peace after the Fall of France. The continuing defiance of Britain meant that the Kriegsmarine needed to be sent into the North Atlantic to attack convoys and the Luftwaffe had to keep forces in France to launch bombing raids on Britain. More seriously, the lack of a western peace forced Hitler to keep army units in France, Belgium, Holland, Denmark and Norway to prevent a British invasion. These were, on the whole, reserve units rather than the elite of the army, but they were nevertheless tied down in the West and were unavailable for the war in the East.

In July 1940 Hitler held a meeting with his senior commanders. He gave a sweeping overview of the strategic situation, then came to a surprising conclusion. "Britain's hope lies with Russia and the United States. If Russia drops out of the picture, America is also lost to Britain because the elimination of Russia would free Japan in the Far East. My decision is that Russia's destruction must be made a part of this struggle. The sooner Russia is crushed the better. If we start in May 1941 we will have five months to finish the job.'

In one sense, Hitler's strategic conclusions were correct. Germany had the vast majority of her armed might in the army, not in the Kriegsmarine or the Luftwaffe. Britain could not be invaded or defeated by the army, so it would be best to use this superb fighting machine elsewhere. The defeat of Russia would, as Hitler argued, totally change the world situation and might very well have brought peace with Britain. But Hitler had not, at this point, undertaken a practical review of what was involved in defeating Russia. The question was, could Russia be beaten?

On February 3, 1941 OKW staff put before Hitler the first draft of the plans for the invasion of Russia devised by the staff officers of the army at Army High Command, OKH, and the staffs of the Kriegsmarine and Luftwaffe. The generals and their staffs who drew up these plans were fully aware that Russia's greatest asset was almost limitless space. The Soviet armies could retreat for hundreds of miles, putting enormous strains on the supply system of an advancing enemy, before turning to counterattack the weakened and over-stretched invader. Napoleon had been defeated in this way in 1812 and the German invasion of Russia in the First World War would have ended in similar fashion if the Russian Revolution had not broken out.

PLAN OF ATTACK

The plans from OKW, therefore, concentrated on the problem of how to defeat the Russian armies without giving them a chance to retreat into the vast Russian interior. It was known that the mass of the Russian army was located within a hundred miles of the Soviet western border. OKW proposed three massive blitzkrieg attacks of combined panzer and Stuka forces to punch through the Russian forces and to encircle them some 150 miles or so to the east. The conventional infantry and artillery would then march forward to crush the Soviets against the panzers to their rear, creating what came to be known as the Kesselschlacht, or "cauldron battle." It was envisaged this phase of the operation would take about a month.

Then the Germans would turn east to capture the cities of Leningrad, Moscow and Stalingrad and the vast open spaces between them. This would, OKW reasoned, paralyze the Soviet government and halt the calling up of the Russian reserves. Four months after the start of the campaign, the Germans would be establishing a firm line from the Caspian Sea to the White Sea. Russia would be defeated.

The war would begin, the plan said, on May 25, 1941 and end in October.

The plans were codenamed *Barbarossa*, yet another example of a German codename giving away the purpose of the plans: Friedrich Barbarossa was a powerful 12th century German monarch who had conquered vast swathes of territory beyond Germany's eastern borders. Nazi propaganda had often portrayed Hitler as a successor to the emperor, and this comparison would hardly have been lost on Soviet Intelligence.

Hitler read the plans with care, then made three decisions which would have a radical effect. The first was to emphasize that the purpose of the first month's fighting was "to wipe out the enemy, not put them to flight." The second was to give the northern attack column the task of capturing Leningrad in the first phase of the campaign, not the second. This division of purpose for the northern attack was, in itself, an unwise dissipation of forces. For Hitler it was a strange decision. In all previous campaigns he had insisted on a ruthless concentration of forces to achieve a key strategic objective. Now he was asking for forces to be divided to tackle different objectives.

The third decision was the most important. There had been a dispute in the OKH about exactly how to handle the main panzer thrusts. Heinz Guderian, the general who had done most to develop the idea of blitzkrieg, and Erich von Manstein, who had developed the plan to invade France, wanted a daring and fast moving attack. They saw the panzers racing as far east as the river Dnieper, taking with them their own motorized supplies, supplemented by air drops, so that they would be self-sufficient. The panzers would then fan out and turn back to attack all the Russian armies from the rear and ensure their annihilation.

The more conservative Keitel and Brauchitsch, however, feared the supposedly self-sufficient panzer units would get cut off and crushed by sheer weight of Russian numbers. They wanted the panzers to turn inward much sooner, encircling the forward Russian units before moving on to those in the rear. Hitler decided in favor of his more conservative generals. Again, this was not like Hitler. He had previously favored the bold and daring solution to a problem.

Hitler's growing tendency to set divided objectives, and then favor a cautious method of achieving them, was to become more pronounced as time passed. And it was to prove a weakness.

This was not, however, clear in the early months of 1941. The Germans knew they could muster 120 divisions for Barbarossa, of which 17 were panzer divisions and another 12 were fully motorized. The Finns had promised to attack Russia north of Leningrad, and Romania was to add forces to the German southern attack. Over 3.5 million men were to be involved in the strike on Russia, backed by 3,550 panzers, innumerable bombers and all the latest war equipment made to excellent German standards.

The only problems the OKW foresaw were those affecting supply. Russian roads and railways were notoriously bad and the rapid advances and heavy fighting would demand thousands of tons of food and ammunition being moved hundreds of miles. In late February Field Marshal Walther von Brauchitsch, the head of OKH, tried to convince Hitler that shifting supplies would present serious problems, but Hitler brushed him aside. The OKH planners decided to reduce the need for trucks and wagons by cutting the estimates of supplies and equipment they would need to transport. One crucial compromise was to reduce the quantities of winter clothing to be sent to the army of occupation. Both Hitler and OKW were adamant the main fighting would be over by autumn and that only a few troops would be needed in the field to mop up isolated Soviet units or put down rebellions. The rest of the German army would be back in Germany or snug in winter quarters. OKH therefore allowed for only 20 per cent of the German army to have winter clothing.

On March 17, Hitler held a meeting with his most senior commanders, including Brauchitsch and Halder from OKH, Keitel from OKW and senior figures from the Luftwaffe and Kriegsmarine. Hitler had more changes to make to the plans. He had been inspecting the maps of western Russia and talking to German officers who had fought in the area in the First World War. These had convinced him that the plans contained a fatal flaw.

In the center of the proposed German line of advance, between Kiev and Minsk, was a vast wilderness area of swamp, lakes and bogs known as the Pripet Marshes. Covering over 14,000 square miles, this area had been written off in the OKW plans as impassable for an army and simply bypassed. Hitler, however, had learned that during the dry summer weather the marshes were passable to infantry and cavalry, though not to heavy artillery or tanks. Hitler insisted that German cavalry be sent into the marshes to root out any Soviet fugitives and that a strong flank guard be posted around the area to stop Russian attacks on German supply lines. In the event, Hitler was proved right and his precautions saved the Germans from an embarrassing defeat.

Hitler also demanded that the southern front should be extended to capture for Germany the rich agricultural and industrial resources of Ukraine and, beyond them, the oil fields of the Caucasus. This was yet another strategic objective, further diluting the concentration of force needed to achieve the objectives already set.

Having persuaded his senior commanders to adopt these changes, Hitler called a conference on March 30 for the 200 senior commanders who would lead the invasion. Most of them did not even suspect that Russia was the next target and none knew the war would start so early. Hitler spoke from a podium with a large map of Russia on the wall to explain the plan. He began by explaining his reasons for the war, then ran through the outline of the revised OKW proposals. He ended by acknowledging that there would be supply problems then added that many of these were "caused by the problem of what to do with the Russian prisoners." Then he went on: "The war against Russia will be such that it cannot be fought in a chivalrous fashion. This struggle is one of ideologies and racial differences and will have to be conducted with unprecedented, merciless and unrelenting harshness."

The generals present knew what Hitler meant, though he had not actually spelled it out. Most were aware that the SS had followed the German army into Poland and carried out mass executions. Some knew that the extermination of the Jews, clergy and upper classes in Poland was proceeding by means of mass murder. The army had refused to have anything to do with such crimes in the Polish campaign and many lower ranking officers and men had known nothing about them. Now, the commanders feared, Hitler was asking the army to commit mass murder of prisoners. None of them spoke up openly at the conference on March 30, but they soon began voicing their opposition to each other and to their superiors.

On May 15, Hitler was holding a meeting with his senior staff to discuss final arrangements for *Barbarossa*. He suddenly broke off from talk of logistics and maneuvers to rage at the assembled military men. "You will have to rid yourselves of your outmoded ideas of warfare. This is to be a war of unprecedented harshness. I know my way of thinking is beyond the comprehension of my generals—and that makes me so angry—but my orders must be carried out." He threw down his pen and stormed out.

Brauchitsch assured the generals that Hitler was merely upset and did not mean what he had said. Even if he did, Brauchitsch explained, the army would not have to get involved. The SS could handle Hitler's plans. In the event Brauchitsch was proved wrong. The army was ordered to carry out executions without trial, mass killings and the most brutal of reprisals for guerrilla activity. Some units obeyed the orders enthusiastically, some reluctantly and some found excuses not to do so.

To face this vast and unrelenting tide of invasion, the Soviets had their own enormous armed forces. The Soviet dictator, Josef Stalin, had 170 divisions and 12,000 tanks in the field and about another 200 divisions and 14,000 tanks as reserves. These vast forces were, however, dangerously weak. Most of them were supplied with obsolete equipment, in particular the tanks and anti-tank guns, which would have been well matched to the Panzer I, but were hopelessly outclassed by the Panzer III and Panzer IV. Moreover, Stalin had spent the later 1930s purging the army of officers he thought disloyal to his regime. Thousands of experienced commanders had been shot, sent to the slave camps or given jobs on farms and in factories. Huge though they were, the Russian forces were in no fit state to stand up to blitzkrieg.

But before Hitler could attack Russia he had to solve other problems.

In October 1940 the Italian dictator Benito Mussolini had taken advantage of the victorious war Hitler waged in the west to mount his own war of conquest by invading Greece. The Italian attack had become bogged down, however, and by Christmas 1940 was locked in stalemate in northern Greece. In January 1941 some Australian and New Zealand troops arrived to aid the Greeks. Until this event, Hitler had been content to let his Italian allies suffer for their ambitions. But the arrival of British troops and RAF squadrons made him suddenly nervous. He did not want to invade Russia if powerful British forces were going to attack from the Balkans. In January Hitler offered Mussolini help.

Hitler told his generals to divert troops from the planned *Barbarossa* campaign to the Balkans, but to rest assured that they would be back in time to attack Russia. On March 27 the detailed plans for an attack on Greece through the territories of Germany's allies Romania and Bulgaria were issued. This was after Yugoslavia had been persuaded to agree to neutrality in the coming conflict. That very day, however, a military coup in Yugoslavia took place and the new regime repudiated the agreement with Hitler. Hitler at once ordered the German plans to be changed to include the invasion of Yugoslavia.

On April 6 German troops poured into Yugoslavia and Greece. On April 17 Yugoslavia surrendered and six days later Greece followed suit. The war had been short, but for Hitler it was deeply damaging. He had lost few men, but was now forced to station more German troops in the Balkans to support the Italian occupying forces. Moreover he had been obliged to send a panzer division and an infantry division under Erwin Rommel to North Africa to help the Italians in their campaign against the British in Egypt. Both moves were a drain on his manpower.

A German Sd.Kfz. 251 halftrack leads infantry into Athens

More dangerously, the attack on Russia had been delayed until June 22.

Hitler no longer had five months before the dreadful Russian winter came, but just four months. It had been Hitler's personal decision to allow five months of good weather to defeat Russia. Now it had been his personal decision to reduce the time to four months. Had the diversion to the Balkans been necessary, the delay might have been worth it. But the attacks were not, strictly speaking, needed. Mussolini's troops had been holding their own and could have guarded against a flank attack on the *Barbarossa* campaign. Hitler may have been prompted by loyalty to his Italian ally or by caution about a vulnerable flank, and he was later to give both these excuses. But whatever his reasons, the action proved the first mistake of the Russian campaign.

The attack on Russia finally began before dawn on Sunday June 22, 1941. Unlike previous aggression by Germany, Hitler had not bothered to fabricate an excuse for his actions by allegations or demands. As a result, the Russians were totally unprepared for the attack. Stalin himself was so taken aback that he refused against all the evidence of his front line commanders to believe that the Germans were attacking, and ordered Soviet troops not to open fire. Even those who had foreseen that Germany would invade at some date were taken by surprise. The Russian air force was destroyed on the ground within days, giving the Luftwaffe complete control of the skies and, with it, the ability to cooperate closely with the army.

To the south of the Pripet Marshes Army Group South, under Gerd von Rundstedt, had 59 divisions, including one panzer group of five panzer divisions and three motorized divisions concentrated together as the First Panzer Group, commanded by Kleist. To Rundstedt's south nine Romanian divisions invaded along the Black Sea coast. The objective of Rundstedt's southern attack was to destroy the Russian armies to their front, then drive on to capture Kiev and reach the River Dnieper. Rundstedt got off to a flying start and his right wing was leaping forward toward the Crimea, but only slow advances were made on his left wing, towards Kiev.

In the north was Army Group North under von Leeb, which fielded 26 divisions including the Fourth Panzer Group under Höppner. Leeb's task was to overrun the Baltic states and capture Leningrad. Like Rundstedt in the south, Leeb made good initial progress but he was brought to a halt in front of Leningrad.

The main weight of the German attack fell in the area immediately north of the Pripet Marshes. Army Group Center was commanded by von Bock and had 51 divisions as well as the Second and Third Panzer Groups under Guderian and Hoth respectively. This was the elite of the German army, commanded by the most able generals.

Bock made rapid progress forwards, capturing almost 300,000 prisoners at Minsk on July 2; a month later nearly 400,000 were taken at Smolensk. By this time, however, both Guderian and Hoth were forced to remove their panzers from the front lines. The strains of driving hundreds of miles and fighting dozens of battles had taken their toll and repairs were necessary.

The pause in the panzer advance gave Hitler and his generals time to assess progress thus far. The German forces had advanced hundreds of miles. Over a million Russian soldiers had been killed, captured or surrounded. And yet the war was not going well for the Germans. Although the Russians had suffered terrible losses, they still had intact armed forces. Many hundreds of thousands of Russians had retreated faster than the Germans advanced, escaping the panzer pincers. More and more reserves were being mobilized and pushed into the fighting. The Germans had not achieved their principal strategic objective of crushing the Red Army, nor had they captured Leningrad or Ukraine.

While the panzers were being repaired, Hitler and his commanders debated what to do next. The majority of the generals, including Guderian, Bock and Brauchitsch, wanted to attack Moscow. They argued that the capture of Moscow would destroy the industrial and communications heart of Russia. Moreover—and Brauchitsch was especially enthusiastic about this point—the Soviets would fight hard to defend Moscow, allowing the Red Army to be destroyed, not merely chased further to the east.

Some of the 25,000 Russian soldiers captured at Minsk, part of 290,000 captured in the Battle of Bialystok–Minsk

German troops take a break in Russia, July 1941. The panzer thrusts were frequently held back so infantry could catch up

Hitler, however, disagreed. He pointed out that Napoleon had captured Moscow in 1812 and little good it had done him. Much better, Hitler said, to concentrate on Ukraine and Crimea with their huge coal reserves and agricultural lands and, at the same time, cut off the supplies of oil from the Caucasus to the Red Army. On August 21 the decision was made. Hitler ordered Guderian's panzers to drive south to help Rundstedt.

Guderian fought his way south with his customary skill and flair while Kleist came north with equal determination. On September 14 the two panzer forces met at Lokvitsa, far to the east of Kiev. Over 600,000 Russian prisoners were taken and Ukraine fell to the Germans. It was a major success at the tactical and strategic levels, but it proved to be yet another illusory victory. The Red Army was still in the field and the war went on.

By October 2 Guderian was back with Bock. Hitler now agreed to a drive on Moscow and unleashed Army Group Center. Within eight days another 600,000 Soviets had been surrounded and captured. It looked as if Brauchitsch's plan to destroy the Red Army in front of Moscow was going to become reality. The diversion had cost valuable weeks, however, and the Russian weather, never really acknowledged as a factor in *Barbarossa*, took a hand. At the end of October the autumn

rains came, and with them the rasputitsa, the season of mud which turned most of the country into one vast, unpassable quagmire. The supply trucks could not move and the German advance ground to a halt.

THE WAY FORWARD

Again, Hitler used the enforced delay to rethink his strategy and, again, he changed the objectives. Instead of concentrating all his forces on the Moscow attack, as Brauchitsch again urged, Hitler divided the replacement panzers and his reserves between the three army groups. Bock was ordered to capture Moscow, though he doubted he now had the forces to do it. In the north Leeb was ordered to capture Leningrad, which he had now surrounded and cut off from supplies. In the south Rundstedt was ordered to advance beyond Rostov to take Stalingrad and the Caucasus oilfields.

When Rundstedt was handed the instructions from Hitler's command post he laughed out loud and congratulated the signals officer on a splendid practical joke. Only after he was shown the original encrypted message did Rundstedt accept the orders were genuine. He was amazed, for they were far beyond the resources he had available. He ordered an advance, but only got as far as Rostov.

In the center, Bock was having more luck. He got to within 20 miles of Moscow and, in a determined attack after the frost froze the ground, got in to the city suburbs on December 2. Unfortunately for Bock, he also had Hitler close at hand.

In the preparations for Barbarossa, Hitler had established himself in a forward command post in East Prussia at Rastenburg. The elaborate complex of bunkers, radio communications and living quarters was dubbed the *Wolfsschanze*, or Wolf's Lair. Hitler had intended to stay here during the Russian campaign, keeping in daily contact with his commanders by radio. He had followed this pattern in the earlier campaigns, but this time things developed differently. After the crisis of early August, Hitler spent more and more time at the headquarters of the Army Group commanders, especially at Bock's. Hitler pestered Bock with questions, queried his decisions and interfered in quite minor decisions. He was still there when a fresh crisis broke.

The Russians launched a counterattack at Moscow. That the Russians were capable of such a move came as a nasty surprise to the Germans, and to Hitler personally. Even more of a shock was the arrival of a new weapon on the field of battle, the Russian T-34 tank. This tank was ahead of its time to the extent that it outclassed the Panzer IV, the mainstay of the German army. It was equipped with a powerful 76mm gun as well as two machine guns, and could travel over 180 miles without refueling. The armor was not only thick, but cleverly shaped and rounded to ensure that incoming shells were deflected without exploding.

The standard German anti-tank gun was almost useless.

CREEPING PARALYSIS

With their new weapon and plentiful reinforcements, the Russians drove the Germans back from Moscow. The German front began to crumble. A sense of panic swept the senior staff at OKH and OKW. The military men all knew of the dreadful fate which had overtaken the French army in its retreat from Moscow in 1812. The cold, hunger and relentless Russian attacks had inflicted 90 per cent casualty rates. One army corps had started the campaign with 32,000 men and ended it with just 297 fit for duty. Nor had Napoleon's high command escaped lightly, with 60 generals being killed. Faced with this appalling prospect, Brauchitsch seemed to lose his nerve and a creeping paralysis spread through the German high command.

Russian troops take cover from German artillery near Moscow, autumn 1941

A mounted division of the SS pushes on towards Moscow as the Russian winter closes in

NO RETREATING

It was at this point that Hitler issued what became known as his "Standfast Order." The instruction was simple and clear, but devastating. No German soldier was to retreat at all, under any circumstances. The suffering of men fighting in the bitter Russian conditions without winter clothing was as unimportant to Hitler as were the opinions of his generals. Only one thing was important, that there was to be no retreat, nor even the thought of retreat, and Hitler soon made it clear that he meant this literally.

General Hans von Sponeck pulled his division back after it was outflanked and in danger of being surrounded. Hitler immediately relieved him of command and sent him to a hurriedly convened court martial presided over by Göring. Sponeck was found guilty of cowardice in the face of the enemy and sentenced to death, though he was in fact merely thrown into prison. Even the greatest of soldiers were made subject to Hitler's determination. On December 15, Heinz Guderian

pulled his panzers back from an exposed position to a more easily defended ridge a few miles to his rear. Hitler sacked him on Christmas Day.

There can be no doubt that part of Hitler's reasoning for the brutal simplicity of the Standfast Order came from his experiences in the First World War. Prior to the German retreat to the Hindenburg Line in 1917, Hitler had seen at first hand the way entire regiments could give up the will to fight, once they knew they would soon be retreating. In the desperate circumstances facing the German army in December 1941, Hitler suspected that a retreat could quickly become a rout. Although he had no doubt that his order would lead to the annihilation of some units in isolated positions, Hitler was equally convinced that it was necessary to preserve the army as a whole: he was probably right. Although many of his generals opposed him at the time, most accepted in hindsight that his Standfast Order saved the German army.

The month of December saw a large scale

Field Marshal von Reichenau died of a heart attack in Russia, 1942

clearing and replacing of the senior commanders. Rundstedt offered his resignation rather than carry out the Standfast Order and was promptly replaced by Walther von Reichenau. Bock gave way to Hans von Kluge and Leeb was replaced by Küchner. Further down the lines of command other generals were ousted if Hitler had any doubts as to their loyalty.

ANOTHER CASUALTY

The single most far-reaching command replacement came at OKH. Under Brauchitsch the Army High Command had remained a bastion of tradition and of excellent, if cautious, staff work. The logistics of supply were accurately assessed as were roads, railways and river crossings. But Brauchitsch had been won over to Hitler by an act of personal generosity in the pre-war years, not by any great admiration for his political or military skills. Throughout the long summer and autumn of 1941, Brauchitsch had disagreed with Hitler's strategy and tactics on more than one occasion. In early December, Brauchitsch suffered a mild heart attack. On December 19, sick and exhausted, he resigned and retired to his family home for the rest the war, dying of a heart attack in 1948.

With Brauchitsch gone, Hitler appointed himself as the new Commander in Chief of the Army. The move was to have profound consequences. Until the summer of 1941 Hitler had been the guiding strategic hand of the Wehrmacht. He had decided to send troops into the Rhineland in 1936. He had authorized the military march into Austria in 1938. As time passed he had become inclined to get involved with the planning of operations and his interventions at a detailed level in the planning of the attacks on Poland and France had been considerable. But

Hitler had usually stood back from the actual conduct of military campaigns.

When Hitler made himself Supreme Commander in Chief in 1938 he had taken the OKW as his personal staff. This gave him secure control of overall strategy for the Wehrmacht, on land, on sea and in the air. He had used this power, for instance, to force an unwilling army to accept Manstein's plan for the invasion of France. At this level, there can be little doubt that Hitler had a flair for choosing the right men for difficult jobs and had a capacity to grasp the potential of a radically unorthodox idea.

CONTROL FREAK

The decision in August 1941 to divert Guderian's panzers to the Ukraine had been the first major operational decision taken by Hitler in the course of a campaign. Thereafter he became increasingly interested in what was going on lower down the command structure and showed a growing tendency to interfere in the operational commands of his generals. By taking the position of Commander in Chief of the Army, Hitler formalized this interference and gave himself the powers to issue orders of increasing tactical detail. This revealed Hitler's military weakness. He simply did not have the patience for the detail of staffwork. He had no idea of the sheer complexity of the logistics needed to back up a sweeping new battle plan, and he had no intention of learning.

During the grinding winter of 1941–42 these drawbacks would not matter too much. But as Hitler took ever-increasing control, treating generals as his tools, his failings at an operational level became more important. And the campaigns to come would reveal those failings in the stark form of dead soldiers and lost battles.

GERMAN ASSAULTS ON
STALINGRAD: 1942

- - - - Front line
━━━▶ German offensives

11

THE EASTERN FRONT

Having failed to subdue the Soviets in 1941, Hitler hoped to do·so in 1942 with a swift advance in the south. However, his obsession with Stalingrad caused him to ignore opportunities for victory elsewhere and led to his first great defeat

Hitler's first real opening move affecting the Eastern Front in 1942 took place in Berlin. By this time Hitler held three crucial positions in the military hierarchy of the Third Reich. He was the head of the army and so had control over the planning staff of the army at OKH. He was the supreme commander of the armed forces, giving him control over the global strategy planned by the general staff at OKW. Thirdly, Hitler was the Minister for War in the civilian government.

It was as Minister for War that Hitler appointed a new Minister for War Production and Armaments in February 1942. The man was Albert Speer, an architect who had been responsible for building the arena for the Nuremberg rallies, the new Reich Chancellery and other major buildings. As an outsider to the Nazi Party, Speer was unpopular with Nazi veterans such as Himmler and Göring, but his·undoubted gifts as an architect and organizer made him invaluable. As Minister for War Production, Speer turned German industry over totally to the war effort, boosting production of tanks, aircraft, submarines and all the impedimenta of war with consistent efficiency through to 1944.

In October 1942 German attacks finally reached the Volga and most of Stalingrad was in German hands

Albert Speer (center dark overcoat), Minister for Armaments, views a panzer in the field in Russia to ascertain maintenance needs

It was Speer in Berlin who told Hitler some unpleasant truths early in 1942. Blitzkrieg had failed to crush Russia in the five months Hitler had hoped for. As a result, said Speer, Germany had to plan for a war of at least two or three years' duration, making it essential to secure for Germany a steady supply of oil. No less essential was the disruption or destruction of the Russian arms manufacturing capacity.

This struck an immediate chord with Hitler. A few weeks before he appointed Speer, Hitler had received a report on the Soviet war capacity. The report stated the Soviets would have 1.7 million men under arms by March 1942 and that the Soviets were producing 1,200 tanks a month. Halder, the chief of planning at OKH, was present and recorded "Hitler flew with clenched fists and foam in the corners of his mouth at the man who was reading the statement and forbade such idiotic twaddle."

Hitler never did like bad news and would increasingly ignore it. But in March 1942 the bad news he was receiving fitted in with his own ideas and influenced the strategic and tactical plans for the campaigning summer season. The oil Speer wanted for Germany could be found in the oilfields of the Caucasus Mountains and much of the Soviet industrial plant that needed to be destroyed was in the valleys of the Donetz, Don and Volga rivers, particularly around the city of Stalingrad.

Hitler wanted a grand, dramatic campaign that stood a chance of defeating Russia in 1942 or, at least, of setting the groundwork for a victory in 1943. This, Hitler thought, could be achieved by a large-scale assault on the Russians in the south to destroy the main center of Soviet war production, capture the oilfields and put the German forces in a position to surge north up the Volga to take Moscow from the rear and so finally destroy the Soviets.

At first, Hitler hoped to complete the southern advance by early September, giving the Germans two months of good weather to march up the Volga. Halder and the generals, however, thought the southern conquests themselves were ambitious enough to consume the whole summer. They prevailed on Hitler to draw up detailed plans for the first stage of the attack only. The Volga attack could wait.

Using his new position as head of OKH, Hitler involved himself as never before in the detailed planning for the 1942 summer offensive. But detail was not Hitler's strength, so he treated the task with contempt. He told Halder, "This little affair of operational command is something anybody can do." It was not so easy and Hitler's refusal to give the task due priority was to cause problems.

Nevertheless, the plans were drawn up. Army Group South was divided into two huge units, Army Group A in the south beside the Black Sea and Army Group B in the north, along the Don. Of the two, Army Group A had further to travel, but was expected to meet the lesser resistance. Army Group A consisted of the Seventeenth Army and the First Panzer Army and was put under the command of List. His task was to race southeast to take the oilfields and reach the Caspian Sea, securing the foothills of the Caucasus. Army Group B was under the command of von Bock, and was made up of the Sixth Army and the Second Army together with the

Fourth Panzer Army. Their task was to drive down the Don, capture Stalingrad and secure a defensive line along the Volga behind which the Germans could prepare for the march north.

MORE MANPOWER

In planning this mighty assault, Hitler came up against a problem. The German army simply did not have enough men and equipment to succeed. To remedy this shortfall, Hitler embarked on a series of determined diplomatic missions to his allies. Large numbers of Italians, Romanians and Hungarians were sent, at Hitler's insistence, to form the reserve forces of the great assault. As preparations for the attack became complete, Hitler moved to yet another forward command post. This time it was located at Vinnitsa in the Ukraine and was dubbed *Werwolf* (Werewolf).

Soviet troops watch German shells fall on Sebastopol, spring 1942

As in the previous year, the German attack could not begin as soon as the spring weather settled over Russia. First the mighty fortress city of Sebastopol had to be captured in the south, and then a Russian attack near Kharkov had to be defeated. Hitler's great sumer offensive did not begin until June 28, a week later in the year than *Barbarossa* had been launched.

As in 1941 the German attack began well. The panzer spearheads thrust deep into Soviet territory while the following artillery and infantry dispatched isolated and surrounded Russian troops. As in 1941, however, the Germans did not move quite fast enough to ensure that all the opposing Russians were captured or killed, many thousands of them escaping eastward to fight again. Meanwhile, the panzers surged forward across the seemingly endless grainfields of southern Russia.

The speed of the advance in the north was discussed at a meeting at Werewolf on July 10. Hitler was in optimistic mood, believing the Soviet forces in the south had been crushed and were in full flight. Halder, ever cautious, thought they had merely been defeated and were retreating in good order to defensive positions beyond the Don River. Halder was, in fact, deeply worried by the way the attack was progressing. His aide noted that, unlike in previous discussions with Hitler, Halder got so agitated that he completely forgot to address Hitler as "mein Führer."

Hitler swept aside Halder's comments and issued new orders. The Fourth Panzer Army of General Hermann Hoth was to be removed from Army Group B and sent south to help Army Group A, now given the additional task of conquering all Russian territory south of the Volga. The task of capturing the Don valley and Stalingrad was given to General Friedrich von Paulus and his unmechanized Sixth Army. "You may shake your head now," said

Hitler to Halder, "but you will see that everything is going to work out very well." Halder considered resigning, but decided to stay on in the hope that he could persuade Hitler to change his mind.

General von Paulus (right) lands to inspect units near Stalingrad, November 1942

In fact, Hitler's decision to send Hoth and his panzers south ensured things did not turn out well at all. Without the panzers and motorized units, Paulus made slow progress towards Stalingrad. Instead of taking it in mid-August, as he might well have done with Hoth, Paulus was still trying to reach the suburbs in early September. Hitler then transferred Hoth back northward from the attack on the Caucasus. It was too late. The panzers would have been useful in pushing across the open country of the Don at high speed, but were useless in the street fighting developing in Stalingrad. Meanwhile, the move meant that they were no longer able to help capture the oilfields. Hundreds of panzers had, effectively, spent most of the summer driving back and forth behind German lines without attacking the Russians.

On September 24, with the prospect of winter closing in before the main objective of the 1942 offensive had been gained, Hitler removed troops from in front of Moscow to join the attack on Stalingrad. Halder objected more forcefully than usual, and was sacked by Hitler. Like so many others, Halder retired to his home for the rest of the war. He was arrested by the Gestapo in 1944 after the bomb plot to kill Hitler, but as we have seen, persuaded them of his innocence. He was cleared of war crimes by the Allies after the war and spent the post-war years working on various military history projects. He died in 1972.

Halder was replaced at OKH by General Kurt von Zeitzler, an expert at logistics and supplies. Zeitzler was a younger and less experienced man than Halder and Hitler was confident he could overawe him.

MAJOR MISTAKES

It was at this time that General Adolf Heusinger, who had long had doubts about Hitler's abilities in the field, confided to a colleague, "He's the supreme commander, and that is the problem. He suppresses all individual initiative, he is suspicious of anyone whose opinion differs from his own. He tells the generals only what it is absolutely essential for them to know. This is bound to lead to trouble." It was an accurate assessment.

Hitler had been wrong to send Hoth's panzers south but, having done so, he then compounded the mistake by sending them back north. Halder had been right both times, and Hitler could not forgive him. Other generals saw what happened to Halder and learned the lesson. If they wanted to keep their jobs they had to agree with the Führer.

Meanwhile, the attack on Stalingrad was moving slowly. By early October it was clear the city would not be captured before the snows came.

But Hitler was determined that the city would fall. It was essential that the Germans be poised ready for the attack north along the Volga the following spring and for that they needed Stalingrad. Hitler also came to regard the city as a major morale factor. It bore the name of the Soviet leader and had become something of a personal battle between Hitler and Stalin: its capture would surely break the Soviet will to resist. For this reason, Hitler continued to order Paulus' Sixth Army to attack long after they should have broken off the engagement.

In October, with the winter weather closing in, Hitler abandoned Werewolf for his more congenial headquarters at the Wolf's Lair in Prussia. He left Zeitzler in the Ukraine, but kept in constant touch by radio and refused to allow Zeitzler or Paulus to take any decisions without his express approval. One of Zeitzler's first actions after Hitler left was to undertake a review of the German defensive lines either side of the Sixth Army attacking Stalingrad. These were actually held by Romanians, Hungarians and Italians. Zeitzler was appalled by the haphazard state of defenses and in particular by the poor state of the

Soviet infantry inch forward in the ruins of Stalingrad, autumn 1942

supply system. He sent a message to Hitler stating that the area was vulnerable to Soviet counterattack and needed to be strengthened with German units or properly engineered defenses. Hitler replied that the Russians were finished.

On November 19 the Russians attacked just where Zeitzler had feared they would, on the weakly-held flanks of the Sixth Army. Just three days later the Soviet pincers closed and Paulus with most of the Sixth Army was surrounded in Stalingrad. Hitler's first decision was to sack the entirely blameless General Heim, whose panzer division happened to be the closest to the Soviet breakthrough. In giving the orders to Keitel, Hitler announced, "I want my generals to understand once and for all that they're expected to do their duty like everyone else. If not, they will be held responsible for their actions."

Nobody present pointed out that the reason Heim had not moved his tanks was that Hitler had given orders that no panzers were to move without his authorization, which had not been given.

On November 24, Zeitzler was in the *Wolfsschanze*, the Wolf's Lair, along with most of the senior OKH and OKW staff discussing the situation at Stalingrad. General Paulus had requested permission to break out of the closing Russian pincers to rejoin the main German forces west of the Don. Zeitzler read out Paulus' message and concluded by expressing his own opinion in favor of the move. "Never!" snapped Hitler and demanded of Zeitzler what could be done.

True to his background in logistics, Zeitzler's reply was based on the fact that the 300,000 Germans and Romanians cut off in Stalingrad would need 300 metric tons of supplies a day just to survive the winter. At this point Göring stepped in to promise that his Luftwaffe would have no trouble getting such a quantity of supplies into

Stalingrad. Göring failed to mention that to do so the Luftwaffe would need access to Stalingrad airport. If the airport was lost, so was Stalingrad. In fact, the Luftwaffe managed to supply more than this bare minimum on only three days during the siege, achieving on average no more than seventy metric tons in any one day; nor was there ever any likelihood of their being able to do so: Hitler took Göring at face value more through loyalty than any objective logistical assessment.

Nevertheless, Hitler agreed with Göring's proposal, then added his own touch. Erich von Manstein, the master of maneuver, was recalled from his work elsewhere and put in charge of the Third and Fourth Romanian Armies and Fourth Panzer, with orders to reach Stalingrad by Christmas. At first Manstein was optimistic that he could reach Stalingrad and strengthen the defenses so that the city could be held through to the spring. But by December 10 he had changed his mind. With only Hoth's 17th and 23rd Panzer Divisions reinforced by the 6th Panzer hurriedly brought by rail from France, Manstein thought he would be lucky to do as much as open a corridor to Stalingrad along which Paulus could retreat.

Manstein's attack, codenamed *Winter Storm*, was launched on December 12. On December 18, Manstein sent a message asking Hitler to order Paulus to make an assault on the Russians from his side so that the two German forces could link up south of Stalingrad. Hitler refused to give an answer. On December 19, Manstein asked again. He asked again the next day, and the next. But Hitler still gave no answer. On December 23, Manstein asked Paulus directly if he could break out. The gloomy reply was that the Sixth Army had enough fuel and ammunition to advance about 20 miles towards Manstein. The gap between the two forces was 35 miles. Paulus was also extremely reluctant even to make the attempt without a direct order from Hitler; an order which Hitler simply would not give. The following day Manstein had to pull back to respond to a Russian attack on his flank.

On January 10, 1943 the Soviet attack on the isolated German Sixth Army began. Ten days later Paulus knew that he was finished. German units began to surrender to the Russians. In desperation Paulus flew out a trusted staff officer, Major Zitzewitz, to describe conditions to Hitler and beg for help. Hitler listened to Zitzewitz, then dismissed him without a word. Minutes later Hitler sent a message to Paulus, "Surrender out of the question. Resist to the end."

On the same day Hitler sent Paulus the order not to surrender, he received news that his nephew had been wounded in Stalingrad. Paulus offered to send the young man to an improvised air strip if Hitler sent a light aircraft to pick him up. Hitler refused. "Leo is a soldier" was his only comment.

On January 30 Hitler promoted Paulus to the coveted rank of Field Marshal. The message giving Paulus the news was followed by another which noted that no German field marshal had ever surrendered to the enemy. There was, however, little Paulus could do. His men were throwing down their weapons. On January 31 Paulus surrendered. The Russians had taken 91,000 prisoners, including 24 generals, but many thousands more had died.

Hitler's reaction to the disaster was to fly into a rage with the absent Paulus. Hitler accused him of cowardice, of treachery and of disobedience, before stating it would have been better all around if Paulus had shot himself.

Soviet infantry in winter camouflage open fire across Stalingrad

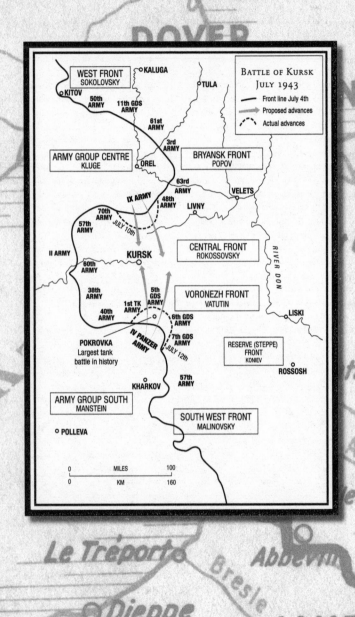

12

KURSK

By the summer of 1943 the German invasion of Russia had clearly failed, but Hitler was determined to seek victory in one last great offensive. Events would prove the German army no longer had the strength to mount such a campaign

In the wake of the disaster of Stalingrad, Hitler began holding two military conferences each day instead of one. He distrusted his generals and staff officers even more than before, blaming them for the fact that his grand plan for 1942 had not been successful. Hitler insisted that all decisions of any importance had to come to his conferences for approval by himself. This inevitably slowed up the pace at which decisions could be made and led to some decisions being put off day after day as more urgent matters took precedence on the agenda. Slowly the German command structure was becoming paralyzed by indecision.

The man Hitler distrusted more than any other was Göring. The two men had been firm allies since the earliest days of the Nazi Party in the wake of the First World War. Göring had been wounded in the failed putsch of 1923 and later used his contacts in business and the armed forces to smooth the path for Hitler's rise to power. He had built the Luftwaffe up from scratch in the 1930s and supervised the supine Reichstag in the pre-war years, being rewarded with the unique title of *Reichsmarschall*. But he had failed Hitler

The German plan for Kursk involved an ambitious double envelopment of Soviet armies

During the struggle for Stalingrad, German troops set up their mortar in the shadow of an abandoned Soviet T-34

in the Battle of Britain and now failed again at Stalingrad. Despite his close friendship and past loyalty, Göring was ousted from Hitler's inner circle. He retired to his extensive hunting estates and lived a life of luxury amongst his looted treasures until arrested for war crimes in 1945. After dominating the Nuremberg war crimes trials with his wit and charm, Göring was condemned to death, but committed suicide first.

Hitler began laying plans for the defense of his vast conquests, but he still had a taste for the grand scheme and innovative strategy.

The crushing of the Sixth Army at Stalingrad had done nothing to dampen Hitler's belief in his own ability to achieve a single war-winning master stroke. In 1943 he looked to the area around Kursk for that great victory.

Before he began planning Operation *Citadel*, the name for the attack at Kursk, Hitler realized he had to make some serious strategic decisions about the war. He tore himself away from his operational responsibilities at OKH and reapplied himself to his tasks as Defense Minister and strategic commander at OKW.

His first task as Defense Minister was to order new weapons able to combat the surprisingly advanced Soviet T-34 tank. In December 1941, as soon as the T-34 had emerged as a problem, Hitler had ordered design work to begin on a similar German panzer, the Panzer V Panther. As usual the army put out performance specifications and asked different manufacturers to come up with designs. The contract was won by the conglomerate Maschinenfabrik Augsberg Nuremberg, better known as MAN, and in June 1942 the tank prototypes were put through extensive tests.

A column of Panzer Mk V Panthers with infantry riding on board moves through snow on the Eastern Front, probably early 1944

IMPROVED ARMOR

The Panther proved to be a revolutionary vehicle. It copied from the T-34 the concept of sloping armor to cause incoming shells to bounce off. Also copied from the Soviet tank were the wide tracks and large road wheels which gave better traction on snow and mud, both of which had caused problems for the Panzer IV. The Panther took the ideas further by mounting a powerful engine and advanced gear box along with a robust suspension system. Together these allowed the Panther to move cross-country at a much greater speed than any other tank on the battlefield. Also better than anything else in action at the time was the tank's 75mm gun, which had been designed specifically to punch through armor.

In July 1942 Albert Speer presented Hitler with the finished prototypes of the Panther. The Führer was impressed, but his attention was distracted by the developing offensive in southern Russia. He approved an order for 1,000 Panthers. By January 1943, however, Hitler's priorities were changing and he took a much closer interest in the Panther. He demanded that 250 of the new tanks be ready by May, another 750 later that summer and another 1,000 in time for the summer of 1944.

Also tested in prototype form in June 1942 was the Panzer VI Tiger, perhaps the most famous, and the most fearsome, tank of the war. The Tiger had been conceived in May 1941, even before the attack on Russia began, as a heavy tank with impenetrable armor and the most effective gun on the battlefield. Designed to be invincible, the Tiger turned out to be almost unbeatable, but was never produced in enough numbers to turn the tide of war. The prototypes tested in the summer of 1942 had heavy armor, able to withstand most armor-piercing shells of the time, and were equipped with the famous 88mm gun as well as with machine guns. The engine and gearbox, however, were below standard and broke down with distressing regularity.

ENTER THE TIGER

Even while changes to the Tiger were under way, Hitler ordered that the new weapons be deployed on the Eastern Front. Predictably they broke down and some were captured by the Soviets. By the spring of 1943, when over 200 Tiger tanks were ready for action, the element of surprise had been lost. Nevertheless, the Tiger was to prove a major advantage to the Germans in their battles against the Soviets, and they were even more effective when deployed in the West.

SS-Leibstandarte Tiger, Normandy 1944

Hitler's role as head of OKW and the global strategic overview that it brought him were also causing problems in the first months of 1943. In North Africa, Rommel with his Afrika Korps and Italian allies had been defeated at El Alamein and were in headlong retreat. Rommel's skilful use of his panzers delayed the Allied victory in North Africa, but it was clearly inevitable. In March 1943 Hitler recalled Rommel and was shocked to find the general in defeatist mood. He told Hitler that not only was North Africa lost, but that Italy was on the verge of collapse. Hitler's response was to send more German troops to Italy and the Balkans to guard against an Allied invasion from North Africa. This, of course, reduced the German forces available to fight the Russians.

In February Hitler made some changes to the command structure in preparation for the coming summer campaigns. He summoned Manstein

to the Wolf's Lair and gave him command of the entire southern front in Russia. Hitler gave Manstein a free hand to conduct the war in the area as he wished. Manstein was taken aback by the apparent freedom of action he was being given and specifically asked if he could undertake tactical withdrawals if necessary. Hitler agreed. In the event Manstein was not to enjoy a completely free hand for Hitler was to issue direct orders from time to time, but he had more freedom than most.

Guderian was the next to be summoned to see the Führer. General Heinz Guderian had been at the forefront of the development of blitzkrieg ideas in the 1930s and was one of the most respected panzer commanders. Nevertheless, he had been sacked over a year earlier after he broke Hitler's "Standfast Order" in the winter of 1941. Hitler's opening words amazed Guderian, long accustomed to Hitler's refusal to accept criticism. "Since 1941," said Hitler, "our ways have parted after numerous misunderstandings at that time which I now much regret. Please come back. I need you."

GUDERIAN'S RETURN

When told that he was to be put in overall charge of the armored troops, their training, equipping and tactical development, Guderian leapt at the chance. He knew about the new Panthers and Tigers and was keen to be involved. Equally surprising, and more worrying, was Hitler's physical appearance. "He has aged greatly," noted Guderian. "His manner is less assured than it was and his speech was hesitant. His left hand trembled."

The third general to be subjected to the new, reasonable face of Hitler as a military commander was Zeitzler. At the very end of February, Hitler ordered that the exposed salients which pushed deep into Russian lines between Leningrad and

Moscow were to be abandoned. The army, he declared, was to pull back to a new and much shorter defensive line running from Kirov, through Smolensk to Lake Ilmen. One of the positions abandoned was the town of Demyansk, the site of a supremely heroic resistance by Waffen-SS units in the face of overwhelming Russian numbers. If Hitler was willing to relinquish such a position to gain a better defensive line, some generals hoped, perhaps he was becoming more reasonable at long last. They were to be disappointed.

SECRET WEAPON

With an army equipped with new tanks and top class generals at his side, Hitler faced the task of planning the war for 1943. In February Manstein launched an attack with the new panzers, which captured the city of Kharkov. This convinced Hitler that the new panzers were the secret weapon he had been waiting for. He dismissed the cautious defensive plans of the staff officers and instead looked for an opportunity for a major offensive that would knock the Russians out of the war before the Allies could attack in the Mediterranean or across the English Channel.

Hitler took up a plan first mooted by Zeitzler, who had noted that no less than five entire Soviet armies were grouped together to defend the strategic rail and road center of Kursk, south of Moscow. There was a bulge forward in the German line to the north of Kursk at Orel and another to the south at Belgorod, offering the possibility of launching a double envelopment to cut off the armies in Kursk and destroy them. On March 13, Hitler ordered Zeitzler and the OKH staff to draw up plans for a giant pincer attack around Kursk for mid-May.

Once again, however, Hitler undermined his chances of success by dividing his objectives and

his forces. Not only was Kursk to be attacked, so was Leningrad. As before on the Eastern Front, Hitler was so confident of success that he dissipated his forces between two objectives instead of concentrating them against one. As a result he lost both and gained nothing.

The forces mustered to attack Kursk in Operation *Citadel* were, arguably, the finest fighting force the Germans assembled in the entire war. Half a million men were gathered for the assault, made up of the best units drafted in from other commands and other areas. There were a total of 17 panzer divisions, including the elite panzer units of the Waffen-SS—the Leibstandarte, Das Reich, and Totenkopf divisions. All of them were concentrated on a narrow front to achieve a single objective, unlike the wide-front assaults of the previous two years. Nor was equipment anything but the best. The attack was to be mounted with the latest artillery, assault guns and, crucially, panzers.

On May 4 Hitler met with his senior generals in Munich to discuss the details of the imminent attack. Manstein and Kluge, who would be commanding the troops on the ground, wanted to start operations on May 20. They argued that the best chance of success was to move as soon as the mud of the spring thaw had dried out, but before the Soviets could prepare any serious defenses. Zeitzler, however, argued that victory would be more likely if the new panzers were present in large numbers. Problems with production meant that the Panther and Tiger would not be ready en masse until mid-June. At this point Walter Model intervened. As commander of the Ninth Army, he was under Kluge's orders and would be leading the bulk of the non-panzer units in the northern pincer. He agreed with Zeitzler that it would be better to wait for the new tanks.

Hitler had great faith in the new panzers, the first of his "secret weapons" to enter service, and he had respect for Model. He ordered the *Citadel* attack to take place in mid-June, as soon as the panzers arrived. In the event the Panthers and Tigers did not arrive with the front line units until the very end of June. *Citadel* began on July 5.

From the moment the attack began, it was clear things were going badly for the Germans. The delay had given the Russians time to prepare defenses against the attack their scout planes and British intelligence had warned was coming. Over a million men were entrenched behind mines and gun emplacements, and they were supported by vast swarms of tanks. The German attack made little headway, and casualties were high. The men being lost were the trained, veteran elite of the German army and they were irreplaceable.

On July 12 a vast tank battle, the largest in history, took place at Prokovka when 450 panzers ran into 800 Russian tanks. The Soviets lost more than 400 tanks, the Germans just 100. But the Germans had been stopped. The action at Kursk stalled. On the following day Manstein asked Hitler for permission to stop the attack. Hitler was furious. "These generals calculate and examine

every aspect of a problem, but never take action!" he raged. "When things don't go quite as well as they'd hoped, they want to give up immediately. I can't trust Manstein. He is intelligent, but he is not a National Socialist. These generals have no stomach for a fight." That evening, however, as he read the reports coming in from the front line, he accepted reality and called a halt to the operations.

Stalingrad had shown the Germans could be halted. Kursk showed that they could be beaten. After Kursk there were to be no more bold, daring projects with the expectation of outright victory to the Germans. There was only to be a long, deadly grind as the Soviets brought their massive superiority in numbers to bear on their invaders. By the autumn of 1943 the Soviets believed they had a superiority of about four to one.

The Soviet attacks began the day the Germans' stopped. The first strike was on Orel, then five days later came an assault on Belgorod. As these offenses began to slow down, a new one took place further south as the Russians crossed the Donetz river.

The pattern for the next two years was being set. The Soviets could amass in any area an attacking force so overwhelming that it could drive through the German defenses, but their logistic back up was so poor that they were unable to keep an advance supplied for more than two or three weeks. As a result, startling breakthroughs of the type the Germans had achieved in 1941 and 1942 were beyond the abilities of the Red Army. Instead, the Russians pushed one attack until it ran out of supplies, then built up another in a different area. In this way, the Russians kept up continual pressure on the Germans, forcing them

An infantryman of the 3rd SS Division, known as "Totenkopf" from their death's head badge, on the Eastern Front

A shattered Soviet T-34 tank wrecked during the Kursk offensive

to move reserves back and forth between danger points. It was no way for the Russians to win the war quickly or easily. But Stalin had vast reserves of manpower and was willing to lose hundreds of thousands of his men in the slow grind that promised ultimate victory.

On the German side, Hitler had his attention engaged elsewhere. In July 1943 Mussolini was ousted as dictator of Italy by his own Fascist Party, which promptly made peace with Britain and the USA. Allied troops poured into southern Italy. Hitler's longstanding fear that southern Europe would prove his weak spot was becoming reality. He organized a swift and successful capture of many of the Italian armed forces, some of whom were shot by the Germans, and also the strengthening of the defenses in Italy and Greece.

On November 3, 1943 Hitler issued War Directive 51. Most of it was concerned with the war in the Mediterranean and the West. The Eastern Front, where the bulk of German forces were engaged, merited just one sentence. "In the East, the vast extent of the territory makes it possible for us to lose ground, even on a large scale, without a fatal blow being dealt to Germany."

INEVITABLE DEFEAT

The trouble for the German generals on the Eastern Front was that when they tried to put this policy into action, Hitler intervened. Manstein wanted to evacuate his men from beyond the Dnieper, but Hitler refused permission until it was too late. Thousands of men were killed or captured who could easily have escaped the closing Russian trap.

By the end of 1943 the majority of the generals and professional army officers realized that the war was lost. In 1918 the army had reached the same conclusion and informed the civilian government that peace should be made as quickly as possible to avoid useless casualties, foreign invasion and the utter ruin of the Fatherland.

In 1943 Hitler's secure grip on the military command structure and on civilian government made such a move impossible. Some officers tried to persuade Hitler, some simply did their duty. But some began to consider a radical alternative: the assassination of the Führer.

Battle of the Bulge: December 1944–January 1945

.... Front line December 16	- - - Front line December 20	—— Front line December 25

13

THE WESTERN FRONT

Hitler avoided making decisions on the Western Front, as his main attention was focused on the Eastern Front. When he did finally intervene in the fighting in France it was with disastrous results

As 1944 opened Hitler was faced by serious military problems which would have daunted almost any other military commander. Hitler, however, was so convinced of his own superiority and ultimate victory that he simply refused to believe that Germany was in serious trouble and, instead, looked for a way out of his difficulties.

Hitler looked to the past and the future for solutions. In the past he found the figure of King Frederick the Great of Prussia, a man with whom he was increasingly coming to identify. Frederick had won a series of brilliant victories in the mid-18th century before finding himself faced by a monumental coalition of forces in the Seven Years War, which began in 1756. By 1762 Prussia was facing invasion and crushing defeat when the Czarina Elisabeth suddenly died. Her successor pulled Russia out of the anti-Prussian coalition, allowing Frederick to defeat his remaining enemies and win the war by 1763.

The German advance into Belgium in December 1944 proved to be a costly failure, for which Hitler must take the blame

A King Tiger tank in Paris, summer 1944

As 1944 progressed Hitler was to refer to Frederick time and again as an example of how a leader can snatch victory from defeat. His comment to Rundstedt in July was typical: "Under all circumstances we will continue this battle until, as Frederick the Great said, one of our damned enemies gets too tired to fight any more."

FORMIDABLE NEW WEAPONS

But Hitler did not look only to the past, he was also looking to the future. In 1943 Hitler had unleashed the new panzers, the Panther and the Tiger, which were proving to be the best tanks in the world. In January 1944 a new panzer began to roll off the production lines. This was the Panzer VI Königstiger, or King Tiger, a radical upgrade of the Tiger. The new tank was bigger, heavier and equipped with thicker armor, and it had the powerful 88mm L71 tank gun, able to knock out any enemy tank at a range of over a mile. This formidable new weapon entered front line service in time to take part in the battles on the new Western Front, opened up in 1944. Fortunately for the Allies, the King Tiger was never produced in great enough numbers—less than 500 between January 1944 and the end of the war.

Hitler also had other weapons in planning and production, and he referred to these darkly as his Vengeance Weapons. The first of the V weapons to go into action was officially known to the British as the V1, but those who were on the receiving end knew it as the doodlebug. The Germans named it the FZG-76. This was, effectively, an unmanned aircraft powered by a simple ram jet and carrying a warhead of 2,000 pounds of high explosive. The guidance system was crude, but effective. The V1 was launched from ramps which pointed in the rough direction of London, after which gyroscopes linked to the rudder kept it flying in a straight line. It fell to the ground and exploded when the fuel ran out. The damage these bombs could inflict was terrible, but their low speed and low height made them vulnerable to both barrage balloons and fighter aircraft. Of the 12,000 V1s launched against cities in southern England, only about 3,500 reached their target.

More dangerous was the V2. This was a ballistic rocket, the ancestor of the missiles which dominated the Cold War: its inventor, Werner von Braun, was to play a large part in the development of the US ICBM arsenal after the war, as well as the NASA space program. The V2 was capable of carrying a 2,000 pound warhead over 225 miles. Unlike the V1, the V2 was invulnerable to defenses as it flew on a parabolic arc over 50 miles high and fell almost vertically on to its target. The only warning experienced by victims was a sonic boom seconds before impact. Fortunately for the intended victims, the V2 suffered from difficulties with accuracy caused by electrical problems in the gyrocompass guidance system. Nevertheless many arrived in suburban England. Some 1,100 V2s were fired at Britain, and hundreds more were fired at the advancing Allies after D-Day.

Potentially more deadly still was the atomic bomb being developed by the Germans. Before the war began, German skill in theoretical physics was among the best in the world. Hitler established a top secret team of scientists, under Werner Heisenberg, to look at nuclear physics research and decide what, if any, of it could be used to benefit Germany. At first the team worked on producing a nuclear electricity generator, but later began to explore the possibilities of an atomic bomb. In late 1941, Hitler ordered funding for the research to be cut drastically. The German army had acquired vast coalfields by conquest from Russia and had access to the Romanian oilfields, so nuclear energy was simply not necessary. Nor, since Hitler thought he had won the war, was a nuclear weapon needed.

By late in 1943, after the German defeats at Stalingrad and Kursk, the need for a devastating weapon was growing and Hitler's thoughts returned to the atomic bomb. Heisenberg and his team were still struggling with the practical problems of controlling a chain reaction of nuclear fission. They replied that a bomb would take at least three years to develop and would cost a vast sum of money. Aware of the problems they were encountering, they told Hitler that the Allies could not possibly develop an atomic bomb for many years. The whole idea was shelved.

An A4 rocket is tested on the island of Peenemünde. The later military version would be known as the V2

IMMINENT INVASION

By the spring of 1944 it was obvious that all the weapons which had been developed would be needed to face the expected assault on Western Europe by the British and American allies. Hitler actually welcomed the prospective invasion, as it suited his strategic view of the war in the early months of 1944. Some 60 German divisions and numerous Luftwaffe squadrons were tied down in

France waiting to face the Allied attack. Hitler was confident the coming invasion could be defeated, as had the Allied landings at Dakar and Dieppe. He discounted the successful Allied landings in Sicily and North Africa as these had been virtually unopposed. Once the landings were thrown back into the sea, Hitler reasoned, the Western Allies could be pummelled by the new V weapons. They would be unable to launch another attack for at least a year. He could then move his divisions to the Eastern Front to destroy the Soviets.

As so often before, Hitler had a firm grasp of the strategic needs of Germany. But by 1944 the Wehrmacht was not the all-powerful force it had been. Hitler's success would depend on defeating the Anglo-American invasion of France and that meant correctly foretelling the answers to two questions and solving a problem. Hitler needed to anticipate where and when the attack would come, then formulate plans to defeat it.

Occupied France and the Atlantic defenses were under the command of Field Marshal Gerd von Rundstedt, though the armies along the north French coast were under the operational command of Field Marshal Erwin Rommel. The two commanders agreed that the Allied attack was most likely to occur in May or June and that it would be launched in the area around Calais where the sea route to Britain was shortest and landing beaches were available. They also agreed that supply logistics would be crucial to the Allies, so the major ports in the area were fitted with demolition charges to be blown if there was any danger of them being captured.

Beyond that, Rundstedt and Rommel disagreed profoundly about how to defeat the invasion. Rundstedt had little faith in fixed fortifications, preferring to fight with panzers and infantry. He saw the coming invasion in terms of a land battle fought some miles back from the sea. As a consequence, Rundstedt wanted relatively few men on the coast, instead massing his forces inland ready to deliver a powerful counterattack which would overwhelm the landing forces.

Rommel, on the other hand, believed the invaders would be most vulnerable on the beaches. He wanted to fortify all possible landing beaches with mines, pill boxes and artillery to slow down the initial disembarkations. Any bridgeheads established would then be attacked later that same day by whatever panzers could reach the beaches. The panzers would throw the invaders back into the sea before they could pour ashore in dangerous numbers. Such a plan required the armored units and reinforcements to be divided up and placed close to possible landing sites.

Unable to resolve their differences, Rundstedt and Rommel put their ideas before Hitler. Hitler's growing indecision and his refusal to make difficult choices was reflected in the way he solved the dispute. Rommel, he said, should fortify the possible landing beaches and was allocated the money and weapons necessary for the job, but the panzers would be held back. Moreover, Hitler insisted, the panzers would not be allowed to move without his personal approval. Hitler was concerned that the first landings might turn out to be a feint to divert the panzers away from the real landing grounds. By attempting to find a compromise between the two plans, Hitler managed to throw away the advantages of both.

In late March, Hitler went even further in reducing the Germans' ability to defeat the coming invasion. He moved three panzer divisions and one infantry division from France to the Eastern Front to defend the passes through the Carpathians and so safeguard the precious Romanian oil for the German war effort.

In May, Hitler interfered again, though this time to better effect. On May 2 the Führer sent a message to Rundstedt and Rommel announcing that the Allies would attack in Normandy and instructing them to make their preparations accordingly. In particular, Hitler decreed that three crack panzer divisions were to be moved to Normandy from Calais. Hitler gave no reasons for this change, and it remains unclear whether this was simply one of his inspired guesses or if he had firm knowledge of Allied plans.

Although Hitler had correctly anticipated the Allied invasion plans, when he went on to make relevant decisions, he once again compromised. When Rundstedt objected to the redeployment on the grounds that the main attack would be near Calais, Hitler allowed him to keep 15 infantry divisions in the Calais area. And when Rommel asked for the panzer divisions to be moved close to the most likely invasion beaches in Normandy, Hitler refused on the grounds that the panzers might need to race back to Calais after all. He then compromised again by moving the 21st Panzer Division to Caen, but holding the rest in reserve to the south.

On June 4, 1944 the weather in the Channel was windy and the sea was rough. Deciding that no Allied invasion was likely for several days, Rommel left his command post and travelled to Germany for his wife's birthday. Likewise the panzer commander, General Leo Geyr, slipped off to take part in a staff training exercise in Belgium.

THEY'RE HERE

Just past midnight on June 6, Allied paratroops began to land in Normandy and seized bridges and road junctions from the German garrisons. German commanders on the spot organized localized counter attacks, but more and more Allied troops arrived by parachute and by glider. As dawn broke a vast armada of ships was seen in the Channel. Battleships and cruisers opened up with gunfire aimed at Rommel's beach defenses and by the time it was light hundreds of Allied landing craft were coming ashore with thousands of troops.

At 4am a telephone call reached Rommel from his headquarters. Rommel told his staff to use infantry reserves to oust the Allied airborne units and to send the panzers to the beaches. Then he got in his car and raced back to Normandy,

stopping at frequent intervals to get radio and telephone updates. Rundstedt, meanwhile, was also busy. As well as trying to gain a true picture of what was happening, he was responding to the various landings being reported to him.

By 6am, Rundstedt was convinced that he was faced by a major landing, if not the full invasion force, not by just a large raid or feint. He ordered his chief of staff, Gunther Blumentritt, to call Hitler for permission to move the panzer reserves forward to Caen. Hitler was at his mountain retreat in Bavaria, the Berghof, above the village of Berchtesgaden. As usual, the combined staffs of Germany's armed forces, OKW, were installed in temporary accommodation close to Hitler.

Blumentritt's call was taken by General Alfred Jodl, the chief of staff at OKW. In response to the request, Jodl asked Blumentritt to ascertain the true situation before calling back. As the hours ticked by, the situation in Normandy became increasingly clear to Rundstedt and to Blumentritt. Phone call after phone call was made to OKW asking for the panzer reserves to be unleashed, but Jodl simply asked for more details before the Führer could make a decision.

General Dwight Eisenhower pays a final visit to American paratroops in southern England just before D-Day

In fact, Hitler was not even aware that Blumentritt was calling. He had been up until 3am enjoying the company of Josef Goebbels, Eva Braun and others. Jodl was reluctant to wake Hitler unless he had firm news to give him. It was not until 9.30am that Jodl finally accepted that the landings in Normandy were serious and large scale in nature. Even then he did not dare wake Hitler until almost 11am. At first Hitler, like Jodl, suspected the landings might be a trick to draw German reserves away from the real landing area. He demanded more reports and more information.

It was at a conference of OKW staff that Hitler finally approved the release of the panzers. It was 2pm and it was already too late. The 21st Panzer Division had shown what could have been achieved. Attacking directly towards the British landing on Sword Beach the panzers crashed into the advancing troops, driving them back to the sea in the area around Luc-sur-Mer before swinging left to take the Canadians landing on Juno Beach in the flank. It was a crucial moment, but unsupported by other forces the 21st Panzers had to fall back.

TIRADE OF ABUSE

By nightfall on June 6, 130,000 Allied soldiers were ashore. Rommel's attempts to defeat them on the beaches had failed. Two weeks after D-Day it was clear that Rundstedt's plan to defeat the Allies once they were ashore was also failing. Montgomery had 20 divisions ashore in Normandy, while his old adversary Rommel had just 18 to oppose him. On June 17 Hitler visited Rommel and Rundstedt at Marginal, ironically at the command post built in 1940 for Operation *Sealion*, the invasion of Britain. Rundstedt had barely begun explaining the situation when Hitler interrupted and began a long tirade of abuse at the way the campaign had been conducted.

Canadian soldiers advance across Juno Beach

When Rundstedt asked for the 15 divisions around Calais to be moved to Normandy, Hitler refused on the grounds that they were needed to guard the bases of the V weapons. "Perhaps," said Rommel, "it is time to end the war." Hitler turned pale with rage, and stormed out, hurling abuse at his favorite general.

For the following month the battle to contain the Allied landings continued unabated. On July 1, Rundstedt sent Rommel his last reserves, but the Allied advance continued. Rundstedt had lost 90,000 men. He phoned OKW to tell them that he could keep the Allies penned in Normandy for only a few more days. After that, said Rundstedt, it would just be a matter of a slow retreat eastward and an inevitable Allied invasion of Germany itself.

"My God," replied Jodl. "What can we do?"

"Make peace, you idiot!" replied Rundstedt and slammed down the phone. Next day Hitler removed Rundstedt from his command and replaced him with Hans von Kluge. On July 17 Rommel was injured when his car was strafed by an RAF fighter. Operational command passed to Kluge.

Despite the change of high command, the campaign in France went very much the way Rundstedt had predicted. Hitler's continued interference consistently made things worse than they might have been. At Cherbourg, Hitler ordered the besieged garrison commander von Schlieben to abandon the inner defenses for the outer defense perimeter which had been ordered, but never completed. Once again, Hitler was refusing to allow a tactical withdrawal to prepared defenses. The lessons he had learned in the trenches of the First World War had become an obsession. The result was a foregone conclusion. Cherbourg, which could have held out for weeks, was overrun in eight days. The German garrisons in Lorient and St Nazaire stuck to their prepared

defenses and held out until the end of the war.

In early August, Hitler intervened again. With the Americans racing into Brittany and south towards the Loire, Kluge wanted to fall back to the line of the Seine River, a more easily defended position than the open fields to the west. Hitler refused and instead told Kluge to launch an attack from Falaise to drive through the base of the American advance and so cut off the armored spearhead from their supply base in Normandy.

This order shows a new side to Hitler's increasingly desperate plans drawn up in the safety of OKW, far from the harsh reality of the battlefield. Hitler allocated Kluge no less than six panzer divisions for the attack. The combined paper strength of the divisions was 1,500 panzers of various types. But in fact Kluge had just 185 tanks in his strike force.

The policy of keeping divisions in existence when their fighting strength had been severely reduced by casualties, detachments and sickness had begun in Russia in 1942. At first the policy had been undertaken for the very good reason that the Soviets were able to identify divisions, but not their strength. So keeping a high number of divisions masked the true weakness of the German forces. It did have a drawback in that the divisional support staff stayed the same irrespective of the number of front line troops. By keeping the number of divisions while reducing the numbers of men there developed a serious skew in the ratio of front line troops to support staff. By 1944 the depletion of the divisions had created a much more serious and unforeseen problem. It was becoming almost impossible for the planning staff at OKH, OKW and even more so for Hitler to keep up to date. One division might have as much fighting power as five others combined. Planning operations became fraught with difficulty.

At Falaise, the lack of armored punch in the six panzer divisions meant the attack faltered after just five days. Even worse, the accelerating American advance swooped round to the south and drove north, threatening to trap the German attacking force in a pocket south of Falaise. On August 17, Hitler ordered Kluge to report back to Berlin and replaced him with General Walther Model. Uncertain if he was being recalled to be blamed for the Falaise debacle or because the Gestapo wanted to interrogate him over alleged links to the July bomb plot to kill Hitler, Kluge committed suicide.

Model ordered an immediate retreat from the Falaise Pocket, but the loss of heavy equipment and men had been huge. By the end of August the Germans had lost 450,000 men in France as casualties or prisoners as well as 1,500 tanks and 3,600 aircraft.

German soldiers search British prisoners after Arnhem September 1944.

After Falaise morale collapsed and supplies became almost non-existent. The Germans fled eastward. Hitler tried to intervene again on August 20. Furious as he was at the precipitous retreat of his armies, he did not try to devise a plan to stop the rot. Instead he ordered that the public buildings of Paris be dynamited to destruction and every house set on fire. The German commander of Paris, General Dietrich von Choltitz was appalled by the order. Not daring to refuse, he kept finding excuses to delay the destruction. On August 26 Charles de Gaulle arrived with a division of Free French troops to take the relieved surrender of Choltitz, who was hourly in fear of death at the hands of the SS or Gestapo for failing to carry out his orders.

ON THE MOVE

By the end of August the Germans had been chased out of France and Belgium. The Allies came to a halt, not because of German resistance,

but because of the difficulties of getting supplies from Britain through France to the fighting troops. The Germans had destroyed the dock facilities of Boulogne, Calais and other ports as they retreated and all supplies therefore had to be taken in over the Normandy beaches.

By mid-September the Allies had gathered enough equipment and supplies to make an attempt to get over the Rhine and into Germany before winter closed in. A surprise airborne assault took place to capture the bridges at Arnhem while the British XXX Corps attacked towards Arnhem from Eindhoven. This time the newly reinstated Rundstedt did not need Hitler's orders to move his men to counter the threat. The 2nd SS Panzers were just outside Arnhem and went straight into action. The Allied attack collapsed.

Relieved to have driven off the Allied attempts to invade Germany, Rundstedt reluctantly accepted the loss of the great port of Antwerp. He knew the Allies would be unlikely to launch a major attack before the spring, so he settled down to preparing his defenses in a last attempt to delay the inevitable.

COUNTER-PUNCH

Hitler, on the other hand, had no such ideas of defense. Despite a serious stomach illness in late October, he had been thinking about how to win the war, despite all the odds. And, once again, he had decided that if he could knock the Western Allies out of action for long enough, he could concentrate all his forces in the East to defeat the Russians. Whether the Germans still had the resources to defeat the Russians, even if they concentrated them all in the East, is doubtful. But Hitler believed they did and set about planning a blow to knock his attackers on the Western Front out of action. He called it Operation *Autumn Mist*.

Given the situation on the Western Front in November 1944, Hitler's choice of target could not have been better. He aimed to split the British and American forces, as he had split the British and French forces in 1940, then drive on to capture Antwerp in a lightning 12-day attack. All Allied soldiers caught north of the advance would be captured. As soon as Antwerp was taken, Hitler believed, the Allies would rush troops from other areas of the front in an attempt to retake the city. Once the Allied front line was weakened, Hitler planned to launch a second attack, Operation *North Wind*, further south at Saarbrucken to take the Americans on the right flank and roll up the entire Allied line.

Simultaneously, hundreds of V2 and V1 weapons would be launched against London, as the capture of Antwerp brought them within range. The British, Hitler jubilantly told Goebbels in mid-November, would be forced to negotiate or face destruction and the Americans would have no choice but to go along with the British.

As in 1940 Hitler was planning a massive panzer attack. As in 1940 the attack would go through the Ardennes region. But this was 1944, not 1940, and the world had changed.

The staff at OKW had been at work since the middle of September on *Autumn Mist* and on October 9 the draft plans were presented to Hitler. The Führer made no attempt to contact Rundstedt, the overall commander in the West, nor Model, the operational commander of the armies facing the Allies. Instead he pored over maps of the area, studied the latest panzer production figures and studied the lists of divisions and regiments available for use. On November 1 he sent the revised plans back to OKW. Written across the front cover in Hitler's own handwriting were the words "Nicht Abändern," Not to be Altered.

On November 3, Jodl outlined the plans of *Autumn Mist* to Rundstedt, Model and their divisional commanders. The generals listened in amazement. Though impressed that so many reserves had been built up in the face of Allied bombing, they were unanimous that Antwerp was an unobtainable objective. "If we reach the Meuse we should go down on our knees and thank God," was Rundstedt's opinion. Jodl rejected all criticism of the plans. They were, he said, the Führer's own plans and were not to be altered.

The plans envisaged an attack mounted by three armies. In the south at Echternach the Seventh Army, made up of infantry and artillery, was to form a flank guard to keep the US Third Army pinned down. In the center the Fifth Panzer Army was to smash through the front, capture the strategic communications center of Bastogne and drive on to cross the Meuse at Dinant before swinging north towards Antwerp. In the north the Sixth SS Panzer Army was to crush the First US Army, take Liege and Maastricht, then join the Fifth Panzer Army in the drive on Antwerp. Hitler gave command of this northern force to his old favorite Sepp Dietrich. As a junior SS man in 1934, Dietrich had helped Hitler organize the arrest and execution of Ernst Röhm and the leaders of the SA. He had proved to be steadfastly loyal ever since, as well as being a gifted, if ruthless, military commander.

In all, Hitler had allocated 200,000 men and 600 tanks for the operation. The most modern and effective tanks and guns were given to the attacking force. The weakness was in the air. The Luftwaffe was a spent force and the skies belonged to the Allies. It was this that led to the delay in starting. Originally planned for November 27, *Autumn Mist* had needed to be put back because Allied control of the skies had delayed the concentration of armor and men necessary.

On December 10, Hitler was finally confident that everything would be ready for December 16. He travelled to a specially constructed forward command post near Frankfurt am Main, and summoned all the senior officers who would be involved in the attack. As the officers filed into a conference room they found themselves under the guns of an armed SS guard. Then Hitler entered to sit at a desk and read a prepared speech. Hitler was clearly ill. His face was puffy and his shoulders were stooped. His left hand which had begun to shake some months earlier was now twitching almost uncontrollably. Hitler opened his speech with an attack on the alliance facing Germany and why, in his view, it was so fragile, and moved on to give one of his typical diatribes about how wars should be fought. As the speech droned on with no end in sight one officer reached to his

American tanks relieve Bastogne, December 26, 1944

pocket for a handkerchief, almost getting himself shot by the nervy SS guards. Finally Hitler got to the attack plan, which he described as if already a victorious fact.

The attack began at dawn on December 16. The Western Allies were convinced that the German army was on the point of collapse and was quite unable to resist an attack, never mind mount one. The first few days saw easy victories and swift advances. The stretch of line being assaulted was held by four American divisions; Hitler was attacking with twenty-eight. As the panzers surged forward they met unexpected resistance at Bastogne where a single American division refused to retreat. When called upon to surrender, the American commander General Anthony McAuliffe replied simply "Nuts." By holding the vital road center of Bastogne, the Americans slowed up the supplies for the panzers and so slowed the panzers themselves. In the north the British commander Montgomery brought down reinforcements and took command of the Americans. He stopped Dietrich and the SS panzers.

On December 24 the low cloud which had covered the area suddenly cleared. The Allied aircraft swarmed into the skies to bomb and strafe the German columns. The remains of the Luftwaffe came up to fight them off, but were shot from the skies. Two days later the German attack was brought to a halt at Celles. As Rundstedt had feared, they had not even reached the Meuse.

Hitler was not depressed. Despite the fact that the attack had got nowhere near Antwerp, he gave the order to proceed with *North Wind*. It began on January 1, 1945 and failed dismally.

Rundstedt asked for permission to pull the men and tanks back to their start lines, which offered better defensive positions than the exposed areas where the attack halted. Predictably, Hitler

American transports drop supplies into Bastogne, 1944

refused. He demanded that no retreat take place. The predictable result was that the Germans took heavy casualties when the Allied counterattack began on January 14. By the time the Allies called off their attacks the Germans had lost almost 100,000 men as casualties or prisoners together with almost all the new tanks that had been sent to the front.

By then Hitler had other and more pressing worries. Heinz Guderian, who had been left in charge of the Eastern Front, had for some time been sending Hitler messages about the state of the war against Russia. He had received no replies and no instructions. Now Guderian had come to see Hitler in person to tell him the terrible news. The Russians were about to attack and the German armies would be unable to stop them. Total collapse was about to happen.

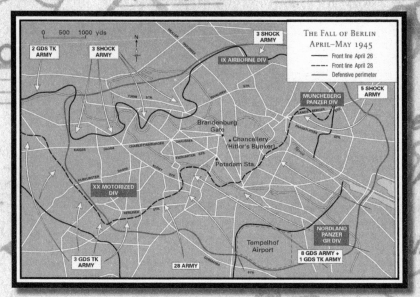

THE FALL OF BERLIN
APRIL–MAY 1945

- —— Front line April 26
- - - - Front line April 28
- —— Defensive perimeter

2 GDS TK ARMY

3 SHOCK ARMY

3 SHOCK ARMY

IX AIRBORNE DIV

5 SHOCK ARMY

MUNCHEBERG PANZER DIV

Brandenburg Gate

Chancellery (Hitler's Bunker)

Potsdam Sta.

XX MOTORIZED DIV

NORDLAND PANZER GR DIV

Tempelhof Airport

3 GDS TK ARMY

28 ARMY

8 GDS ARMY + 1 GDS TK ARMY

0   500   1000 yds

14

ROAD TO BERLIN

As Hitler faced the certainty of defeat his grip on reality weakened. He gave orders to units that no longer existed, expected generals to carry out impossible orders and refused to accept that he had failed

After the failure of the German attack at Kursk in the summer of 1943, the Germans were thrown on to the defensive by the Soviet Red Army. Hitler had lost the initiative and was merely responding to Russian attacks. The problems were manifold, but all came down to the fact that Hitler no longer had enough men or equipment to mount a sustained assault with any real chance of success. The distances were too great and the Red Army too numerous for that.

But Hitler did not give up his ambitions nor his faith in the ultimate victory that would be Germany's, increasingly invoking the memory of Frederick the Great. He also began to make statements to his generals of mystical importance: "Providence will bestow victory on the people that has done most to earn it," Hitler announced on January 1, 1944. His generals would have preferred to hear more solid reasons for believing in ultimate victory.

The final Russian assault on Berlin cost the lives of 82,000 Russians and 95,000 German troops

Although he was not going to tell the generals, Hitler did have solid reasons to hope for victory. His increasing paranoia, however, was to do much to undermine the efforts that were going well. Hitler had long been talking about secret weapons which he would unleash on his enemies at a time of his choosing. In 1943 the Panther and Tiger tanks had been used on the Eastern Front. Although they were undoubtedly the best tanks in the war, they did not have the impact they could and should have had, because they were committed before adequate numbers became available, a mistake made by the British in the First World War, and explicitly cautioned against by Guderian in his book *Achtung—Panzer!*

Despite this, Hitler retained his blind faith that the next generation of secret weapons would turn the tide of war. All that was needed was the time necessary to develop the weapons and then manufacture them in large quantities. It was to gain that time that Hitler drew up his plans for the Eastern Front for 1944.

For the first time since 1937 Hitler planned no major summer offensive action for the Wehrmacht. Instead his plan was to fight tenaciously for every inch of ground, retreating only when absolutely necessary. The Germans still held vast swathes of western Russia, from the suburbs of Leningrad in the north to Crimea in the south. There was, Hitler thought, plenty of space with which to play.

The Russian attacks came in a succession of local waves, flung forward one after another. This policy was dictated to the Soviets by their generally bad level of supply logistics. It took some weeks to transport to an area enough men, guns, tanks and supplies for an attack, and once the attack was launched the supply system was totally unable to keep up with the advancing divisions. The men subsisted on what they could carry with them, but

once the ammunition or food began to run out, the advance would come to a halt. Meanwhile, the men and matériel for another attack had been built up elsewhere and this would be launched as the first came to an end.

In this way the German commander on the Eastern Front, Field Marshal Erich von Manstein, was kept guessing about what the Soviets would do next, and was forced to rush his reserves back and forth along the front, using up precious oil and gasoline which the Germans no longer had to spare. For the Germans the situation was made worse by Hitler's insistence that no position be abandoned until the last possible moment.

In March of 1944 Hitler's refusal to allow Manstein to pull divisions out of Korsun when a Soviet attack threatened to outflank them led to 60,000 men being surrounded. Manstein sent a strong force of panzers to drive through the Russian lines and open a corridor along which the Korsun divisions could retreat. He extricated 30,000 of his men, but the rest were left dead or prisoners.

Suffering from eye trouble, Manstein went back to Germany and took the opportunity to visit Hitler. Able to confront Hitler face to face after months of futile messages and phone calls, Manstein told Hitler in no uncertain terms how self-defeating the orders not to retreat were proving to be on the Eastern Front. After a blistering row, Manstein was sacked. He was never to serve in the German army again. In 1945 he surrendered to the British and was imprisoned for eight years for allowing the SS to carry out war crimes in his area of command. Released in 1953, Manstein retired to write his memoirs and play a role in various veterans' associations. He died in 1973. With Manstein gone Hitler had lost his most talented strategist just when he would have needed him most.

Marshal of the Soviet Union Georgy Zhukov led the final Soviet offensive that captured Berlin

In March Soviet Marshal Zhukov reached the Carpathian Mountains, threatening the Romanian oilfields on which Germany depended. In response, Hitler sent divisions from France to the area. This action fatally weakened the defenses of France, allowing the Allies to land successfully on D-Day in June.

This was a crucial moment in the war, and Hitler knew it. Whatever his faults as a military commander, and they were many, Hitler at his best was one of the finest strategists of the 20th century. During 1943 he stated on several occasions that 1944 would decide the war and that the decisive moment would be that of the Anglo-American invasion of France. If that could be defeated, Hitler argued, he would be able to move the many divisions he was forced to keep in France to the East and so be in a position to defeat Russia, or at least force a peace. If, on the other hand, the invasion was successful then

Germany would be facing a war on two fronts without enough resources to fight it. It would only be a matter of time before defeat became inevitable.

The assistant chief of OKW in the autumn of 1943 was General Walter Warlimont. In his recollections written after the war, Warlimont recorded that Hitler had told him several times that if the Western Allies got ashore in France in 1944 the war was effectively lost.

RED ARMY RAMPAGE

When the Allies did manage to land successfully in France in June 1944 Hitler by his own admission, must have known Germany was defeated. In the opinion of many leading generals, the time had come to sue for peace. Field Marshal Rundstedt said as much and was sacked for it.

If the critical danger was not clear after D-Day, it soon became stark enough for all to see. On June 23, the Red Army opened up with a vast artillery barrage along 150 miles of the Eastern Front east of Minsk. They then unleashed four massive assault columns consisting of 1.7 million men, 2,700 tanks and 25,000 guns. The defending Germans were outnumbered by more than two to one and had hardly any tanks.

On the first day of the Soviet attack 30,000 Germans were trapped around Vitebsk and 20,000 at Bobruisk. A week later the Russians had raced the 100 miles to Minsk to surround another 100,000 men. Hitler ordered the trapped forces to hold on, but they had been taken by surprise and lacked the stores to survive. Some managed to break out to the west, but most were killed or captured. In all the Germans lost 200,000 men in the month of fighting. Army Group Center had effectively ceased to exist. The battle, the beginning of the Russian Operation

Bagration, was the key which unlocked the way to their continued advance. By the end of August the Soviets had pushed forward into Romania and Bulgaria in the south, while in the north they were almost at the German border.

In the midst of these disasters to east and west, Hitler made it clear that he was not going to follow the advice of his generals and sue for peace. He had made some serious mistakes as a military commander before, but this was the greatest of them all. There was no longer any realistic chance of victory, but Hitler chose to continue the war. This decision to carry on fighting led to the attempt on July 20 to assassinate Hitler. Plots had been cobbled together before, but this came closest to success. It was backed by large numbers of senior army officers who now realized that Hitler was determined to fight until he had brought about the bitter and crushing defeat of Germany. The assassination plot failed and thereafter there could be only one end to the war, the final battles around Berlin in 1945.

TRIUMPH OF THE WILL?

The reasons why Hitler chose to fight on in the summer of 1944 were varied. He continued to speak about destiny and fate, about the miraculous escape of Frederick the Great, and there can be little doubt that he believed in such things. Above all he believed in the force of will power. After the Normandy landings and as the Eastern Front was rolled back, Hitler told Jodl, "My task, especially since the year 1941, has been never to lose my nerve under any circumstances." It was willpower that had turned the half-blind, gassed and penniless ex-soldier of 1918 into the dictator of Germany. His faith in willpower had been reinforced by the success of his Standfast Order in the winter of 1941. By 1944 his confidence in it was absolute.

There has been much speculation about Hitler's use of astrology both in the early days of power and, more significantly, as the war moved towards defeat. Astrology was very popular in Germany in the 1920s and 1930s. Many astrological readings and predictions were about politics and some were remarkably accurate. In 1934 it was made illegal for any horoscopes to be printed that related to Hitler or the Nazi Party. Some have seen this as a move to monopolize astrology, but it is just as likely that Goebbels wanted complete control of information published about Hitler.

Rudolf Hess was certainly a firm believer in astrology. It is likely that his surprise flight to Scotland in 1941 was prompted, at least in part, by an astrological reading he had which predicted defeat for Germany unless peace came before November 1942.

In 1941 the OKW hired an astrologer named Karl Krafft to produce birth charts on the Allied commanders the German generals were facing in the hope of gaining an insight into their characters. Krafft was also tasked with producing astrological predictions of German success that could then be used in the German press or leaked to foreign astrological circles. This news prompted the British high command to hire their own astrologer to produce identical charts so that they would know what information, true or otherwise, the Germans had at their disposal. The British later expanded this program in order to explain how they could predict German actions. In fact the information came from the Ultra project, the breaking of German military codes.

What remains very unclear is exactly how much of all this Hitler actually believed, or indeed heard about. In the early years, the influence of astrology was probably slight. But by 1944 Hitler was willing to grasp at straws. An astrological prediction of victory would have been very welcome.

On July 9, 1944, Hitler told his senior staff that the war would be won early in 1945. The key factor in the recent defeats, Hitler argued perfectly correctly, had been the Allied control of the air. This, he announced, was about to be ended. The coming success would be guaranteed by yet another secret weapon. This time it was an aircraft named the Swallow, or Messerschmitt Me262.

The Messerschmitt Me262 jet fighter came too late to save Hitler

The Swallow had a troubled history. It had been conceived in 1938, but the primitive jet engines then available were neither powerful enough nor reliable enough for combat service. By spring 1942 a new engine, the Junkers Jumo 004, had been developed. These built up to a thrust of 15,600lbs and could power the aircraft at an astonishing 540mph, at a time when the leading Allied fighters could manage only 400mph. Unfortunately the engines had an alarming habit of suddenly blowing up unless stripped down and thoroughly cleaned after every 50 hours of flying time. As with many other projects, funding was cut off as Hitler believed the war was almost won.

Not until the summer of 1943 was the Swallow project revived. Despite the engine problems, in autumn 1943 Hitler ordered the aircraft to enter production under the strictest security measures.

He instructed that the aircraft be developed as a bomber, able to deliver two 500lb bombs with great precision, then escape before the enemy fighters could arrive. Göring as head of the Luftwaffe had other ideas. His ace pilot Adolf Galland had flown a prototype and declared it essential that fighter squadrons be equipped with the aircraft as soon as possible.

In May 1944 Hitler learned that the Me262 was being developed as a fighter. He flew into a temper and gave instructions the aircraft was to be built as a bomber only. He was angered more that his orders had been disobeyed than by the fighter design itself. Aviation experts put forward the reasons why a fighter version was not only more useful in combat but easier to produce. Hitler brushed their comments aside. It was to be months before he could be persuaded to allow development of the fighter version as well. By then months of lost production had slipped by and Allied bombing was making manufacture difficult.

In the event only 300 of these superb aircraft entered service. Allied pilots had real difficulties facing the Me262 in combat. But due to Hitler's meddling the aircraft appeared in such small numbers that its impact was insignificant and did nothing to stem the collapse of the German armed forces. Other secret weapon projects, such as the Komet rocket plane, were similarly delayed by Hitler's intervention and also had little effect on the war.

There was also a terrible, dark reason why Hitler could not surrender. He knew that he was ultimately responsible for the murders of millions of Jews, Gypsies and Slavs. The horrors of the slave camps, death camps and concentration camps were, in the summer of 1944, only guessed at by most Germans and carefully hidden from the Allies. Hitler knew that he could expect little in the way of mercy if Germany were to surrender.

He and many of his top Nazi aides would have only execution to look forward to once the secret of the Holocaust was revealed. With death his only reward for surrender, why not continue fighting? He may have been throwing away hundreds of thousands of lives, but they belonged to other people. His own life was already forfeit and he must have known it.

Hitler had always had a liking for Wagnerian opera. By bringing about the total ruin of Germany and as much of Europe as he could engineer, Hitler would be creating his very own nightmare of destruction. His own *Twilight of the Gods.*

And so the war went on, even though it was already lost.

Hitler continued to grasp at straws, however, whether they promised an illusory chance at victory or simply served to delay the Allied advance and so give time for the development of more secret weapons. As 1944 advanced Hitler came to place increasing reliance in the concept of the "fortress wavebreak." The thinking behind this idea was tactically sound. Towns or villages in the path of the advancing enemy which served as important road or rail centers were fortified with bunkers, pill boxes, tank traps, heavy artillery and the like.

These fortresses would then be held for as long as possible after the enemy army swept through the open country around them. By denying the enemy the transport junction, the logistics and supplies of the advance would be seriously disrupted. At the same time, the enemy would be obliged to use combat units to reduce the fortresses, taking forces from the advancing front to do so. These factors would tend to slow or temporarily halt the advancing enemy.

CRUMBLING RESISTANCE

In the event, the fortress wavebreak system proved far less effective than Hitler had hoped. In some instances the supposed value of the transport center was greater than its actual worth to the enemy. In such cases, the fortress was simply bypassed and a few reserve forces set to watch the German defenders until they surrendered through lack of food. Those fortresses which were assaulted were quite often lacking the heavy artillery or prepared defenses to withstand a full attack. The resistance crumbled in a few days, not the few weeks that Hitler had anticipated.

Typically of Hitler by this stage of the war, he seemed blind to the fact that the soldiers left in the fortresses were being abandoned to death or capture with no hope of relief. He simply did not care about the fate of these men. In Hitler's eyes their duty was to fight for *Volk* and *Fatherland* and he expected them to do so until they died.

Although the fortress wavebreak tactic failed time and again, Hitler continued to place great faith in the idea. He blamed its failures not on a lack of defenses or supplies, but on a lack of fighting spirit in the commanders of the fortresses. From Hitler's point of view this was very often

Jubilant American troops display war trophies at Saarbrücken

true. The commanding officers knew that they and their men faced only death or capture in the cause of a war that was already lost. Very often the commanders made a show of resistance, then negotiated surrender terms. Hitler was predictably furious when this happened. The commanding officers were routinely condemned to death for cowardice in the face of the enemy, though as they were prisoners the sentence could not be carried out. Realizing this, Hitler began ordering the imprisonment and even execution of the families of the officers who surrendered.

A tactically sound idea was being turned into a ruinously costly strategy of failure by Hitler's blindness to the realities of the German military situation. The armed forces no longer had the resources to make a reality of Hitler's ideas.

In January 1945, as Hitler played desperately for time, the Allies were standing on the borders of Germany in both the East and the West. The final thrust into the heartland of the Reich was just a matter of time.

Heinz Guderian, now a Field Marshal, was chief of staff at OKH. During December he had been compiling intelligence on the state of the Eastern Front and sending a stream of reports to Hitler. Getting no reply from the Führer, Guderian travelled personally to Berlin to see him. He presented a report stating that the Russians had 225 infantry and 22 tank divisions poised to attack the German line held by just 50 infantry and 12 panzer divisions. Hitler listened to Guderian with barely concealed contempt, then threw the report back at him. "Who produced this rubbish?" he demanded before launching into his own analysis of the situation with its usual reliance on the coming secret weapons, the imminent collapse of the enemy alliance and other fantasies.

Guderian travelled back to his headquarters.

When he arrived Guderian found that while he had been travelling, Hitler had called OKH and personally ordered the only two remaining reserve panzer divisions to be sent south to launch an attack aimed at relieving the 140,000 German and Hungarian troops trapped in Budapest. The attack proved to be a costly failure with the panzers suffering heavy losses and the Budapest garrison being forced to surrender. Guderian now had no reserves to meet the coming Soviet attack.

That attack began on January 12, 1945. With the opening assaults the Germans received a shock even more unpleasant than they had anticipated. The Russian attack was spearheaded by large numbers of a new tank, the Josef Stalin, which had very thick armor and was armed with a powerful 122mm gun. Only the German King Tiger stood a chance against this monster in combat, and the Germans had few such panzers on hand.

Within three weeks the Soviets captured over 100,000 prisoners and leapt forwards to reach the Oder River, deep within Germany, near Guben. The rapidly advancing tank columns of Marshal Zhukov's army reached Kustrin, just 40 miles from Berlin, early in February. For once, however,

At the Yalta Conference in 1945 Churchill (left), Roosevelt (center) and Stalin agreed the post-war face of Europe

Hitler's fortress wavebreak doctrine was working effectively. The garrison at Poznan held out for several weeks and effectively disrupted the Soviet supply system, which was not very good at the best of times. As a result the Russian advance came to a halt on the Oder. The Soviets spent the next few weeks capturing fortresses and advancing on the flanks to Vienna and Danzig.

BUNKER MENTALITY

In his bunker in Berlin, Hitler inspected the maps marked with flags giving the positions of German divisions, few of which were up even to half strength, and the supposed positions of the enemy forces. In the West, in December 1944, Hitler's maps showed the Americans seriously weakened by the *Autumn Mist* offensive, known to the Americans as the Battle of the Bulge. Convinced the Western Allies would be unable to launch an attack for some weeks, perhaps months, Hitler shifted divisions from the Rhine to the Oder. He was convinced the main attack would come from the Russians and he was mustering his forces to face it.

February passed relatively quietly for Hitler on the military front. The Allies held a conference at Yalta where Churchill, Roosevelt and Stalin agreed to partition Germany and impose the payment of serious reparations after they had gained victory. Hitler and Goebbels used this decision in their propaganda aimed at stiffening German resistance. Germany had to fight, they argued, or be destroyed by the Allies.

Hitler then had a row with Guderian. Hitler had appointed the head of the SS, Heinrich Himmler, to command a proposed offensive against Zhukov's Russians. Convinced the attack would fail, Guderian wanted the reliable General Walter Wenck in charge rather than the fanatical Nazi Himmler. After a shouting match lasting over two hours, Hitler agreed to a compromise with Himmler in command and Wenck as his deputy. Unknown to either man, Himmler was even then engaged in secret talks with Swedish diplomats to try to secure a last minute peace deal with the Allies.

On March 7 the long-expected Allied attack began. But it was the Americans who launched the assault, not the Russians. Within three days the Americans were on the Rhine and had even captured an intact bridge at Remagen. Hitler promptly sacked his commander in the West, Field Marshal Rundstedt, who had been reinstated the previous November. Hitler then travelled to the Eastern Front to address his commanders facing the Russians.

He appeared a physical wreck when he met them. When he entered the room, Hitler had to be supported by an assistant, for his left leg was useless. His left arm jerked and twitched throughout the meeting. For the first time, Hitler's gifts of

The bridge at Remagen was captured intact by the Americans

oratory failed him. His voice barely reached above a whisper as he instructed the commanders to halt the Soviet advance or, at least, delay it long enough for the secret weapons to be deployed. Few of the officers were convinced, but the ever present SS men made sure that orders were followed. It was the last time Hitler would leave Berlin, and probably the last time he stepped outside the area immediately around his command bunker in the grounds of the Chancellery.

When Hitler got back to Berlin he ordered the total destruction of the Ruhr industrial area, which lay in the path of the advancing Americans. On March 22, Hitler ordered that "the battle should be conducted without consideration for our own population" and that "all industrial plants, all electricity works, waterworks, gas works and all food and clothing stores are to be destroyed."

Hitler's minister of production, Albert Speer, was horrified. He secretly contacted the senior officers in the West, begging them not to obey the order. He then sent a memo to Hitler asking for the orders to be rescinded as the German people would need these basic services once the war was over. Hitler summoned Speer and delivered a chilling lecture.

"If the war is lost," Hitler told Speer, "the people will be lost also. It is not necessary to worry about what the German people will need for survival. On the contrary, it is best for us to destroy even these things. For the nation has proved to be the weaker, and the future belongs to the stronger Eastern nation. In any case only those who are inferior will remain after this struggle, for the good have already been killed."

As a strategy plan for the final weeks of the war such a view was disastrous. Apparently no longer interested in winning the war, nor even in gaining a peace, Hitler was determined to destroy as much of Germany as possible.

The senior German commanders could not, of course, see things in this light. On March 28 Guderian again came to Berlin and descended to the bunker where the increasingly infirm Hitler waited with his maps and battle plans. Guderian was determined to get a decision from Hitler on the fate of 200,000 German troops trapped behind Russian lines at Kurland. Guderian either wanted an attempt to be made to evacuate the men by sea, or authority for them to surrender and so save lives. After some preliminary debates about the defense of the Oder, Guderian asked about the evacuation of the Kurland troops. "Never!" shouted Hitler and a bitter argument followed.

Finally Hitler told Guderian that he was looking ill and should take six weeks' leave. "Find somewhere to rest," urged Hitler in a sudden rush of conciliation. "In six weeks the situation will be critical and I shall need you."

"I'll try to find somewhere that won't be captured by the weekend," remarked Guderian icily as he left. The two men never met again.

With Guderian gone, Hitler's fragile grip on reality seemed to vanish completely. His maps were populated with German divisions which were not just below strength but entirely phantom. Units which had surrendered en masse to the Americans were shown as still in combat. Rail links that had been bombed to oblivion were shown as still functioning perfectly. Never leaving his bunker, Hitler sent out a stream of orders to non-existent units or to commanders quite unable to fulfil his demands.

Then, on April 12, Hitler's hoped for miracle seemed to arrive. American President F. D. Roosevelt died in the midst of a heated dispute with Stalin over procedure for a German surrender. To Hitler this was a direct comparison with the death of the Russian Czarina which had saved the

American and Russian troops met near Torgau on April 25, 1945

Prussian King Frederick the Great in the Seven Years War two centuries earlier. Hitler was radiant. "It is the turning point," he told his staff. He was convinced the grand alliance against him would collapse now that one of its principal architects was dead. He called in his Foreign Minister, Joachim von Ribbentrop, to discuss the situation. After leaving, Ribbentrop reported, "The Führer is in seventh heaven. What nonsense. How can Roosevelt's death change anything?"

In this mood of hope, Hitler threw himself energetically into a revised war plan for victory. As the last even semi-coherent strategy Hitler was to produce, it was bizarre and based on a set of assumptions and conditions which were not true. It assumed that the anti-German alliance

would collapse within a few weeks of the death of Roosevelt. All Germany needed to do, Hitler believed, was to hold on until the enemy left the field of battle. Hitler called on the units defending Berlin to form an increasingly tight and determined defensive perimeter. This rock of defiance would be bound to bring upon itself the full might of the Soviet Red Army, but to make doubly certain of this Hitler would stay in Berlin himself. Once the Russians were closing in on the city, they would find the task of the attack so great that they would have to divert men and resources from other fronts. This would give the German forces there the opportunity to break out, attack the Russians around Berlin from the rear and destroy them utterly.

It was nonsense, of course. The Red Army was so large that it could attack Berlin without weakening its forces elsewhere, nor did the plan take into account the British and Americans advancing from the West. In any case, most of the German divisions involved in the plan no longer existed.

BATTLE BABBLE

When Hitler's orders went out in the form of an eight page document that was part battle orders and part political pamphlet on April 15 it had a mixed response. Some troops believed the rhetoric and were convinced that Hitler, as so often before, had some surprise that he was about to unleash to defeat his enemies. Others viewed it as the ravings of a man out of touch with reality.

"For the last time," wrote Hitler, "our deadly enemies the Jewish Bolsheviks have launched their attack. Their aim is to exterminate our people. While the old men and children will be murdered, the women and girls will be reduced to barrack-room whores. The rest will be marched off to Siberia. . . . we have foreseen this attack and have done everything possible to construct a strong defense. The enemy will be met by massive artillery fire. Gaps in our infantry have been made good by new units. If every soldier does his duty in the days and weeks which lie ahead, the last assault of Asia will crumple, just as the invasion of our enemies in the west will fail. At this moment, when fate has removed from the earth Roosevelt, the greatest war criminal of all time, the turning point of this war will be decided."

The day after this message went out, Marshal Zhukov began the final Soviet attack of the war. His vast armies surged forward, brushing aside the feeble resistance of the Germans. The Soviet columns dashed onwards, swooping around the German capital and thrusting deep into the heartland of the Third Reich.

Meanwhile, Hitler drew up detailed plans for the defense of Berlin. Where the regiments were to stand, where the guns were to be sited, how many tanks were to be deployed. On April 20, Hitler celebrated his 56th birthday. A string of important visitors came to the bunker to congratulate Hitler, and to urge him to follow one route or another to victory or surrender. Hitler saw all his visitors, told them emphatically that he was staying in Berlin to direct the final battle that could yet save him, Nazism and Germany.

On April 21, Hitler sent a direct order to General Felix Steiner who was commanding a small reserve of Waffen-SS panzers north of Berlin. Steiner was ordered to drive his panzers southeast to fall upon the Soviets behind their armored spearhead where the following infantry would be most vulnerable. He should then encircle the tanks of Zhukov's advance troops and wipe them out. "Officers who do not comply unconditionally with this order are to be arrested and shot," concluded the order. Steiner was a good Waffen-SS Nazi, but he knew the order was militarily impossible. He made a half-hearted attempt at an attack, then withdrew his men in good order and prepared to cover the inevitable retreat. Better, he thought, to surrender to the British or Americans than risk being shot out of hand by the Soviets when they saw the SS uniform.

The next day, April 22, Hitler took his last step as a military commander. He called a conference in the afternoon attended by General Hans Krebs, who had taken Guderian's place, Keitel, Jodl, Bormann and others. Hitler began with an angry tirade about the liars, traitors and cowards who had let him down time and time again. "Where is Steiner?" he demanded. Krebs replied that the Waffen-SS panzer attack had faltered. Hitler collapsed into a chair. His jaw fell open and his eyes glazed over as his face went deathly white.

For some minutes nobody moved. Then Hitler sat slowly upright. "All is lost," he said. "Hopelessly lost. Gentlemen, this is the end. I shall stay in Berlin and shoot myself when the time comes. You must make your own decision on what to do."

Keitel and Jodl both protested that the supreme warlord of the German people could not just stop directing the war. He had a duty to decide whether to surrender or, if not, how to continue fighting. Hitler would have none of it. He refused to give the order to surrender, refused to give orders to defend Germany and refused to appoint anyone else to take the decisions. Keitel and Jodl, Hitler's most loyal and dedicated generals, left the bunker that afternoon and made their way to the front line units. Their last duty was to get as many German troops as possible out of the way of the vengeance of the Soviets and to surrender to the Western Allies. That way at least, lives could be saved.

In the bunker, Hitler was still surrounded by his personal staff. In the field generals and field marshals had no orders other than to carry on fighting. On April 27 General Koller radioed the Berlin bunker from Furstenburg to ask for orders. He spoke to Field Marshal Ritter von Greim, who urged him to hang on to his position as long as possible. "Everything will be well," urged Greim. "I have spoken to the Führer and his confidence has completely inspired me." Koller was incredulous and laid his plans for surrender.

By this time, Berlin was completely surrounded. Savage street fighting was costing thousands of lives, both German and Russian.

Reports continued to come in to the bunker, but Hitler merely raved at the incompetence and treachery of his generals. Hitler gave no orders, though some were issued in his name. He still inspired

Hitler and Ribbentrop compare notes in Poland back in 1939

those around him with hope and determination, his personal magnetism and will power were still working.

By April 29 the Soviets were less than a mile from Hitler in his bunker. Hitler married Eva Braun. The next day Hitler ate lunch while the Soviets battled down the street next to that under which the bunker had been built. At about 3:30 that afternoon, Hitler killed his new wife, then himself. Berlin surrendered first, then Germany. Hitler's career as a military commander ended in final and total defeat.

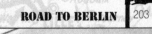

CONCLUSION

In the final analysis Hitler must be seen as a military failure. His military career ended in the ruin of his nation, his dreams and his plans. Few men have seen their careers end in such total and abject disaster.

Yet that is not to say that he was without talent or skill as a military commander. The sweeping victories of 1936 to 1941 are proof that the German military machine was capable of achieving much. As supreme commander, Hitler could justifiably claim some of the credit. Even in 1942 and 1943, when the German war effort was faltering, Hitler was not without some skill and success in maneuvering his armies. Yet, by the autumn of 1943 the war was clearly lost and for that Hitler must, again, take his share of the blame.

Some people have tried to strip Hitler of his credit for the early victories. They argue that it was the concept of blitzkrieg developed by such men as Manstein and Guderian that won these victories, not Hitler. It is understandable that people seek to remove from a man as unspeakably evil as Hitler any credit at all, but the theory does not stand up. The proponents of blitzkrieg had been pushing their views for some years before Hitler came to power, but had been met with resistance or outright contempt by the army high command. It was Hitler who saw the potential of the combined might of panzer and Stuka, and it was Hitler who ensured the necessary government funds and manpower were made available to the army.

Similarly, it has been suggested that it was the army staff which ensured the smooth running of the invasions of Austria, Czechoslovakia, Poland and France. Hitler, it is said, merely accepted the plans of his generals. Again, this is being unfair to Hitler. As supreme commander, it was Hitler's task to choose which plans to approve and which to reject. One could argue that there was as much luck as judgement in Hitler's decisions, but it cannot be denied that the decisions did belong to Hitler.

Conversely those who have sought to excuse Hitler from blame for the final defeats have argued that he was simply overwhelmed by sheer weight of numbers. This is undoubtedly true, but then it was Hitler's decision, against the advice of his generals, to invade Russia before Britain was defeated, a move that has been described as one of the greatest military blunders in history. It was also Hitler's decision to declare war on the United States after Pearl Harbor, a decision taken on the basis of political expediency, rather than on an assessment of the military potential of the US as an adversary. This decision has been described as another of the great military blunders. Hitler it was, also, who chose to fritter away the manpower of the Wehrmacht in several simultaneous campaigns rather than concentrating them on a single objective.

As this book has shown, Hitler had many successes and many defeats. We have explored why he took different decisions and how they affected the outcome of the war. We have looked at Hitler in good times and in bad, how he interacted with his closest military advisors, how he behaved in victory and how he reacted to defeat.

In conclusion, the author believes that Hitler was a one trick general. Although his plans took many forms, they all conformed to a single pattern. He would identify a weak point and then unleash the greatest force possible against it. It was good trick and it worked well for several years. But once his enemies realized what Hitler was doing, the game was up.

Late in 1940 Churchill took the decision to hold out in Egypt, goad Hitler's Italian allies in Africa, intervene in Greece, launch commando raids on France and bomb Germany. The aim was to create a diffuse field of battle on which Hitler could not concentrate overwhelming force on a single weak spot. Instead he had to dissipate his forces to react to a number of small threats. Frustrated and unable to pull off his usual trick, Hitler lost interest in Britain and turned on Russia.

On the Eastern Front the pattern was repeated. Hitler again achieved startling victories so long as the Russians continued to fight the war in a conventional way. When they too learned the same lesson as Churchill, they spread their forces across a wide front, launching a limited attack in one place, then in another. Again Hitler was denied a single weak point that he could exploit.

For all Hitler's undoubted talents as a soldier in the trenches or as a politician, his skills as a military commander were limited. He could achieve great and spectacular victories, but once the enemy learned from their defeats, Hitler was at a loss. Unable to come up with a new war-winning trick, Hitler could only flail about trying to repeat his earlier successes using his earlier tactics, but these had become out of date in a rapidly changing war.

Hitler had been produced by the First World War, and his experiences on a single front, and he developed tactics and strategies to cope with the problems of the First World War. But he could not cope with the Second.

Bundesarchiv—German State Archives: p.10 102-02465 Pahl, Georg; 12 146-1977-065-28 O.Ang; 13 146III-286 O.Ang; 18R 101I-185-0118-14 Neubauer; 20 183-L08129 O.Ang; 21 183-L08126 Schwz; 25 Bild 146-1984-079-02 O.Ang; 28 146-1980-128-63 O.Ang; 30-1 134-B0527 O.Ang; 33 146-1973-077-63 O.Ang; 34T 23-63-21 Klein. A; 34-5 193-04-1-26 O.Ang; 37 146-1990-081-10A Lagemann; 41 119-2406-01 O.Ang; 43 102-04060 Pahl, Georg; 46 183-H26837 O.Ang; 47 183-2005-0103-516 Hoffmann; 48TL 183-C13676 O.Ang; 48BR 183-H13160 O.Ang; 51 102-15573 Pahl, Georg; 52 102-16240 O.Ang; 55 183-R98690 Hoffmann, Heinrich; 56 183 L18802 Röder; 63 104-00879A O.Ang; 68 146-1987-038-29 O.Ang; 69 146-1990-048-29A O.Ang; 72 136-B1049 Tellgmann, Oscar; 73 183-H15617 O.Ang; 74-5 146-1995-066-10A O.Ang; 76 101I-382-0248-33A Böcker; 78 101I-216-0417-19 Dieck; 79 183-97906 Schremmer; 80 101I-127-0391-21 Huschke; 81 183-L18622 Bauer; 82-3 101I-379-0015-18 Rübelt; 87 102-04640A Pahl, Georg; 88T 102-13532 Pahl, Georg; 88B 183-B0527-0001-020 O.Ang; 89 102-15569 Pahl, Georg; 90 227-31 Kamphenkel, Wilhelm; 91 102-13376 Pahl, Georg; 93 192-250 O.Ang; 94T 146-1972-026-11 Sennecke, Robert; 94-5 183-1991-0319-501 O.Ang; 96 183-R99230 O.Ang; 99 102-18088 Pahl, Georg; 100 183-S04233 O.Ang; 105 183-1987-0922-500 O.Ang; 109 183-S56768 O.Ang; 114-5 101I-121-0010-11 Boesig, Heinz; Ehlert, Max; 117 101III-Moebius-029-12 Moebius; 118-9 DVM 10 Bild-23-63-09 Klein. A; 126 183-H01757 O.Ang; 127 101I-769-0229-11A Borchert,Erich (Eric); 129 183-H28715 Hoffmann, Heinrich; 130 146-1977-136-13A O.Ang; 131 146-1978-062-24 O.Ang; 134-5 146-1971-086-06 Schmidt; 138-9 183-M1112-500 O.Ang; 144 101II-MW-5675-29 Engelmeier; 145T 101I-402-0265-03A Pilz; 145B 183-L09712 O.Ang; 146 146-1971-011-13 O.Ang; 149 101I-785-0287-08 Otto; 156 101I-164-0357-29A Rauch; 157 146-1991-060-36A Weidner; 160T 101I-140-1226-06 Cusian, Albert; Scherl Bilderdienst; 160B 183-R63745 O.Ang; 164 146-2004-0018 O.Ang; 165 262 Grund, Horst; 166 101I-021-2081-36A Mittelstaedt, Heinz; 167 183-R76599 O.Ang; 169 183-E0406-0022-001 O.Ang; 172 Bild-101I-218-0529-17A; 173 101I-664-6759-30 Schödl (Schödle); 177 101I-022-2912-10A Horster; 181 B0791-42 BSM O.Ang; 186 101I-497-3529-22 Jacobsen

ED Archives: 42T, 42B, 58-9; 65; 111; 147; 183, 188; 189; 195; 196; 197; 198, 200; 203

NOVOSTI London: 159 RIAN_633408; 193 RIAN_60714

Getty Images: 8-9

Corbis: 26

Imperial War Museum: 36

Australian War Memorial: 52T

Shutterstock: 19, 122-3

Robert Hunt Library: 14, 15, 16, 17, 18L, 17R, 22T, 22B, 23, 32, 38, 44, 54, 60, 70, 83, 84, 86, 116, 132, 137, 158, 174, 176, 180

Wharton Military Collectables: 154

Cartography © Peter Harper